DECEMBER 2000

TO MY FRIEND JIM, WHO IS
NOT 'SWIFT' BUT IS CERTAINLY
A 'TRAITOR'... UM, '..TRADER'..

Dave

Swift Trader

Perfecting the Art of Day Trading

Charles Kim

Prentice
Hall
Canada

A Pearson Company

Toronto

Canadian Cataloguing in Publication Data

Kim, Charles
    Swift trader: perfecting the art of day trading

Includes index.
ISBN 0-13-026680-9

1. Electronic trading of securities. 2. Stocks - Data processing. 3. Investment analysis. I. Title.

HG4515.95K552 2000   332.64'0285   C00-930129-1

ISBN 0-13-026680-9

Editorial Director, Trade Division: Andrea Crozier
Acquisitions Editor: Nicole de Montbrun
Copy Editor: Bruce McDougall
Production Editor: Jodi Lewchuk
Art Direction: Mary Opper
Cover and Interior Design: Dwayne Dobson
Cover Image: Author Photograph
Production Manager: Kathrine Pummell
Page Layout: B.J. Weckerle

1 2 3 4 5 F 04 03 02 01 00

Printed and bound in Canada.

This publication contains the opinions and ideas of its author and is designed to provide useful advice in regard to the subject matter covered. The author and publisher are not engaged in rendering legal, accounting, or other professional services in this publication. This publication is not intended to provide a basis for action in particular circumstances without consideration by a competent professional. The author and publisher expressly disclaim any responsibility for any liability, loss, or risk, personal or otherwise, which is incurred as a consequence, directly or indirectly, of the use and application of any of the contents of this book.

Visit our Web site! Send us your comments, browse our catalogues, and more. **www.phcanada.com**.

A Pearson Company

DISCLAIMER

The author and his company in no way encourage or actively solicit any Canadian to invest in the speculative nature of the stock market and/or day trade. The author has witnessed and experienced many a trade gone quickly bad and watched as thousands of dollars disappeared right off his and other traders' trading terminals in less time than it takes to read this disclaimer. Day trading is highly speculative and inherently risky. It is not investing. People wishing to begin day trading should use risk capital only. Trade only that which you can afford to lose.

The author assumes no responsibility or liability for any financial losses related to decisions made by the reader as a result of reading this book. Readers are further advised that the information contained in this book is written solely for informational purposes and is not to be construed as stock purchasing advice. The opinions and analyses included are based on sources believed to be reliable and have been written in good faith, but no representation or guarantee, expressed or implied, is made as to their accuracy, completeness, or correctness. Please check with your own broker/dealer before making any investment decision(s).

Contents

ACKNOWLEDGMENTS

I would like to extend my sincere gratitude to Nicole de Montbrun at Prentice Hall for seeking me out and providing me with an opportunity to share this book with the rest of Canada's population interested in the art of day trading, which seemed to me at last count to be everyone I've met. Thank you, Nicole, for your unending patience and wisdom.

I'd like to express a heartfelt thank you to my partners and friends Peter Beck and Joseph Ianni who manage Canada's first and largest day trading firm. Guys, this is as much your book as it is mine. I have to add my thanks to the Admin & Bridge staff for putting up with us traders, the entire Technical Department for the same reason, Simon, Perry, and their staff in the software department, and Remarkable trainers Ron Brown, Matt Zylstra, and Eddy "Bucketshop" Stewart in the original Training Department. Your dedication to customers and the company was and is truly outstanding.

I would never forgive myself if I didn't take the time to acknowledge and thank all the full-time traders at Swift Trade in Toronto for picking up the slack while I've been busy trading full time and writing this book down in the States. The "oldtimers" Tom, Mark, Samuel, the David(s), Steve(s), Peter(s), and Ben(s), along with everyone else on that trading floor that I'm leaving out: You people are the best. Here's wishing us many more volatile, profitable trading days!

Thank you to all the day traders across North America who allowed me to visit them in their various cities and who have permitted me to interview, watch, learn, and grow as a trader while having the time of my life.

A word of acknowledgment gratefully goes out to Edgetrade.com and its founders, Joe Wald, Kyle Zasky, and their Number One Samantha Lipnack. You people helped start me out in the wonderful world of day trading.

And lastly, to my eternal friend and mentor, Mr. Peter Beck, from whom I have learned many important life lessons and business skills. Peter, you know how much our friendship means to me and I want to publicly acknowledge and thank you for the sacrifices you've made over the years to help me get here. Thank you, my friend. Without you I wouldn't be where I am today.

Preface: History of *Swift Trader* and Swift Trade Securities Inc.

It was in early 1997 when my close friend and brilliant business partner Peter Beck took the short plane ride from Toronto to New York City to visit some friends. As is his custom on such trips Peter had bought a couple of magazines and was busy digesting them for the short hop. On this trip he was reading *Wired*, the technology and business periodical. I can still vividly remember the excited phone call from New York City when he touched down: "Charles! We have to get into the day trading business!" It seems that he had read a short three-paragraph article on the business of day trading and how small, young, broker-dealer firms were making astounding profits with short-term stock market speculation.

One year later Peter Beck, Joseph Ianni, and I opened the doors to Canada's first electronic day trading firm: Swift Trade Securities Inc. (**www.swifttrade.com**) located in downtown Toronto just a few minutes' walk from the heart of Canada's financial district off Bay Street.

Fast forward to May 2000. Canada's first and only day trading firm has achieved a phenomenal rate of growth. The company has moved twice during the first two years of business, first from a 1,200-square-foot office to 5,000 square feet of trading floor space. Recently, the company finished expanding to the new ultra-modern Canadian headquarters, which includes over 17,000 square feet of trading floor space located on University Avenue in downtown Toronto. Swift Trade started with four floor traders and two staff members back in May of 1998. In May 2000 there are well over 250 traders and over 50 staff members. Additional offices have been opened in British Columbia, Quebec, and Ontario while the other provinces will follow in mid-2000. Thirteen offices in total are planned for Canada, with international growth expected in 2001.

This book is the result of practical knowledge acquired over the three years Peter Beck, Joseph Ianni, and I have spent developing and growing Swift Trade Securities Inc. The information outlined in this first book came from having day traded and executed thousands of trades using real stocks employing the principles of trial and error, as well as having spoken to and trained over 1,000 Canadians who were interested in making day trading a career.

It is our hope that this book will help you decide whether day trading is right for you.

INTRODUCTION

I have arranged the book into five separate parts:

Part One: A Swift Trader Is Born

This first part, entitled "A Swift Trader Is Born," is for those of you who want to know a little bit more about the differences between trading on-line using a discount broker and day trading using a direct access day trading (DAD) firm. It will answer questions such as: "What's the difference between using TD Waterhouse and a company like Swift Trade Securities Inc.?" It will help you decide whether full-time DAD is right for you and how to pick a DAD firm.

Part Two: A Swift Trader Deals with the Execution

The second part is written for people who have decided to try their hand at full-time direct access day trading. It defines and explains the different methods of executing trades using a direct access day trading terminal. Stock execution rules, advantages and disadvantages of one system over another, and examples of what your screen might look like are all included in this section.

Part Three: Swift Trading

This part deals with the daily rules and regulations you need to understand and memorize in order to succeed financially and keep your DAD experience satisfactory. Understanding how to short sell stock, understanding risk management, margin, and the games market makers play on us are all topics of interest to most aspiring direct access day traders and are included here.

Part Four: Before You Start

The final chapters include a bit of relevant personal philosophy as well as a counterpoint to the business of day trading.

Appendices

The appendices are an assemblage of useful lists, addresses, stock indices, and a DAD glossary.

FOREWORD

This is probably the best time in history to focus on financial markets. The investment business—and securities trading in particular—is undergoing a radical change. The "dis-intermediation" of financial markets, which has allowed anyone access to information and trading platforms, has transformed the old-school price club into a vibrant competitive "self-serve" business.

These changes are bringing about new forms of business. Collaborative business models exist alongside rugged individualists using network economics to their best advantage.

Much has been written about the largest visible change: day trading. The rise of day trading is the result of highly efficient auction markets that have enabled shorter and shorter periods to capture profits.

Swift Trader is a thought-provoking guide for anyone considering day trading as an investment strategy. It's also a guide for anyone already engaged in this process since it not only defines and describes day trading but sheds light on market activity. Mortgage rates, housing prices, even the price of fruit at the supermarket, are all determined through various auctions, which take place all day around the globe. Understanding the influence of market activity and using the information and tools outlined in these pages will help readers control risk and amplify returns.

I have spent the better part of my career trading and building trading systems to exploit market inefficiencies. It is my experience that, with consistency of practice, a focus on risk control, and through discipline, day trading *can* be profitable.

Good luck, and don't trade on hope.

Doug Steiner,
CEO of E-Trade Canada

PART ONE

A Swift Trader Is Born

swift ('swift) adj

1. Moving or capable of moving with great speed
2. Occurring suddenly or within a very short time
3. Quick to respond

synonym see FAST

1

Welcome to the Cyber Jungle

You could say that I was reborn as a day trader in 1998. That year I discovered my true calling. Since then, I have executed well over 10,000 trades. And I've done so with success.

As the head trainer/trader of Canada's Swift Trade Securities Inc., I was asked to write a book on the subject of day trading to assist fellow Canadians in following my path to becoming a day trader: investigating the nature of day trading, then making the decision to quit my job to do it full time. With this book, I hope I can help you to avoid many of the costly mistakes I made and skirt the inevitable pitfalls that often accompany such decisions.

This book is an introduction to the business of day trading on U.S. equity markets through direct access day trading (DAD) terminals. Books such as this can never cover all the details of day trading, which grow and evolve continually. It can give readers only a general idea of how the business of day trading works and how to get started in Canada if they wish to trade full time. To keep it short, I have assumed that you've already traded some stocks in the past, that you know the difference between a full-service broker and a discount broker, and that you know the difference between a bid and an offer price.

Much of the information in this book reflects my own opinions and those of other successful day traders. I encourage all of you to do your own research and verify all facts before making any decision regarding the stock market or related fields. It isn't for everybody. In fact, it isn't a business I recommend for most people.

Day trading is an extremely risky business. I've often told a story involving $50,000 in cash, a jug of gasoline, a front lawn, and a lit match. Imagine spreading all that cash on your front lawn, saturating the bills with gasoline, lighting the match, and holding it between your thumb and index finger while standing at the edge of the lawn. I picture people in Canada in such a situation when they decide to trade stocks using the methods and styles that hundreds of others use every day to earn a respectable living. If you aren't in complete control, if the wind catches your match and you make the mistake of dropping it onto the money, your hard-earned cash will disappear faster than the market drops when U.S. interest rates rise a couple of percentage points.

Day traders should be prepared to lose most or all of their trading capital, and you should trade only risk capital. If you lose this money, your lifestyle will not change. You should never use borrowed money or money with which you intend to pay the rent or the mortgage. Some day traders open margin accounts, which give them access to credit secured by their trading assets. In other words, they borrow money to execute trades, and they sometimes sustain losses that exceed their initial trading capital. In plain English, you can lose more than you have! I advise against opening a margin account.

Day traders must also be responsible for their own actions. Each day trader is accountable for every completed trade, even if the trader did not intend to make it. Please, if you are a beginning trader, be extremely careful when executing trades. Innocent mistakes can be costly.

Having said all this, I'd like to state that I've always been fascinated by books that explain get-rich-quick schemes. They are often fun to read, and I end up daydreaming about how my life would change with all that extra money. They're often simply written, and they make me feel that my dreams are within my grasp. Sometimes these books contain great ideas, sometimes they don't, and sometimes they contain partial truths or outdated formulas. Nevertheless, I think they reflect our times and reaffirm something about our basic human nature. I know this from reading get-rich-quick books written at the turn of the century. They show that, for all our technological prowess, human nature has not changed much. People have always felt an urge to trade, to speculate, and to gamble, whether they were swept up by the great tech stock rally of the 1990s or the great tulip rally of 16th-century Holland.

However, this is not a get-rich-quick book. In my time as a day trader, market maker (a term I'll explain in greater detail later), and head trader/trainer at the first and largest direct access electronic brokerage in Canada, I've talked to thousands of people who, like me, have also read all the get-rich-quick books and all the stock-picking books around and who, like me, are interested and even amused by the writings. But in their attempts to better their financial lives, they have never encountered a book that deals with the realities of trading their own account in the digital age. Nor have I. What we have found are unlimited books on stock picking, trading strategies, sophisticated sales pitches, and pompous books by major institutional money managers who manage multi-billion-dollar funds.

In 1998, a plethora of new day trading books appeared on the market. Many of them are helpful, but none seem to deal with the realities of how to buy and sell stock in a fast-moving, electronic market or how to open up a successful day trading account in Canada. To that end, I decided to put on paper what I know about conducting transactions in the electronic marketplace, based on my own experiences and those of people around me. I decided to write about how we as Canadians face additional challenges in using direct access day trading terminals here on Canadian soil. Consider the following: If you own 1,000 shares of EBAY or AMZN or RHAT or CMGI or any of the really volatile stocks, which can drop two points in as many minutes, and you go to sell that stock using the wrong route, the transaction can take several minutes. Several minutes can mean several dollars. On 1,000 shares, this can mean the difference between a healthy profit and a disastrous loss.

So how do you buy and sell stock efficiently? You can hire a full-service brokerage to do it for you, and you can even enter your orders on-line. TD Waterhouse, Charles Schwab, Datek, E-Trade Canada, Action Direct, and many others offer excellent full service online. In the process, you'll incur exorbitant commissions or less-than-stellar execution, sometimes both at once. If you're investing for the long term, you may not mind. But if you actively trade for a living, you'll eventually decide to do it yourself.

Full-service discount brokerages take the other side of your trades; non-discount brokerages rape you with high commissions, then take the other side as well. Eventually, if you trade for a living, you'll get burned enough that you'll want to cut the broker and trader's cost out of the equation. With new laws and technological advances in place, you can do just that. Formerly reserved for market professionals, and available only at a prohibitive cost, direct access to stocks, options, and global currency markets is now available to individuals, for a small and manageable fee. It is indeed a brave new world.

With a computer and a phone line, you can trade directly with a specialist on the floor of the New York Stock Exchange (NYSE). You can appear, along with all other professional participants, on the virtual floor of the NASDAQ, from anywhere in the world. You have the control, you do the execution, and you keep all the proceeds that formerly went to the broker and trader.

But trading your own account directly entails certain responsibilities. Anyone who has ever traded through a direct-access-oriented electronic brokerage knows you don't just buy or sell. The securities markets are exactly that: markets, full of buyers and sellers. If you want to sell something, you need to find a buyer. It's your job as a trader to locate the buyer.

I will assume you have heard of electronic communications networks (ECNs). These online systems enable the trading of shares by individuals outside the stock exchange itself. Orders are completed directly at a fraction of the usual costs, and private investors have direct access to information about buyers and sellers usually reserved for members of the exchange, but at a cost of less than $100 a month. Some brokerages claim their ECN is the best, but why? In what way? Every route of execution works differently in different situations. All are truly amazing, given certain circumstances, and utterly useless in others. The best of the electronic brokerages offer full access to a multitude of routes, so you can point and click to designate one or another. But which route is best to use in which situation? People who do not take this question seriously have obviously never traded their own accounts.

No discussion about which route is the fastest, surest way to transact would be possible without a thorough discussion of the road map of buying and selling: the NASDAQ Level II quotes montage. What is Level II and, more importantly, how do you interpret it? How do you tell what the market makers are doing? And what games and tricks do market makers play? This book is not going to endear me to any market makers nor will it make me friends in the old boys' club on Wall Street and Bay Street, but I'm going to outline just what it is that market makers do, how they do it, and how to spot it. And I don't mind upsetting them, because I'm the least of their problems. The world is changing. An electronic revolution in the truest sense is sweeping the world's equity markets, and many of the financial communities' pillars of strength are reinventing themselves to avoid obsolescence.

This is, therefore, the first Canadian book about the new electronic era of direct access day trading. DAD created the newest breed of traders: the swift traders. These are day traders who take relatively quick profits in short periods using the latest tools. What are the tools and how do you use them?

With a little knowledge and today's technologies you can buy and sell stock faster and with more transparency than professional market makers themselves. It's possible to turn a small trading account of $25,000 into an account worth millions. Many people across Canada and in the U.S. have done just this. But it is more important to note that many more people have been hammered and lost everything on the anvil called speculation. Unscrupulous get-rich-quick schemes can be found in all industries and are especially prevalent in the fields of gambling and stock speculation. These may consist of simple or complex systems, which you can purchase from a so-called expert, or they may come in the form of very expensive courses guaranteed to turn anyone into a successful trader. The least scrupulous ones usually recommend a particular brokerage (which, of course, will give you a huge credit line) and encourage scalping as a business plan for people new to trading. New traders, by the way, are the last people who should use huge lines of credit to scalp. Many traders make great livings scalping, but for reasons to be discussed shortly, it is one of the hardest ways to make a buck over the long term. Scalping with great success requires experience and knowledge. I hope this book will shorten part of the learning curve. But it won't eliminate the need for knowledge and experience, which must be acquired through hard work, practice, and study.

Finally, there is the age-old debate about education and evolution. Are great traders born great or do they become great through practice and hard work? I believe they become great and that those few who turn their accounts into enormous empires worth more than the GDP of many small countries also have a certain gift, a knack for the game. They are persistent. They educate themselves through all means available, including the most effective and relentless school of hard knocks: the stock market.

This book may help you turn your account into just such an empire. But I hope you don't read it with that in mind. I'll leave that to the get-rich-quick books. Trading is a ruthless, competitive game, in which the losses are real and instantaneous. Day trading, in particular, is a tough, hard game. The purpose of this book is not to turn you into a supertrader or to give you some secret that will make you rich overnight. This book is oriented toward the singular purpose of assisting you in deciding whether or not day trading might be a full-time career for you and to help those of you already day trading to become successful, defining a successful trader as one who understands the game and the risks involved and has the necessary skills and tools to minimize risk and implement a trading plan.

That's it. If you are one of the gifted, that's your business. If you are one of the gifted, if you have the persistence to work hard and accept the heartbreak that will come with inevitable loss from time to time, and if you have the foresight to continually educate yourself in an ever-evolving game, hats off to you. For the rest of you, this book may be the start of something new and wonderful in your life.

2

A Good Day's Work: What Is Day Trading?

Simply put, day trading is the practice of profiting from intraday (within a single day) moves in the equity market and closing all positions by end of day. Once in a while, many successful day traders hold a position overnight, and some even hold positions for a few days at a time. But this book will focus primarily on the trading style most widely followed by day traders: momentum, short-time-frame trades primarily on the NASDAQ exchange.

Day trading can be highly profitable. So can scalping—trading quickly for small profits—at least for a time. However, by limiting yourself only to scalping, you take tremendous risk for minimal gain, and you miss the big picture. Many stocks move four, five, or more points intraday. It doesn't make sense to ignore all this potential out and, by scalping, take more risk for tinier profits. (See Chapter 24 on "Risk/Money Management" for an in-depth discussion.)

Securities markets become more volatile every day. Watching the market intraday, you can buy during rallies and sell short on sell-offs, thereby profiting from volatility. (We'll explain the details of selling short later.) In fact, on an awful day like the August 1998 sell-off, prepared traders can reap enormous profits that will change their lives.

Why should day traders close all positions by the end of the day? In a word, protection: By doing this, you can insulate yourself from adverse happenings overnight. Say you own 1,000 shares of a biotech company whose new technological widget is widely expected to win FDA approval. But news about the company comes out after market hours, and it is bad. The FDA doesn't approve the widget. By the market's opening the next day, the price of your 1,000 shares has been cut in half. Similar situations happen all the time. Holding no positions overnight keeps your losses contained. You may lose potential profit as well, and you must decide for yourself if you'd rather be safe than sorry. I don't recommend categorically that you close all positions by end of day. Many of the best profits I have seen came from holding overnight. I just want to discuss the reasoning behind the day trader's approach.

Remember, this book focuses on how you can buy and sell your positions in the fastest, most agile way possible, and how you can determine the approach to execution that best serves your needs at the time. Countless profitable trades have turned into losses because the trader lacked information about the execution systems available.

SCALPING: NOT RECOMMENDED

Likewise, you can profit from scalping. But there are bigger fish in the day trading ocean. In an average day, a scalper may buy a $10 stock and sell it for 10 1/8. An eighth doesn't sound like a lot, but on 1,000 shares it amounts to $125. Since the average scalper makes dozens of such trades a day, those fractions add up fast. (Of course, so do the commissions!)

The best scalpers sometimes trade 100 or more times a day. Like sharks swimming in shallow waters, they wait for a moment of weakness in a stock's price. And those moments occur all the time. However, as I've mentioned, if you concentrate on scalping, you will miss out on major moves, like the price of Yahoo rising from $27 a share to a split-adjusted $340. (Of course, you would have held Yahoo in your long-term investment account, right?)

Day trading involves speculation, and successful traders speculate only with a small percentage of their total account. Because it's highly risky, you should use only the money you can afford to lose when you become a day trader.

As an approach to day trading, I consider scalping to be uneconomical. For one thing, NASDAQ's new order-handling rules make it much more difficult to scalp profitably. Scalping also involves much higher risk, because you need to buy or short more shares to exceed the commissions charged on your trades. Yet the traders who often seem most eager to scalp—trading the most volatile, hardest-to-trade stocks—are often the newcomers to trading. To become a successful day trader, you must avoid get-rich-quick thinking. Scalping in today's market requires real skill. You have to understand fully how each order execution system works, and you need the power to make split-second decisions. You can develop this kind of knowledge with experience, but you won't acquire it from a five-day course or even a single book. In fact, to the best of my knowledge, this is the first book that deals with the way execution systems actually work.

In short, scalping for an eighth of a point in today's markets will prove uneconomical for anyone who is new to trading. You may enrich your broker and seminar instructor, but until you have a firm understanding of the basics of trading, you will likely end up as the one getting scalped.

RIDING THE PENDULUM: SWING TRADERS

Swing traders, on the other hand, tend to take a more conservative approach to trading. They tend to watch a comparatively small number of highly volatile or strongly trending stocks, and they employ strict risk-management controls to keep positions open for periods ranging from a few hours to several days. Compared to scalpers, who often know nothing about the stocks they trade, swing traders become extremely familiar with a few stocks, removing some of the risk associated with day trading. Many of these stocks move several or more points intraday or over several days. In fact, at the time of writing, I can name almost a dozen stocks that move five to 20 points intraday, every day. Swing traders tend to assume positions after they've established the period over which they expect the stock to rise or fall. And just as the best day traders close all their positions every day, swing traders close their positions once they see they've miscalculated their particular time frame.

Some swing traders I know approach trading with a momentum-driven philosophy, buying stocks during periods of unusual buying pressure and holding overnight for potential gap-ups to sell pre-market. Others buy stock splits with the intention of holding several days to capture the speculative price run-up. These sorts of knowledge-driven risk-averse plans, coupled with strict adherence to the rules of money management, are often more easily and safely accomplished.

ASSUME THE POSITION: POSITION TRADERS

Successful traders often take positions for a period of weeks or months based on their observations of short- or intermediate-term trends. "The trend is your friend" is what they'll tell you. Short- to intermediate-term trends are not sexy or exciting, because they don't provide the instant gratification of day trades. But they get results. By making educated decisions based on reason, you can remove as much risk as possible from your trading activities. If you look at the NASDAQ 100 during the second half of 1999, for example, you'll see a trend that presents gold for the taking. Pull up a chart with the symbol QQQ to see the NASDAQ 100 go up over 50 percent during that time period.

SERIOUS BUSINESS: INVESTING

Trading involves taking a specific position with a specific reason. It is not the same as investing.

To trade successfully, you must consider opportunity cost, price, slippage, risk, and a multitude of other factors in real time. In trading, as in speculation, you decide, for various reasons, that X will happen, so you do Y to take advantage of it. If X happens, you get out with a profit. If it doesn't, you get out with a loss. You are actively involved and watching.

Investing, on the other hand, involves much longer periods and complex strategies. You may buy a stock for its earnings record, its growth, or for other reasons. Most important, you own it for a long term of three, five, or ten years, or until you retire. You should invest the majority of your account, and certainly your RRSP.

Despite this advice, some firms allow individuals to actively trade their RRSPs. This seems misguided to me. You'll need your RRSP money for retirement, and you shouldn't do anything risky with it, especially if you are approaching retirement age.

You should consult a professional financial advisor for strategic financial planning before you risk anything in a self-directed trading account. Don't speculate until you truly have identified the money you can afford to lose.

If you are reading this book, however, you've probably already made the decision to actively trade your own account. Maybe you've even started to do this and are considering switching from a full-service brokerage to one that offers direct access to the markets. If so, the following section will be of interest.

3

Strokes and Folks: Different Kinds of Brokers

Should you use an online discount broker or a direct access day trading (DAD) brokerage? The answer, based on the number of trades you do, is fairly simple. If you do only a trade or two a week, you will do fine with one of the better online discount brokerages, for the following reasons:

– **Discounted commissions** (and probably less than wonderful execution). You are clearly not subject to the intraday vagaries of the market, so you probably won't need absolute control of your executions. Direct access trading requires your full attention, and you will need to become an expert trader to enjoy the benefits of direct access. But at this point, you are not trading enough to make the effort worthwhile. Meanwhile, you will probably benefit from the low commissions charged by the discount houses. The money you lose from slippage will probably amount to less than the costs of a top-of-the-line, real-time, front-end order-
execution platform, on a monthly basis.

– **Full, easily accessible information.** Most of the better full-service online brokerages offer news, financial reports, and well-designed account information, all set up for easy access by someone whose life doesn't revolve around the markets. The news may not be real time, but you can probably afford the 15- to 20-minute delay, considering your trading plan probably doesn't include scalping based on news hot off the press.

– **Twenty-four-hour access.** You can peruse your account at leisure from the luxury of your home or anywhere else, over the Internet.

– **You will still be able to work at your job.** Unless you're going to devote yourself to a new career, there's no reason to get a full direct access trading platform. It's overkill.

If you actively trade your account intraday, however, and you are committed to trading full time, you should consider a direct access

- **Control.** The ability to trade anytime, directly, gives you ultimate control. There's no substitute for real-time information coupled with the best and fastest execution systems in existence. Of course, there is a price to pay: you will be truly responsible for your own decisions. Sometimes taking responsibility is not a good thing, if you aren't ready and fully committed. But if you're considering trading direct, then you should be committed. Trading direct requires nothing less. Remember, you're trying to beat the traders at the market-making firms. They are trained, licensed, practised, and sharp. There aren't many professional suckers working for the majors. The high stakes of the game weed them out.

- **Lower costs overall.** Electronic brokerages will charge a hefty data-feed fee and higher ticket charges than a discount online brokerage. However, you will not be subject to the slippage incurred when your online full-service discount brokerage takes the other side of a trade. Remember, nothing in life is free. If the brokerage charges you a discounted commission, the additional money used to pay the broker and trader a living wage has to come from somewhere else, and one way or another, it usually comes out of your pocket.

- If the stock is bid 10 by 10 and you buy it at your discount broker, the broker will take the other side—buy it at 10 and sell it to you at 10. On 1,000 shares, that's $250 they'll keep for their trouble. And when you sell it, they'll do it again. So those two $9 **commissions** really cost you $500. When you add it all up, if you are aggressively trading your own account several times a day, you're missing out on a lot of money.

- **Work from anywhere.** The better direct access brokerages offer remote trading platforms. In other words, you can load the software onto your laptop computer and trade from anywhere as long as you have a good Internet connection. I knew a day trader who was trading on the NYSE directly during a visit to the Great Pyramids at Giza, Egypt. Of course, trading really isn't a vacation. It's a hard, often boring job. The fact that some people have travelled while doing it shouldn't make you lose sight of the rigours. (Nor did I say that the person visiting Egypt made any money, did I?) If it's a vacation you want, take one. But don't imagine that trading your own account will take you to a stress-free Shangri-la. Quite the opposite. With responsibility comes pressure. Putting your butt on the line every day is no joke. The fact that you can do it from home might actually ruin your home as a sanctuary.

No matter what your thoughts on trading, before you open an account at a DAD firm and begin to trade directly, you'll need to get most of the facts. You'll need a firm grasp of reading a Level II screen, the basic interpretation of a Level II screen, and a good understanding of most if not all the execution routes your firm has available.

4

Ten Questions to Ask When Choosing a Direct Access Day Trading Firm

Which firm is right for you? As I'll mention frequently, at the time I'm writing this book, there is only one company in Canada that legally offers DAD execution: Swift Trade Securities Inc. (**www.swifttrade.com**), headquartered in Toronto, so there really isn't much choice. Under current securities law, a Canadian living in Canada can't open a U.S.-based trading account. If you call E-Trade in the U.S., for example, and ask for an information package, you won't get one, because E-Trade in the U.S. can't open an account for someone in Canada.

However, other DAD firms will likely open in Canada. If and when they do, here are ten things you should look for in a direct access day trading firm:

1. Has it attracted successful traders who make money consistently? Any firm you trade at should have many already successful traders actively doing business there. The benefit is that you'll have an opportunity to chat with them, listen to what they say at weekly information meetings (held by most reputable firms), and learn from osmosis. In the world of day trading, success breeds more success. So you should trade where other traders have already found success.

2. Does the firm offer systems for executing trades such as SOES, SelectNet, ECN? (I'll discuss these systems in more detail in Part Two.) If your DAD firm offers only one or two execution systems, you will be at a serious disadvantage compared to your colleagues around the world who have access to multiple execution platforms. The more ways you can buy stock quickly and cheaply, the better chance you will have to make profits. Also, execution systems and platforms tend to go down or break from time to time. For example, if your firm offers only the SOES

execution system, and that part of the NASDAQ breaks for a few minutes or for the rest of the trading day, you will have no mechanism for buying or selling stocks. If, on the other hand, your firm offers three or more execution systems, you can continue to trade on the other trading platforms when one goes down.

3. Are the firm's commissions competitive with other firms? Current rates are charged either per trade or per share. The current average is $17 to $29 per 1,000 shares. Note that if you start at a firm that charges by the ticket or trade, your commission charges will be very high when you first begin trading with smaller lot sizes.

4. Who does the firm's clearing? Is your money held by a large, established, and reputable clearing firm? Examples of established day trading clearing firms are Southwest Securities (Dallas, TX) and Spear, Leeds, Kellogg (New York, NY). Newer and smaller clearing firms are, in my opinion, too risky to trade with.

5. Does the firm offer extensive training or just hand you a software manual and tell you to read it? Swift Trade, for example, offers a six-week full-time day trading course that covers theory and practice. Other firms offer weekend and weeknight courses ranging from two to 30 days. Costs vary from $1,500 to over $5,000 per course.

   Look for firms that will rebate or refund your course fees if you decide to trade with them. Also ask if the course is tax-deductible and if the firm is registered with any government bodies as a provider of registered educational courses. Firms registered as providers of certified educational courses and that offer a rebate on your training-course fee after you begin trading with them are probably looking after your best interests. Companies that offer two-day courses are most likely just generating revenues. After all, how can you learn a complicated subject such as day trading in a mere two days?

6. How long has the company been around? At firms that are just starting out, you'll tend to encounter many more technical glitches and problems than you will at firms that have been around the block a few times. Technical problems that remain unsolved

can cause you thousands of dollars in losses if they prevent you from executing your trade.

7. Are you getting direct access to the markets or do you have to use the Internet, which delivers slower execution and quotes? If you trade through the Internet, I guarantee you'll receive slower quotes and slower execution times than you'd get through a company with direct access via private communication lines.

8. Does the firm use the latest technology? Are its computers, monitors, and internal office networks up to date? Does it use the latest Pentium technology or a computer system that's generations old?

9. Does the firm provide you with your own trading terminal, your own charting and real-time news software, and your own Internet connection? Or do you have to share with fellow traders? Having your own terminal is definitely an advantage. It enables you to sit in the same spot every day, and you don't have to worry about finding a place to trade, even if you come in at noon.

10. And lastly, does the firm promise you the world and present day trading as an easy activity? If it does, run!

PART TWO

A Swift Trader Deals with the Execution

swift ('swift) adj

1. Moving or capable of moving with great speed
2. Occurring suddenly or within a very short time
3. Quick to respond

synonym see FAST

5

Ground Zero: A Primer on Execution Platforms

The tools available for execution fall into three main groups: market systems, electronic communication networks, and exchange facilities. All the routes work differently from one another, and all have specific advantages and disadvantages, given certain circumstances. The circumstances may be determined from a quick perusal of Level II, once you understand what to look for.

Part Two explains how each route works and identifies the particular situations that will bring out the best and worst in each route. You should check for updates as routes change their operating structure and add new functionality and as new systems come online. It also explains the NASDAQ quotes montages and provides examples of some typical situations you'll find on the Level II quotes montage.

In Chapters 13 to 20, I'll describe each specific route, first with a brief historical perspective, then by the way it works. Next I'll present a summary of advantages and disadvantages, and some personal anecdotal experiences I've had with the route. Finally, a graphical profile summarizes all this information.

Keep in mind that there are no hard and fast rules for what works in all situations. The markets are dynamic and fluid, and they change constantly, even as you place your order. The best you can do is learn how the routes work and when the routes will function in the manner intended.

Armed with this knowledge and your understanding of Level II as it relates to execution, you can feel confident in your ability to determine in real time the route that will best help you to achieve your goal, in all types of markets.

The proper tool for the job is nowhere more important than it is in the cyber jungle of the trader. You might use a steak knife to turn a screw, and it will work, eventually. You might also cut a steak with a screwdriver, and it will also work, eventually. But there are better ways to do the job.

Likewise, new tools for buying and selling stocks are now available. Using the old tools is like using a steak knife to fasten a screw. The SuperDot, for example, the execution vehicle long used by institutions and brokerages for trading on the New York Stock Exchange directly, is now available for personal use in Canada. With tools such as Level II, SOES, SelectNet and ECNs, you can buy at the bid, sell at the ask, and participate in the NASDAQ market at dealer prices. If you have command of such new and affordable tools, you can trade just as a market maker does, but without the market maker's legal responsibilities.

These tools enable an individual trader to move in and out of positions with greater speed and agility than market makers themselves. (We discuss market makers and what they do in Part Three.) No wonder market makers don't want you to have access to these tools.

These chapters will discuss all the new ways that individuals can purchase and sell listed and over-the-counter securities. Until recently, many of these methods were available only to institutions. But because of changes in the law and in attitudes, they have now been made available to individual traders.

Additionally, this section will deal in depth with the Level II montage, the order book of the NASDAQ. It will give the reader a thorough understanding of Level II, how it works, how to interpret it, and why an individual might want to have access to it if engaged in the trading of over-the-counter stocks. This understanding, coupled with a thorough understanding of the methods, routes, or tools with which one can buy and sell securities, will enable you to buy at the bid, sell at the offer, ascertain in real time the strength and direction of a stock before it moves, and enter and exit positions with greater speed and agility than market makers themselves.

6

Hi-yo, Silver: Waging the Level II Campaign

When you trade your own account, you will face periods when it seems impossible to sell or buy stocks, no matter what you do. In fact, in certain situations, which you can readily identify if you understand Level II, some order entry routes have distinct advantages over others.

An understanding of Level II and how it works is a prerequisite for understanding various tools such as SelectNet, SOES, SuperDot, and the ECNs. If you understand it, Level II resembles a map, showing you the fastest route to your destination. You then can select the route, and you're on your way.

Some routes will create a nearly instantaneous fill, whereas others, in the same circumstances, will result in nothing done. Understanding just how these tools work and when to use them is an absolute necessity to trading effectively. If you have been trading your own account, then you know there is no single sure-fire way of instantaneously entering or exiting a position. Depending on the situation, some work better than others. This section will provide you with an understanding of how all the tools work and when to use them.

Fortunately, there are only a few routes. You can master them all quickly and easily. Once you understand them, you can then distinguish their advantages from their disadvantages in a particular situation as easily as you distinguish a steak knife from a screwdriver.

Now for the hard, boring stuff.

There are three levels of quotes in the NASDAQ market. Brokers generally have access to Level I. Level I is also called the inside market. When you ask your broker for a quote, it's given from Level I. If you ask for a quote in Microsoft (MSFT), for example, your broker will say, "Microsoft is currently bidding 93 13/16 by 7/8" or "Microsoft is bid 93 13/16, offered 93 7/8." This means that a market participant is willing to pay $93 13/16 to buy a certain number of shares, and that a market participant (maybe the same one) will sell a certain number of shares at $93 7/8. So if you want to sell MSFT, you can currently sell it at $93 13/16 per share; if you want to buy it, you can, at $93 7/8 per share. You'll get similar quotes from Yahoo or any full-service traditional or online brokerage.

But Level I is only the very tip of the iceberg. Level I tells you the best bid and offer (offer = ask), that is, the highest price at which you can sell shares and the lowest price at which you can buy them. But you can get access to much more information. Suppose you could tell that, in the next few moments, the price would probably go up? Or suppose you could tell it would probably go down? To get this information, you don't need a crystal ball. But you do need practice, knowledge, and, most importantly, Level II.

MSFT	Last	93 7/8				15:57	----15:57----
High	94 1/16	Low	91 51/64	Tot Vol		17991500	93 7/8 100
BID ↓	93 13/16	ASK	93 7/8	Close		92 1/4	93 7/8 1000

NAME	BID	DIR	SIZE	#BEST	NAME	ASK	DIR	SIZE	#BEST
ISLD	93 13/16	+0	83	576	INCA	93 7/8	+0	37	378
INCA	93 13/16	+0	42	576	MWSE	93 7/8	-1/16	11	22
NITE	93 13/16	+0	22	180	SBSH	93 7/8	+0	10	51
FBCO	93 13/16	-1/16	10	19	REDI	93 15/16	-1/16	10	146
MSCO	93 13/16	+1/4	10	63	ISLD	93 15/16	+0	73	562
BEST	93 13/16	+1/8	10	32	MONT	93 15/16	-9/16	10	14
SLKC	93 13/16	+3/16	10	69	MSCO	93 15/16	+0	10	51
SBSH	93 13/16	+0	10	69	WARR	93 15/16	+1/16	10	9
EVRN	93 13/16	+0	9	2	GFIN	93 15/16	+1/16	10	31
ARCA	93 13/16	+1 13/16	2	40	AGIS	94	+0	10	37
GSCO	93 3/4	+1/8	10	39	PRUS	94	-1/2	10	25
PWJC	93 3/4	+1/4	10	24	HRZG	94	-1/2	10	25
DKNY	93 3/4	+0	1	6	MHMY	94	-1 1/8	10	1
JPMS	93 11/16	+0	1	6	GSCO	94	+1/8	10	37
REDI	93 5/8	+0	40	163	NFSC	94	+0	5	20
MLCO	93 5/8	+1/4	10	21	NITE	94	+0	3	127
PRUS	93 5/8	+1/4	10	23	LEHM	94	+0	1	11
BRUT	93 5/8	+3/8	2	22	SELZ	94	-1/16	1	3
LEHM	93 5/8	+0	1	31	MADF	94	+0	1	50
BTRD	93 9/16	+0	10	30	BRUT	94 1/16	+0	1	49
MHMY	93 9/16	-5/8	1	6	MLCO	94 1/8	-1/16	10	27
AGIS	93 9/16	+0	4	1	BTRD	94 1/8	+1/4	30	18
GFIN	93 9/16	+0	2	0	EVRN	94 1/8	+0	10	3
WARR	93 9/16	+0	1	0	SHWD	94 1/8	+0	1	1

Right side time/price list: 93 7/8 100, 93 7/8 1000, 93 7/8 300, 93 7/8 100, 93 7/8 1000, 93 7/8 4000, 93 13/16 10, 93 7/8 1000, 93 7/8 1200, 93 7/8 300, 93 7/8 200, 93 7/8 3600, 93 7/8 1000, 93 7/8 3600, 93 7/8 1000, 93 7/8 1000, 93 7/8 1100

NASDAQ Level II Quotes Montage

The screen capture on the previous page shows a Level II snapshot of Microsoft and all the market participants. Although NASDAQ market makers use Level III screens, the information on a Level III NASDAQ workstation screen is fundamentally identical to Level II. In other words, if you have Level II, you have access to the same information as the market makers.

This explains why NASDAQ market makers are so miffed: Their playing field has been levelled, and now any Tom or Jane (or Dick or Harry) can compete with them on nearly equal terms.

Life was hard enough for market makers before, but at least all the professional participants followed an unwritten practice of maintaining nice fat spreads. But now, in come Tom and Jane (and Dick and Harry). And Jane's not so greedy.

Jane is willing to make only an eighth or even a sixteenth, and on only a few shares. And with the increased liquidity of Tom and Jane, the market makers can no longer make their big fat spreads. This hurts them. For a while, traders at major firms raise their hands to the sky and bellow, "Where'd all the money go?!" There are layoffs. Firms close their doors permanently, and compensation packages at major firms are substantially reduced.

After all this, market makers can't make their big, fat spreads anymore. They have to split it with Tom and Jane (and Dick and Harry). Market makers have big mortgages and car payments, just like anyone else (well, maybe a little bigger) and now it's much harder for them to make a buck.

But Darwinian law rules the so-called cyber jungle. The market-maker system must adapt or pass out of existence. For now, at least, the individual has access to powerful tools that have never before been available to the nonprofessional trader.

The rest of this section is devoted to those knives and screwdrivers, arrows and blades of successful trading. Keep in mind that a quiet war is raging. Market makers are fighting for their very lives. And since we know they won't go gently into that good night, we must educate and train ourselves to play the game at its highest level. It's a zero-sum game: Somebody wins, somebody loses. In this context, scalping and getting scalped become distinct possibilities.

With all this in mind, you have to examine Level II, the virtual battlefield where great trading campaigns are waged. You must give careful consideration to Level II if you hope to see the market for what it is and not be distracted by the melee. You must understand Level II if you want to profit from the madness of crowds.

Sounds exciting, huh? It gets exciting, but first you have to slog through a bit of tedious information, presented in the next chapter.

7

Battle Stations: Mapping the Level II Battlefield

Before we begin, examine the capture below, which represents a Level II screen shot of Microsoft (MSFT), then review the definitions further in the chapter. The Level II screen below is officially called the NASDAQ Level II quotes montage.

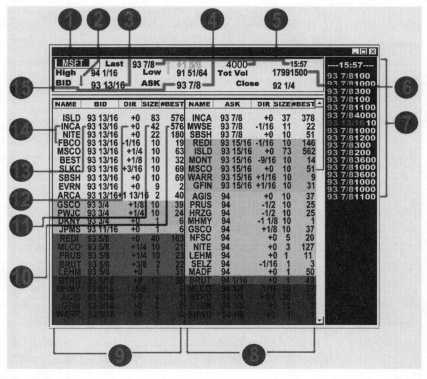

NASDAQ Level II quotes montage

Level II (L2) shows the current bids and offers of all market participants in a chosen stock. It updates dynamically, as market participants change their price and desired transaction size. The Level II quotes montage of a very busy stock will be in a constant state of frenzied flux; for an illiquid stock that few people care about, it will often remain static and unchanged for much of the day. Many of the smaller, less active stocks attract only a few market participants. But as many as several dozen individuals participate in more heavily traded stocks, such as Microsoft. The screen shot was taken at 15:57 (3:57 p.m.) EST, on a Wednesday. As you can see from the volume indicator (item 6), Microsoft has traded almost 18 million shares on the day.

During pre-market hours, particularly in the moments just before the market opens, prices often seem bizarre, with bid prices often higher than offers; this is because the market is not yet open, and some participants have not yet changed their price and size from the day before. In addition, market participants jockey around, raising and lowering their prices before the market opens to shake out the more desperate buyers or sellers. You should keep in mind that any pre-market displays by market makers are just that: pre-market. They are under no obligation to honour their displayed intentions until the market opens.

The pre-market machinations of market makers resemble the activities of banks on opposite sides of the street. At 6:30 a.m., the president of one bank comes in and sees that the bank across the street has posted a new, higher rate of interest. So the president at the first bank raises the rate, too, and a bidding war ensues, until one or the other, unwilling to do business beyond a certain price level, will go no higher. At this time of the day, the doors of the banks are still closed, and neither bank is open for business. Once the banks actually start transacting with customers, no one knows where they will set their rates.

Generally, Level II will be organized in the way displayed on the previous page. Different colours represent a different price level. There is no special significance to the colours themselves. They simply provide a quick visual indication of the depth of market participants at each price level. Here are some of the words and phrases that appear on a Level II quotes montage:

SYMBOL   The symbol of the stock.

TICK ARROW   This arrow will point down on a downtick, in which the last trade occurs at a price the same as or lower than the previous trade; it will point up on an uptick, in which the last trade occurs at a price equal to or higher than the previous one. This is important information, especially when trying to sell short.

BID   This is the best bid, i.e., the highest price at which a market participant will buy a stock. Also known as the inside bid, it is the bid price your broker will typically quote to you.

ASK/OFFER   This is the best offer, the lowest price at which any market participant will currently sell. Also known as the inside offer, it is the offer price typically quoted by a broker.

LAST SALE   Just as it says, this indicates the time of the most recent sale of a stock. In the screen capture, MSFT last traded 4,000 shares @ 93 7/8, and the trade occurred at 15:57, or 3:57 p.m. EST.

VOLUME   This is the number of shares traded so far today.

TICKER   The ticker provides simple sales data: time of sale, price of sale, and size of sale. The complete Time of Sales reports, which I will describe in detail later, contain much more information regarding a stock's activity. But as a quick reference, many traders find the ticker invaluable.

OFFER SIDE   This side of the quote montage contains the postings (not unlike the postings found in a newspaper) of all market participants wishing to sell. Notice that the very best price—the lowest price at which anyone will sell—is at the very top of the montage. Remember, each colour represents a price level.

BID SIDE   This side of the quote montage contains all the postings of all market participants currently willing to buy stock. Note that the highest price anyone will currently pay for stock is found at the very top of the montage.

So, the left side of the Level II montage represents the bid (buyer) side of the participants' quote. Everyone on the left desires to buy at the prices and sizes noted. The right side is the offer (selling) side, displaying everyone's intentions to sell.

If you wish to buy stock, and you have direct access to the market, you can do it in two ways: You can either take the inside (best) offer and buy the stock right away, or you can join the market participants bidding for the stock and perhaps buy the stock cheaper, when someone decides to hit your bid. You would then keep the spread for yourself.

IMPORTANT TERMINOLOGY: You hit bids; and you take offers. If you tell a trader to "hit the offer," the trader will not understand whether you want to buy or sell. This will wind up in confusion at best and, at worst, maybe even a sell when you really wanted a buy. Of course none of this will have any significance at a full-service brokerage; the brokers there don't even know the difference—they are salespeople, not traders. When you want to buy through a full-service brokerage (like Merril Lynch, for example) you'll get the best offer. But, of course, their traders take the other side. If possible, they will buy the stock at the bid and keep the difference.

NUMBER BEST   Also called "hammer," this is an optional informational item found in the better direct access trading platforms. It tells you the number of times in the current trading session that a market participant has remained at the best bid/offer after everyone else has left. I consider this feature nearly indispensable: It clues you in immediately to who the size buyer/seller may be.

If the montage shows someone bidding for only 100 shares, at a price only 1/16 above everyone else, while everyone else is bidding for similar size, you might not think twice about it. But if you found out that the person at the best bid has been there 132 times today, and nobody else has been there more than ten times, you might conclude that the person is a buyer of size. If this happened during a huge increase in volume on the day, you could form a strong impression of what's happening. I find the number best/hammer feature delivers very valuable information.

SIZE   This is the number of shares the market participant will transact at the displayed price. Your L2 (Level II) screen may be configured to show size in multiples of ten, so ten therefore represents 100 shares, as in the screen capture. Or you may configure it to show actual size, so that 100 represents 100 shares.

DIRECTION/CHANGE   This is also a very valuable feature, since it shows you whether the market participant has recently raised or lowered a bid or offer. Suppose you look at a stock and you notice that, in the last minute or two, nearly all the market participants on the bid side have raised their price, meaning that now, for whatever reason, they're all willing to pay more for the stock than they were five minutes ago. Then you notice that on the offer side, nearly all participants have raised their offers too, indicating they're not willing to sell so cheap anymore. Direction/change is a valuable indicator of short-term trader sentiment. Some trading platforms offer you a plus (+) or minus (–) indicator. Others, like the screen capture example, offer plus or minus and the amount by which the participant has changed the price.

PRICE   This is the price that the market participant presents to the world. Participants can change the price at any time, provided they are fulfilling their liabilities and duties as either market makers or ECNs.

MARKET PARTICIPANT   This is the firm that is bidding or offering the stock. It will be identified by a four-letter acronym. Examples: GSCO (Goldman Sachs), SBSH (Smith Barney), and MASH (Meyer, Schweitzer). ECNs are also market participants: ISLD (The Island), ARCA (The Archipelago), INCA (Instinet), etc. (I'll provide detailed information on the ECNs later in this section.) The participants highlighted in the screen capture are INCA (InstiNet) and FBCO (Credit Suisse First Boston). INCA is an ECN and FBCO is a market maker. For reasons soon to be discussed it is necessary to memorize the symbols for the ECNs so you can readily distinguish them from market makers. This won't be hard. There are only a dozen or so. Memorizing the market makers is also important, but it will take you much longer. (I have included a list of significant ones in an appendix.)

Keep in mind that each market maker must maintain a firm, two-sided quote. That means they must always stand ready to buy and sell at their displayed prices and sizes during market hours. Note that the market maker's bid price and offer price may be very far apart. This is the market maker's spread. Of course the market makers may change the price and size whenever they like, so the market maker's individual spread will vary throughout the day. Note also that the quote is two-sided. That is, the market maker may only appear at one place at a time on each side of the market. NOTE: ECNs are not market makers and are therefore not required to maintain two-sided quotes. (See the passage on ECNs later in this section.)

INSIDE MARKET   This is what your traditional broker quotes you. The difference between the bid and the offer is referred to as the spread. Note that unless brokers have access to Level II (and most don't), they will see only the best bid and offer, but not any of the actual montage. In fact, many traditional brokers don't even know what Level II is.

8

Clock Watching:
The Time of Sales Report

Time of Sales reports are not part of the NASDAQ Level II montage, yet these sales data are absolutely necessary to understand and monitor your interpretation of Level II information and executions. (We'll see an example later, when we discuss SelectNet, in Chapter 14.)

Time of Sales reports are also called Time and Sales reports, Print reports, Sales Data reports, and Sales reports. Of utmost importance to the trader, Time of Sales lets you know whether the print received was in line with all the transactions at the time of execution. It also gives you additional information such as whether that last print-point above the market was really a print at that price or whether it was simply a record of a transaction that occurred earlier.

Time of Sales differs from a simple stock ticker. It includes a time-stamped record of all the bid/offer changes of the market participants, as well as records of every transaction executed. If you place a stop loss or even a market order in an extremely liquid stock with your broker or directly online and receive a print that looks out of line with other trades at the time, Time of Sales enables you to see if the execution price is fair and equitable. It is especially valuable when considering prints on the NYSE. For example, if the price is the only print at that price, and every other print is half a point higher, there may be very good reasons for this. But then again, something may have gone awry.

At your request, your broker is required to represent you in an investigation of the print. This will involve filing a complaint with the regulatory organization governing the exchange where the trade took place. StockWatch keeps thorough time-coded records of every transaction and bid/offer in every stock. If there is a questionable print, StockWatch and the regulatory organizations will support your investigation of the trade. Ask your broker to advise and assist you in investigation of the print. Remember, you are a client, and it is in the broker's best interest to keep happy clients. They will be glad to assist in any investigation of a seemingly unreasonable print. If they're not, then report them and change brokers.

Please keep in mind that a print with which you may not be happy is not necessarily a bad trade. Trades that are clearly erroneous are generally bad, and a quick investigation of Time of Sales will clue you in to possible causes for the print. For example, a client once called me and said he had just bought 300 shares of an NASD National Market (NM) security at market. As he placed his market order, the prints were going off at 14 1/4. About twenty seconds later, he received his print: 14 3/4! Then he saw prints at 14 1/4 again! He called me screaming bloody murder since it looked like he had just paid half a point more for the stock than he should have. So I looked at Time of Sales, which indicated that just before he entered his order (and I mean seconds before), the offer changed to 14 3/4. And 5,200 shares printed at 14 3/4. It was the high of the day. It was very close, so I offered to investigate. I was told by NASDAQ that indeed, several seconds before my client placed the trade, the one market maker offered out at 14 3/8 moved his quote. Next in line was another market maker, at 14 3/4. He was happy to sell there, and when he moved his market, the next market maker was happy too. So, I had to give my client the bad news: All in all, it was a bona fide trade.

If my client had entered a limit order (an order to buy or sell a stock at a given price only, then this would not have happened. But as a market order (an order to buy or sell a stock at any price), it executed immediately. He was legitimately peeved, but the print was good.

The screen shots that follow show two Time of Sales reports for a listed stock and one for an over-the-counter (OTC) stock. Please note the different identifiers. They'll come in handy when examining a report:

TRADE   This indicates that an actual trade took place at the time shown.

IRG TRADE   This identifies an irregular trade, likely reported out of sequence or occurring on another exchange. For example, InstiNet trades are reported as irregular trades.

EXCH   This refers to the exchange where the trade took place. NYS is New York Stock Exchange. The rest are regional listed exchanges. In certain situations, listed stocks can trade on the NASDAQ, provided the firms trading them have met certain qualifying criteria. You will see the identifier NAS in the exchange field for NASDAQ trades.

BID/ASK You will encounter moments when no trades take place, but the specialists on the exchange change their price/size. Every change in price/size is time-coded and noted.

BEST BID/BEST ASK When a price is quoted that creates a new inside market, you will see the identifier "best..." showing that a new price/size has been entered, changing the inside market.

CLOSING/OPENING On the listed exchanges, during opening and closing procedures, specialists match the largest number of trades possible. The determined price will serve as the opening price and the closing price for market-on-close or market-on-open orders.

SLD/SOLD This refers to the fact that the trade being reported actually occurred at least twenty minutes ago.

FORMT/.T This refers to the fact that the trade occurred after-market, between 4:02 p.m. and 4:39 p.m.

INTRA This designates a trade that took place during the course of the day.

Date	Time	Price	Volume	Exch	Type	Bid	BSize	BEx	Ask	ASize	AEx	Cond
9/3/99	16:00	97 1/16	1000	NYS	Trade							
9/3/99	16:00	96 3/8	300	NYS	lrg Trade							Intra
9/3/99	16:00	96 3/8	2000	NYS	lrg Trade							Intra
9/3/99	16:00	96 3/8	200	NYS	lrg Trade							Intra
9/3/99	16:00	96 3/8	200	NYS	lrg Trade							Intra
9/3/99	16:00				Bid	96 1/2	100	PHS	97 3/16	100	NAS	
9/3/99	16:00				Ask	96 1/2	100	PHS	97 1/2	100	PHS	
9/3/99	16:00				Bid	96 7/8	100	NAS	97 1/2	100	PHS	
9/3/99	16:00				Ask	96 7/8	100	NAS	97 3/16	100	NAS	
9/3/99	16:00				Best Bid	97 1/16	1000	CIN	97 3/16	100	NAS	
9/3/99	16:00				Best Ask	97 1/16	1000	CIN	97 3/16	100	NAS	
9/3/99	16:00				Bid	96 15/16	1000	NYS	97 3/16	100	NAS	
9/3/99	16:00				Ask	96 15/16	1000	NYS	97 3/16	75000	NYS	Closing
9/3/99	16:00	96 3/8	3000	NYS	lrg Trade							Intra
9/3/99	16:00				Bid	97 1/16	1000	NYS	97 3/16	75000	NYS	
9/3/99	16:00				Ask	97 1/16	1000	NYS	97 3/16	75000	NYS	Closing
9/3/99	16:00				Bid	96 7/8	100	CSE	97 3/16	75000	NYS	
9/3/99	16:00				Ask	96 7/8	100	CSE	97 3/8	100	CSE	
9/3/99	16:00				Bid	96 15/16	200	CIN	97 3/8	100	CSE	
9/3/99	16:00				Ask	96 15/16	200	CIN	97 1/4	600	CIN	
9/3/99	16:00				Best Bid	96 15/16	700	BSE	97 1/4	600	CIN	
9/3/99	16:00				Best Ask	96 15/16	700	BSE	97 3/16	100	NAS	
9/3/99	16:00	96 1/2	4400	NYS	lrg Trade							Intra
9/3/99	16:00	96 1/2	2000	NYS	lrg Trade							Intra
9/3/99	16:00	96 1/2	1000	NYS	lrg Trade							Intra
9/3/99	16:00	96 1/2	200	NYS	lrg Trade							Intra
9/3/99	16:00	96 1/2	200	NYS	lrg Trade							Intra
9/3/99	16:00	96 1/2	1000	NYS	lrg Trade							Intra
9/3/99	16:00	96 1/2	200	NYS	lrg Trade							Intra
9/3/99	16:00	96 1/2	100	NYS	lrg Trade							Intra
9/3/99	16:00	96 1/2	1200	NYS	lrg Trade							Intra

AOL Time of Sales

A Time of Sales report for AOL is shown on the previous page. The elements found in Time of Sales for listed stocks are very similar to the elements found in a NASDAQ Time of Sales report. The time I have chosen for this report is the closing minute. Why the close? Because several items of interest appear only at time of close, including the closing price of the stock and the modifiers describing when the trade actually took place. Compare this to the NASDAQ Time of Sales report for MSFT (below).

```
MB Trader - (Untitled) - [*MICROSOFT CORP]
Page   Design   Time & Sales   Window   Help
         ||—MICROSOFT CORP—
```

Date	Time	Price	Volume	Exch	Type	Bid	BSize	BEx	Ask	ASize	AEx	Cond
9/9/99	15:59				Best Ask	94 1/16	20000	NAS	94 1/8	7000	NAS	up
9/9/99	15:59	94 1/8	2800		Trade							
9/9/99	15:59				Best Bid	94 1/16	25000	NAS	94 1/8	7000	NAS	
9/9/99	15:59				Best Ask	94 1/16	25000	NAS	94 1/8	7000	NAS	up
9/9/99	15:59	94 1/16	1000		Trade							
9/9/99	15:59	94 1/8	2200		Trade							
9/9/99	15:59				Best Bid	94 1/16	27000	NAS	94 1/8	7000	NAS	
9/9/99	15:59				Best Ask	94 1/16	27000	NAS	94 1/8	7000	NAS	up
9/9/99	15:59	94 1/16	500		Trade							
9/9/99	15:59				Best Bid	94 1/16	29000	NAS	94 1/8	7000	NAS	
9/9/99	15:59				Best Ask	94 1/16	29000	NAS	94 1/8	7000	NAS	up
9/9/99	16:00	94 1/8	100		Trade							
9/9/99	15:59				Best Bid	94 1/16	30000	NAS	94 1/8	7000	NAS	
9/9/99	15:59				Best Ask	94 1/16	30000	NAS	94 1/8	7000	NAS	up
9/9/99	16:00	94 1/8	800		Trade							
9/9/99	16:00	94 1/8	500		Trade							
9/9/99	16:00	94 1/8	2000		Trade							
9/9/99	16:00	94 7/64	100		Trade							
9/9/99	16:00	94 1/8	3000		Trade							
9/9/99	16:00	94 1/8	1000		Trade							
9/9/99	16:00	94 1/8	1000		Trade							
9/9/99	16:00	94 1/8	2500		Trade							
9/9/99	16:00	94 7/64	1000		Trade							
9/9/99	16:00	94 1/8	300		Trade							
9/9/99	16:00	94	300		Trade							
9/9/99	16:00	94 1/8	400		Trade							
9/9/99	16:00	94 1/8	2000		Trade							
9/9/99	16:00	94 1/8	2000		Irg Trade							FormT
9/9/99	16:00	94 1/8	1000		Irg Trade							FormT
9/9/99	16:00	94 1/8	5000		Irg Trade							FormT
9/9/99	16:00	94 1/8	100		Irg Trade							FormT
9/9/99	16:00	94 1/8	700		Irg Trade							FormT
9/9/99	16:00	94 1/8	1000		Irg Trade							FormT

MSFT Time of Sales report

There are several other optional items of limited interest found in most Level II setups. They are not relevant to Level II and of limited use.

The capture on the next page shows an over-the-counter bulletin board (OTCBB) stock. The larger issues in the bulletin board market display their quotes in the NASDAQ OTC Bulletin Board System. But these stocks are not NASDAQ stocks. Different order-handling rules apply to bulletin board stocks because of their exchange status, and they are not eligible for electronic trading. You cannot trade a bulletin board stock over your computer. The easiest way to identify a bulletin board

Name	Bid	Size	#Best	Name	Ask	Size	#Best
XDSL		9.187 ↓ +.031		1000	Kk 10:31		
High	9.375	Low	9.187	Acc. Vol.	66100		
Bid	9.156	Ask	9.250	Close	9.156		

----10:31----
9.187 1000

Name	Bid	Size	#Best	Name	Ask	Size	#Best
NITE	9.156	0	0	SHWD	9.250	0	2
USCT	9.125	0	3	ERNS	9.250	0	2
PCOS	9.125	0	4	MHMY	9.312	0	1
HILL	9.062	0	1	ALEX	9.375	0	0
MHMY	9.062	0	1	NITE	9.406	0	0
FRAN	9.000	0	0	POND	9.437	0	0
WIEN	9.000	0	1	KBRO	9.500	0	0
MASH	9.000	0	4	FRAN	9.500	0	0
FAHN	8.968	0	0	WIEN	9.500	0	1
HRZG	8.937	0	0	USCT	9.531	0	1
ERNS	8.937	0	1	HILL	9.562	0	1
ALEX	8.875	0	0	MASH	9.562	0	2

OTC bulletin board stock

stock is by the size of bid offered, which is always zero. The reason for this is that the quotes are subject and not firm. (With a firm quote, the market maker is liable to transact at the quoted bid/offer; a subject quote has to be confirmed with the market maker.) Since you cannot trade them over your computer, you usually need to call a trader at your brokerage to conduct trades in these issues on your behalf.

And that's it. If you know and understand the material above, you will have a good basic understanding of Level II and how to review sales data to learn about what actually occurred. You can become familiar with all this information with a few readings of a Level II quotes montage. However, it may take some time to develop your interpretive skills involving Level II. Don't worry. It's not brain surgery, but it is more complex than it appears, and it requires some careful real-time observation to perfect. You must perfect your understanding of Level II if you plan to trade actively.

9

Dead Giveaways:
Interpreting Level II

Now that you recognize all the stuff on a Level II screen, let's look at what it means. I'll deal with some of the trickier aspects of this subject in the section called "Games People Play" (Chapter 25), which deals specifically with activities of market makers. Here, I'll present the basics: conventional Level II interpretations, and how they apply to getting your order filled.

To understand what's going on in a given stock, you must watch it and know the participants. Market participants resemble horses in a race. Just because a horse is favoured to win (and everyone knows it, because the odds are published) the horse won't necessarily win. Nevertheless, you must know the participants to form your own interpretation of a given situation and to remove from the equation as much serendipity as possible.

For example, it may surprise the uninitiated that, in many stocks, one or two market makers trade a disproportionate amount of the stock's volume. When you think of these 800-pound gorillas, names like Goldman Sachs (GSCO) and Salomon Smith Barney (SBSH) come to mind. This is important, because market participants watch each other and follow each other's cues.

A great game of follow the leader is afoot every day in most stocks, and knowing the key market maker in a stock, commonly called "the axe," will help you determine a stock's short-term direction. The axe often directs the movement of a stock's price. If Goldman Sachs (GSCO) is on the bid, for example, has been on the bid all day, and is the axe in this stock, it may influence the timing of your current sell decision.

Laws of supply and demand suggest that if demand outstrips supply, the price will go up; if supply outstrips demand, the price will go down. Conventional wisdom says, "Don't trade against the axe." If the axe is a seller, you don't want to be a buyer, and vice versa. But this conventional thinking often does not go far enough. In today's market, the axes are fully aware of their reputation. This means they will use the public's perception to their advantage, trying to disguise their real intentions. (I'll deal with this in more detail in Chapter 25.)

It isn't enough simply to know the huge firms that trade the majority of a stock's liquidity. In a particular stock, the axe may change from day to day or even from hour to hour. Large institutions and mutual funds may use GSCO or SBSH as brokers to buy or liquidate large positions. When an institution wants out, it wants out for a reason, and will sell a million shares as quickly as possible, yet without causing the market to fall under excess supply.

The extent to which a market maker can buy or sell a huge amount of stock without noticeably affecting the stock's price is a measure of the market maker's skill. Today, a mutual fund may hire Smith Barney to sell 100,000 shares and be done; tomorrow, the same mutual fund may hire Herzog (HRZG) to buy 50,000, and so on. You never know how many shares the axe has been ordered to buy or sell, but there is a way to determine that a market participant is a buyer or seller of size.

This is important information. If you want to buy a stock, and the axe has been selling huge amounts of stock today, and furthermore, the axe is on the offer, you may want to reconsider. This, obviously, is information available only on Level II quotes, not Level I; in other words, your broker, using Level I quotes, won't be able tell you. (Remember, brokers are salespeople, not traders.)

Most Level II quote screens come with a configurable option of #Best. (Please refer to the RealTick diagram on page 24 for a further description and to see where on the screen it will appear.) This option refers to the number of times in the current session that a particular market participant has been on either the best bid or offer after everyone else has left. The market participant that has been willing to buy more stock at a particular price than anyone else or to sell more stock than anyone else is called the axe.

The identity of the axe can be critical not only when making a decision about taking a position, but also about how you enter or exit the position. (I'll cover this in more depth.) If the price of a stock rises throughout the day, or if it falls throughout the day, an examination of #Best will help you to determine if there is a buyer or seller of size on the day. If, for example, you determine that a certain market maker is buying a huge amount of stock on the day and is currently on the best bid, you might think twice about selling now. The laws of supply and demand suggest that, as long as the market maker is buying, the price may continue rising.

ODETA				11 1/4	↓	+1/16		200		Ot		14:10
High		11 7/16		Low		10 7/8		Acc. Vol.		15300		
Bid	↓	11 1/4		Ask		11 3/8		Close		11 3/16		

Name	Bid	Chg.	Size	#Best	Name	Ask	Chg.	Size	#Best
CWCO	11 1/4	+0	1	7	MASH	11 3/8	-1/8	23	4
INCA	11 1/8	+1/8	10	5	REDI	11 7/16	+0	5	1
SHWD	11 1/8	+0	1	1	RILY	11 1/2	+0	10	0
ALLN	11	+1/8	10	0	HRZG	11 1/2	+0	1	0
CRUT	11	+1/2	4	0	SLKC	11 1/2	+1/4	1	0
BTRD	10 7/8	+0	10	0	ALLN	11 13/16	+0	38	0
HRZG	10 7/8	+0	1	0	NITE	11 7/8	-1	10	1
RILY	10 3/4	+0	10	0	CRUT	12	+0	1	0
ISLD	10 3/4	+1/8	2	0	CWCO	12	+1/4	1	0
NITE	10 5/8	+0	1	0	SHWD	12 1/2	+0	1	0
SLKC	10 5/8	+0	1	0	BLUE	13 1/4	+0	1	0
AVLN	10 1/2	+0	1	0	AVLN	17 1/2	+0	1	0
BLUE	10 1/4	+0	1	0	INCA	0	+0	0	0
MASH	10	+0	3	0	ISLD	0	+0	0	0
REDI	0	+0	0	1	BTRD	0	+0	0	0

Level II screen shot showing the axe, under #Best

Please take a look at the above screen shot, which represents an L2 screen. Note how the buyers/sellers of size on the day are easily identified here using #Best/hammer. This is somewhat exaggerated in this illustration, and you will rarely find such a clear indication of the axe. That's because market makers fully appreciate the appearance created by those numbers, and they will go to great lengths to disguise their intentions.

If market makers hop on and off the bid/offer to change those numbers and put people off the scent, then what use is #Best/hammer? In my opinion, it still has value. But you must interpret what you see. (When you have read Chapter 25, "Games People Play," you will have a clear understanding of just what it is that market makers do, and so you will be in a better position to interpret these kinds of numbers.)

So why are the market makers in the L2 screen in this example displaying their intentions so clearly? The answer is simple: The security quoted above is not an actively traded security. Most trades in this security involve institutional and retail investors, who are interested in this stock over the long term. Nor does this stock show much relative volatility, so it does not attract intraday speculators. So market participants may feel comfortable trading this stock in old-school ways, showing size and intentions, because there simply are no day traders waiting to pick them off and cut into their profits.

Is it advisable to day trade a stock like this? Probably not. Time spent trying to affect orders in an illiquid stock with little volatility or speculative interest and whose market participants are familiar with one another is probably time better spent elsewhere. An illiquid stock with low to no beta (a measure of a stock's volatility) does not provide a friendly environment for active intraday speculation.

I chose to present this screen for two reasons: first, to show clearly how #Best/hammer works; and second, to show that size bids and fat spreads don't necessarily mean a stock is suitable for speculation.

There have been countless situations in which #Best and a little interpretation have been invaluable, even in stocks with scores of participants, where numerous market makers show large numbers. Here's an example, from my own experience: There was a buyer of size in a stock in which I was long in anticipation of a run-up. At a particular time in the day, the price of the stock was up about one point from where I had bought it, giving me a healthy profit on my 1,000 shares.

Then I noticed that the axe, whom I had identified using #Best and a careful observation of the trading in this stock, had dropped its bid. Now the axe appeared on the offer, showing larger size offered as well. At the same time, I noticed that InstiNet appeared on the best bid. A number of trades went off at the bid, and I was considering liquidating my long position. (If the axe was done buying, and its buying was the reason for the run-up in price, then the moment the axe disappeared would be the moment I'd sell). But I soon noticed the appearance of several more sellers, as well as some ISLD and ARCA offers at prices in between the spread. They were either liquidating their long positions or selling short in front of the axe, whom they thought was a seller. And InstiNet was soaking up all the shares that were being sold.

I surmised that the InstiNet bid might really be the axe in disguise. I waited, deciding to risk a little profit. Several moments later, InstiNet left and the axe appeared again on the best bid, disappearing off of the offer. The price of the stock paused for a moment, then rocketed up. Many prints hit the tape, as I assumed the axe was taking the offers.

It had become apparent that the axe, a size buyer on the day, wasn't really finished buying. It just wanted to let the stock breathe for a few moments. By offering out shares (perhaps the axe had a client who wanted to sell too?) it hoped to induce sellers so that it could buy the stock more cheaply. When no real sellers emerged, it decided just to buy the stock and finish the order. From the look of things, the axe just started taking the offers. Several large prints hit the tape and, moments later, I got out—of a point higher because I had pegged it accurately as a buyer of size who wasn't finished.

This sort of interpretive manoeuver requires careful study of the stock and the market maker, and it's not foolproof. Careful observation and practice help, but #Best in and of itself is not sufficient to see you through successfully each and every time. (Later, in Chapter 25, I'll help you develop a better understanding of market maker behaviour so you can interpret it more accurately.)

10

Nothing Up My Sleeve: Level II Situations & Their Interpretations

Now that you understand Level II and the items you can find on it, let's examine what you should look for when determining how to enter and exit positions. You look for the same things when deciding to enter or exit positions as you do when identifying movers, but with a different emphasis.

This chapter identifies what you should look for when you enter an order. It will also help you identify the stocks that will move and whether they will go up or down. Ultimately, it will help you execute with the greatest of speed.

YAHOO INC								
YHOO 173 3/16 ↓ -11/16 100 Ot 13:32								----13:32----
High 177 Low 172 3/16 Acc. Vol. 5834800								173 1/4 400
Bid 173 3/16 Ask 173 1/4 Close 173 7/8								173 1/4 600
								173 1/4 100
Name	**Bid**	**Size**	**#Best**	**Name**	**Ask**	**Size**	**#Best**	173 1/4 100
ISLAND	173 3/16	400	1	MONT	173 1/4	300	9	173 1/4 200
ISLD	173 3/16	400	592	ISLAND	173 5/16	294	0	173 3/16 100
INCA	173 3/16	300	589	ISLD	173 5/16	200	613	173 3/16 300
BTRD	173 3/16	200	112	ISLAND	173 7/16	300	0	173 1/4 100
ARCHIP	173 3/16	200	1	ISLAND	173 15/32	100	0	173 1/4 300
ARCA	173 3/16	200	47					173 1/4 300
AGIS	173 3/16	100	36					173 1/4 100
REDI	173 3/16	100	77					173 3/16 100
MWSE	173 1/8	1000	7					
ISLAND	173 1/8	6	1					
ISLAND	173 1/64	100	1					

Conventional Level II screen: buyers versus sellers

Conventional Level II interpretation centres itself on a supply-and-demand price model: If there is a lot of demand relative to supply, the price should move up. Likewise, if there is a lot of supply relative to demand, the price should fall.

Conventional interpretation provides a very good starting point for making a decision, but you should never use conventional interpretation in a vacuum to determine strength and direction. In the Level II quotes montage on page 42, for example, you can compare the number of buyers relative to sellers and tell, in theory, that the price will move up faster than it will move down because of the number of shares bid for versus offered. In this case, however, the stock went down several moments later. There were many reasons for this: For one thing, the markets were strongly down on this day. In addition, Yahoo had just reversed a very nice run.

The point is that Level II may provide the data you need to make an accurate interpretation of the market, but you must also learn *how* to make an accurate interpretation. Conventional approaches to interpretation often fall short. This chapter tells you what to look for and, more importantly, why you need to look for certain things when interpreting Level II. Combined with later chapters on execution routes and market maker games, it will give you a good understanding of how to execute with confidence.

Using conventional interpretation you can examine data to identify stocks on the move. But you still need more. Who is on the bid/offer? Is it the axe or the axe in disguise (as an ECN) or is it simply a market maker fulfilling their duty of providing liquidity in the stock? Perhaps it's an ECN or market maker showing a complete natural customer order?

This process of identification affects your plan of execution in entering an order. For example, some routes work very well against ECNs; others do not work at all against ECNs. So an understanding of just who is bid/offered is critical to your choice of route.

Additionally, your decision will depend on the participant on the other side of the market. Are there already many orders working for the stock you are trying to trade? For example, if you are trying to sell 100 shares of a stock that currently has only 100 shares bid, and there are already ten orders entered (with an aggregate size of more than 2,000 shares) you know right away that your order has little hope of filling. So you can make alternate plans and save time that would otherwise have been wasted.

As I mentioned, this chapter covers conventional approaches to interpreting data before executing an order. In subsequent chapters, I'll discuss the means of execution: the routes. In Chapter 25, I'll deal with advanced Level II interpretation and market maker tactics. After reading this chapter, you'll recognize the situations you might encounter in which you will have to make fast decisions that take risk and other factors into account.

	E-NET INC									
ETEL		5 11/32	↑	+2 11/32		500	Os	9:46		
High	5 1/2	Low	4			Acc. Vol.	1370800			
Bid	5 23/32	Ask	5 3/4			Close	3			

	Name	Bid	Chg.	Time	#Best		Name	Ask	Chg.	Time	#Best
p	ARCHIP	5 3/4	+0	9:47	1	P	ARCHIP	5 1/2	+0	9:47	0
P	ARCHIP	5 3/4	+0	9:47	1	O	HRZG	5 3/4	+0	9:47	0
P	ARCHIP	5 3/4	+0	9:47	1	O	USCT	5 3/4	+0	9:47	2
P	ARCHIP	5 3/4	+0	9:47	1	O	SLKC	5 13/1(	+1/8	9:47	0
O	ARCHIP	5 3/4	+0	9:47	1	O	INCA	5 7/8	-3/8	9:47	0
P	ARCHIP	5 3/4	+0	9:47	1	O	MASH	5 7/8	-1/8	9:47	3
P	ARCHIP	5 3/4	+0	9:47	1	O	BRUT	5 7/8	-1/8	9:47	0
O	ISLD	5 23/3(	+0	9:47	14	O	ISLD	5 7/8	+0	9:47	7
O	NITE	5 23/3(	+0	9:47	1	O	FAHN	5 7/8	+7/3	9:47	4
O	REDI	5 11/1(	+3/1	9:47	2	O	GRUN	5 7/8	+0	9:47	1
O	ARCA	5 5/8	+0	9:47	9						
O	ARCHIP	5 5/8	+0	9:47	1						
O	ARCHIP	5 5/8	+0	9:47	0						
O	ARCHIP	5 5/8	+0	9:47	0						
O	ARCHIP	5 5/8	+0	9:47	0						
O	SHWD	5 5/8	+0	9:47	1						

High buying pressure on ETEL

In the Level II screen above, you'll note high buying pressure on ETEL. Yet the stock is still bid 5 23/32, offered 5 3/4. All the ARCHIPs you see reflect the individual orders in the ARCA ECN. (See Chapter 15 on ECNs for further explanation.)

You should take note of several things: First, there's heavy buying pressure on the bid side. As you can see, many ARCHIPs are bidding for the stock.

(I'll discuss in more detail ARCHIPs and ARCA ECN in subsequent chapters. For the time being, I've used ARCA ECN here simply for explanatory purposes. Several ECNs behave similarly to ARCA, notably NTRD, but more people have access to ARCA than any other similar ECNs.)

In addition to the high number of buyers in this stock relative to sellers, you should also note the direction indicator. Almost everyone has raised their bid and offer recently, an indication of current investor sentiment that the price is going up. Market participants have indicated they will pay more for the stock than they would have paid five minutes ago, and they're also unwilling to sell it as cheaply as they would have recently.

These two factors tell you that, if laws of supply and demand hold up, at least in the very near term, this stock will go up. If you were to decide to sell now, you would have a good chance of offering out and being taken. The Level II screen capture below shows the situation several moments later. You can see that this stock has indeed bid up a little bit. Had you purchased it at the time you first looked at the screen or held off a few moments in selling, you might have been able to offer it out at 6 1/8, for a profit of around 1/4 a share, or $250 on 1,000 shares.

E-NET INC

ETEL		5 31/32	↑	+2 31/32	500	Os	9:53
High	6 1/8	Low		4	Acc. Vol.	2030200	
Bid	5 31/32	Ask		6	Close	3	

	Name	Bid	Chg.	Time	#Best		Name	Ask	Chg.	Time	#Best
P	ARCHIP	6 1/8	+0	9:53	1	P	ARCHIP	5 15/16	+0	9:53	1
P	ARCHIP	6 1/8	+0	9:53	1	O	USCT	6	+0	9:53	2
P	ARCHIP	6 1/8	+0	9:53	1	O	MASH	6	-5/1	9:52	4
P	ARCHIP	6 1/8	+0	9:53	1	O	ISLD	6	+0	9:53	14
P	ARCHIP	6 1/16	+0	9:53	1	O	INCA	6	-1/4	9:52	2
P	ARCHIP	6	+0	9:53	1	O	NITE	6	-1/1	9:52	14
P	ARCHIP	6	+0	9:53	0	O	ARCA	6 1/8	+0	9:53	5
P	ARCHIP	6	+0	9:53	0	O	ARCHIP	6 1/8	+0	9:52	0
P	ARCHIP	6	+0	9:53	0	O	SLKC	6 1/8	+1/8	9:51	0
P	ARCHIP	6	+0	9:53	1	O	ARCHIP	6 1/8	+0	9:52	0
O	NITE	5 31/32	+0	9:52	2	O	FAHN	6 1/8	+0	9:52	6
						O	REDI	6 1/4	+0	9:51	0
						O	HRZG	6 1/4	+0	9:52	1
						O	ARCHIP	6 1/4	+0	9:51	0
						O	PENN	6 1/4	+1/4	9:51	0
						O	GRUN	6 1/4	+0	9:52	3

ETEL a few moments later

If you see an excess of supply or demand for a given security, you should certainly pay attention. Supply and demand are among the many indicators available to pick a stock to trade. When there is an inordinate amount of buying pressure and the directional indicators are almost uniformly positive, as they are above, individuals are willing to pay more to buy this stock and are less willing to sell it cheaply.

You should memorize the way a stock looks when it is under considerable buying or selling pressure. You'll need to appraise situations like this in an instant.

Several points are worth discussing. First, the stock shown on page 45 is on its way up, and shows no sign of weakness. The example that follows below shows a stock that, using conventional interpretation, looks like it is going down.

Name	Bid	Size	#Best	Name	Ask	Size	#Best		
MLCO	172 5/8	100	51	INCA	172 11/16	3500	516	172 5/8	500
MSCO	172 9/16	1000	25	REDI	172 11/16	1000	95	172 5/8	100
NITE	172 1/2	700	66	ARCA	172 11/16	500	95	172 5/8	100
INCA	172 1/2	500	592	ARCHIP	172 11/16	500	1	----13:37----	
MWSE	172 1/2	100	8	ISLAND	172 11/16	200	1	172 5/8	600
SWCO	172 1/2	100	5	ISLD	172 11/16	200	626	172 11/16	300
MASH	172 1/2	100	31	MLCO	172 11/16	100	20	172 11/16	100
ISLAND	172 7/16	1000	0	MONT	172 11/16	100	13	172 11/16	500
ISLD	172 7/16	1000	599	ISLAND	172 13/16	910	1	172 11/16	100
USCT	172 7/16	100	10	AGIS	172 13/16	100	51	172 5/8	100
				BRUT	173	100	27	172 5/8	100

YHOO going down

Note that in this stock there are very few buyers relative to sellers. There is also very little ARCA or ISLD activity, and the direction indicator is not configured. However, there is a lot of volume on the sell side and very little on the bid, and many of the participants on the bid are showing the smallest size possible, only 100 shares each. Meanwhile, several thousand are offered. Again, if rules of supply and demand hold true, this stock is headed down, at least in the short term, unless something changes.

By watching Level II update dynamically, you can gauge the strength and direction of the stock, at least in the very short term. This is not a guide to picking stocks, although, as you'll see, you can make educated guesses about the short-term movement of a stock. This movement will certainly influence your timing and choice of route.

The examples above demonstrate that gauging strength and direction and taking quick positions can generate quick profits. But to do this consistently is much more risky than it looks.

The basic risk is that the party ends the moment you buy: You buy at a higher price than you may have intended, because of the strength, and you sell a few minutes later, at a lower price, because of the supply that comes into the market. The second example (the one on page 44, with all the ARCAs), seems to show a cut-and-dried profit upon first examination, until you add execution to the equation. With such strong upward pressure, just how would you buy this stock? You can see how many bids there are in the ARCA book for stock at 3/4. If you tried to buy stock from USCT of HRZG at 5 3/4, simple addition tells you that you'd never get it at that price, unless something changed. You'd have no chance. To try to buy those 100 shares at 5 3/4 would guarantee you nothing but frustration.

Example two on page 44 shows a dramatic example of upward pressure. You should recognize the telltale signs whether you're picking a stock on the move or choosing your entry/exit strategy. In both the second and third examples (on pages 44 and 45), it would be simple to sell: You could offer the stock at the ask and rest assured you'd be taken. However, buying in a situation like this becomes a little more complicated.

Were you to decide to buy at this point, you might have to go higher, right away.

If you bought right now, at 7/8, you might prevent the sort of aggravation generated by chasing a stock up or down. After all, sometimes it's better to make a decision and stick to it, recognizing the vagaries of the market.

Keep in mind that there is no single route to guarantee a purchase price in a dynamically changing market. You just have to adapt to changing circumstances. However, it's important to realize the seriousness of this situation. If you buy at a higher price, you're taking on much more risk. You should be aware, for example, of the presence of limit orders around round numbers. In this case, at or near six dollars, there may well be many hidden orders to sell. They are hidden because the price has not traded there yet, and trading there will trigger the order. You should consider this possibility when you consider a buy at 5 7/8 and if you want to sell. If you are considering holding off selling or offering out at six, and a seller emerges just shy of six, you may have to re-evaluate your plans.

In later chapters on execution routes, I'll discuss the routes that work in given situations. For now, I'll concentrate on your mindset. You need to judge just what's happening on Level II and estimate your chances of getting executed.

If you happened to be short this stock and it suddenly took off with runaway buying pressure, you'd need to focus so you could see the situation for what it is. Who is bid? Who is offered? How many shares are bid/ offered? Are they market makers or ECNs? Which way is the stock headed?

In addition to simple supply and demand, you must take into account the condition of the market in that security. If many sellers suddenly appear just when you are getting ready to sell your stock, you should be prepared for a fight. The market is indeed a market. If you are a seller, you bear the responsibility for locating a buyer. Offering out in the hopes that someone will take your stock may or may not be the best approach under the circumstances.

So far, you might have found these initial examples a bit difficult to understand. They are not the easy no-brainers that you find in most execution tutorials. They resemble more closely the everyday electronic battlefields where you will fight if you plan to profit by day trading. It would be wonderful if there were always enough stock to go around for everyone. But with the increasing volatility of the markets, combined with the entry of more and more inexperienced players, who buy stock at prices too dear and have to take a loss, it will only get harder to execute as time goes on.

This isn't a game for the faint of heart. Sadly, however, the most inexperienced players, like moths drawn to a lamp, are often attracted to trade these most-difficult-to-trade stocks. By now, you should understand clearly what you face when it comes to getting in or out of positions. It is said that recognizing the problem is the first step toward solving it, and you should definitely learn to recognize situations like the ones I've just discussed.

In later chapters, I'll examine how the routes work in different situations. They will help you to train yourself to face difficult situations with confidence and everyday situations with knowledge and care. Always be prepared.

11

Ups & Downs and What They Mean: More Exercises in Buying and Selling

E-NET INC

ETEL	6 ↑ +3		500	Os	14:23
High	7 5/16	Low	4	Acc. Vol.	17891000
Bid	5 31/32	Ask	6	Close	3

Name	Bid	Chg.	Size	#Best	Name	Ask	Chg.	Size	#Best
ARCHIP	6	+0	9	1	ISLD	6	+0	5	502
ARCHIP	6	+0	5	1	NITE	6	-1/4	1	156
ARCHIP	6	+0	4	1	FAHN	6 1/32	+0	1	53
ISLD	5 31/32	+0	280	410	REDI	6 3/32	+3/3	5	29
ARCA	5 31/32	+0	30	143	ARCHIP	6 1/8	+0	10	0
ARCHIP	5 31/32	+0	10	1	ARCA	6 1/8	+0	10	94
ARCHIP	5 31/32	+0	10	1	GRUN	6 1/8	+0	5	21
ARCHIP	5 31/32	+0	10	0	BACH	6 1/8	+1/8	5	22
NITE	5 31/32	+0	1	192	USCT	6 1/8	+0	2	72
SHWD	5 15/16	+0	5	17	SHWD	6 1/8	+0	1	49
ARCHIP	5 29/32	+0	10	1	MASH	6 1/4	+0	60	83
ARCHIP	5 29/32	+0	10	1	MHMY	6 1/4	-3/8	5	19
ARCHIP	5 29/32	+0	10	1	HRZG	6 1/4	+0	5	42
HRZG	5 29/32	+1/3	10	34	SLKC	6 5/16	+13/	5	22
ARCHIP	5 7/8	+0	10	1	HILL	6 5/16	+0	1	0
ARCHIP	5 7/8	+0	10	1	ARCHIP	6 7/16	+0	12	0
ARCHIP	5 7/8	+0	10	0	ARCHIP	6 1/2	+0	30	0
MASH	5 7/8	+0	10	118	ARCHIP	6 1/2	+0	20	0
SLKC	5 7/8	+13/	5	16	BTRD	6 1/2	+0	5	0
USCT	5 7/8	+1/1	2	48	PENN	6 1/2	-1/4	1	1
ARCHIP	5 7/8	+0	1	1	ARCHIP	6 9/16	+0	25	0
ARCHIP	5 27/32	+0	10	0	BRUT	6 25/32	+0	50	2
ARCHIP	5 27/32	+0	10	0					

Side panel:
6 200 / 5 29/32 10000 / 6 500 / 6 1000 / 6 100 / 6 700 / 6 1000 / 6 500 / 6 500 / 6 100 / 5 31/32 900 / 6 100 / 6 2000 / 6 500 / 6 300 / 6 200 / 6 500 / 6 1000 / 6 500 / 6 300 / 6 600 / 6 300 / 6 200 / 6 300 / 6 500 / 6 100 / 5 31/32 500 / 6 100 / 6 1500 / 6 500

Another stock going up

The above screen shot shows another stock that's going up. Note all the buying pressure in the ARCA book and all the prints going off at the offer price. Notice, too, that there are 1,800 shares bid for at 6, but only 600 offered. If you were to try to buy at 6, how likely is it that you'd be filled? Not likely at all, unless one of the offers is hiding size. Hiding size occurs when a market participant shows a particular size (say 100 shares) but actually transacts much more at that price (say 5,000). In a volatile stock, whose price fluctuates greatly, the market maker might induce selling if it were to show 5,000 shares offered. Instead, to represent its client fairly, it will show as much stock as it feels it can, given current market conditions. The only way to determine this is by watching the stock and the market participant. (I'll discuss hiding size and other manoeuvers in Chapter 25.)

In the previous shot, taken just prior to the screen shot below, there were many participants offered at 6. All of these offers were taken, as you can see reflected on the ticker. Now, all that's left are ISLD and NITE, with a combined total of 600 shares. Clearly, given this situation, this stock is coiled like a compressed spring. How far it will move is anybody's guess, but at the moment, it certainly looks as if there's more demand than supply.

Minutes later, as the shot below shows, the coil has sprung, and the stock is indeed higher. Many limit orders hover at 6 1/2 offered. There is still a lot of buying pressure, but the picture has changed dramatically.

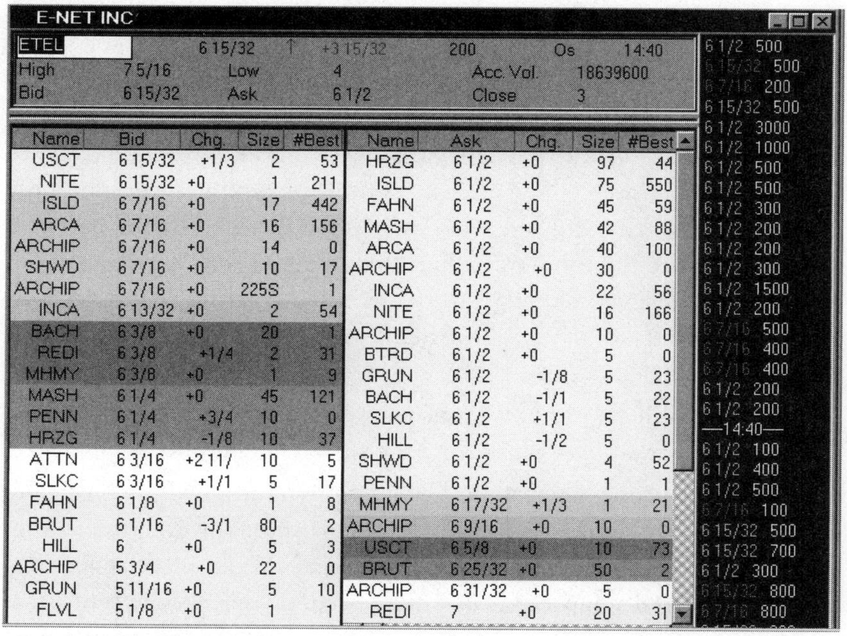

E-NET INC

ETEL		6 15/32	↑ +3 15/32	200	Os	14:40
High	7 5/16	Low	4	Acc.Vol	18639600	
Bid	6 15/32	Ask	6 1/2	Close	3	

Name	Bid	Chg	Size	#Best	Name	Ask	Chg	Size	#Best
USCT	6 15/32	+1/3	2	53	HRZG	6 1/2	+0	97	44
NITE	6 15/32	+0	1	211	ISLD	6 1/2	+0	75	550
ISLD	6 7/16	+0	17	442	FAHN	6 1/2	+0	45	59
ARCA	6 7/16	+0	16	156	MASH	6 1/2	+0	42	88
ARCHIP	6 7/16	+0	14	0	ARCA	6 1/2	+0	40	100
SHWD	6 7/16	+0	10	17	ARCHIP	6 1/2	+0	30	0
ARCHIP	6 7/16	+0	225S	1	INCA	6 1/2	+0	22	56
INCA	6 13/32	+0	2	54	NITE	6 1/2	+0	16	166
BACH	6 3/8	+0	20	1	ARCHIP	6 1/2	+0	10	0
REDI	6 3/8	+1/4	2	31	BTRD	6 1/2	+0	5	0
MHMY	6 3/8	+0	1	9	GRUN	6 1/2	-1/8	5	23
MASH	6 1/4	+0	45	121	BACH	6 1/2	-1/1	5	22
PENN	6 1/4	+3/4	10	0	SLKC	6 1/2	+1/1	5	23
HRZG	6 1/4	-1/8	10	37	HILL	6 1/2	-1/2	5	0
ATTN	6 3/16	+2 11/	10	5	SHWD	6 1/2	+0	4	52
SLKC	6 3/16	+1/1	5	17	PENN	6 1/2	+0	1	1
FAHN	6 1/8	+0	1	8	MHMY	6 17/32	+1/3	1	21
BRUT	6 1/16	-3/1	80	2	ARCHIP	6 9/16	+0	10	0
HILL	6	+0	5	3	USCT	6 5/8	+0	10	73
ARCHIP	5 3/4	+0	22	0	BRUT	6 25/32	+0	50	2
GRUN	5 11/16	+0	5	10	ARCHIP	6 31/32	+0	5	0
FLVL	5 1/8	+0	1	1	REDI	7	+0	20	31

Ticker (right margin):

```
6 1/2   500
6 15/32 500
6 7/16  200
6 15/32 500
6 1/2   3000
6 1/2   1000
6 1/2   500
6 1/2   500
6 1/2   300
6 1/2   200
6 1/2   200
6 1/2   300
6 1/2   1500
6 1/2   200
6 7/16  500
6 7/16  400
6 7/16  400
6 1/2   200
6 1/2   200
—14:40—
6 1/2   100
6 1/2   400
6 1/2   500
6 7/16  100
6 15/32 500
6 15/32 700
6 1/2   300
6 15/32 800
6 7/16  800
```

The coil has sprung: no time to sell!

If you really needed to sell now, would you stand your shares in line with the other 40,700 (!) offered there? To execute in this sort of environment, you must try to stay ahead of the crowd. Things could turn ugly if many of the sellers currently offered at 6 1/2 re-evaluated and sold at 6 15/32, then 7/16, then 13/32, etc. Panic could easily set in and send the stock tanking. If that happened—and it easily could in such a situation—it's better to stay ahead of the crowd.

In this example, if you really needed to be done, right now, you wouldn't offer out along with 40,700 other shares. You might consider selling at 15/32, however, and just be done with it. After all, 1/32 on 1,000 shares equals a difference of around $30. And the peace of mind might just be worth it. At least there is a lot of ECN liquidity in this stock. Execution against an ECN often takes place at electronic speed because there's no human intervention in the transaction. If you decide to be done, chances are you can be—and quickly too. (I'll discuss ECNs in Chapter 15.)

The screen shot at the top of page 53 illustrates the opposite scenario: weakness. Here are some weak stocks without all the ARCHIPs and Archipelago ECN activity. Conversely to a strong up-pressured stock, a down-pressured stock has a lot of liquidity offered out and fewer shares bid for. Ideally, when you look at the direction indicators, you'll see that many of the participants have recently *lowered* their bids and offers. In the first shot below, we see almost 5,000 shares offered out and only 1,000 bid for. At the next price levels, 7,500 shares are offered, and only 1,100 shares are bid for. Under those bids, there is little interest at all. Many participants are bidding 100 shares only. If this stock starts to sell, or if someone hits all the bids, the market could go into panic mode and the stock could tank.

The example at the bottom of page 53 shows another stock with significant downward pressure: Note the similar conditions.

Direction change indicators show uniform minuses. If the change in direction is zero, a plus sign will show. In this case, however, the market participant has not recently changed the price. We also see that 5,900 shares are offered compared to 300 shares bid. If some selling starts, this stock may move down quickly. In fact, if the sizes shown are real (i.e., they're not hiding size) a market sale of only 1,600 shares at this point would drop the price a full point.

CDNW		21 7/8	↑	+7/8		100	Ot t	10:56
High	22 1/4	Low		21 1/8		Acc. Vol.	895000	
Bid ↑	21 3/4	Ask		21 7/8		Close	21	

Name	Bid	Size	#Best	Name	Ask	Size	#Best
INCA	21 3/4	10	38	ISLD	21 7/8	19	30
PWJC	21 5/8	10	11	SHWD	21 7/8	15	1
MONT	21 5/8	1	1	REDI	21 7/8	9	10
BTRD	21 9/16	4	0	OGRU	21 7/8	5	4
NITE	21 9/16	1	3	PRUS	21 7/8	1	5
OGRU	21 1/2	5	0	HRZG	22	23	4
MASH	21 1/2	5	0	NFSC	22	10	0
NEED	21 1/2	1	0	MLCO	22	10	1
VOLP	21 1/2	1	0	PWJC	22	10	0
SLKC	21 1/2	1	0	NITE	22	10	16
JOSE	21 1/2	1	0	PERT	22	5	5
PRUS	21 7/16	1	0	MASH	22	4	5
ADAM	21 3/8	1	0	MONT	22	1	4
CASS	21 3/8	1	0	BEST	22	1	2
USCT	21 1/4	2	0	DEAN	22	1	0
MHMY	21 1/4	1	0	BTRD	22 1/16	1	2
BEST	21 1/4	1	0	SLKC	22 1/8	1	1
MLCO	21 3/16	10	0	BRUT	22 1/8	1	3
DBKS	21 1/8	1	1				
PERT	21 1/16	5	0				
REDI	21	10	0				
HRZG	21	10	0				

These stocks show weakness

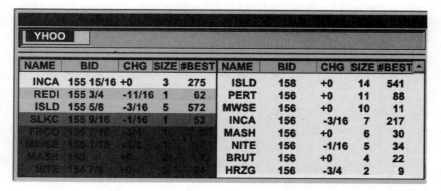

NAME	BID	CHG	SIZE	#BEST	NAME	BID	CHG	SIZE	#BEST
INCA	155 15/16	+0	3	275	ISLD	158	+0	14	541
REDI	155 3/4	-11/16	1	62	PERT	156	+0	11	88
ISLD	155 5/8	-3/16	5	572	MWSE	156	+0	10	11
SLKC	155 9/16	-1/16	1	53	INCA	156	-3/16	7	217
EBCO	155 7/16	-3/4	1		MASH	156	+0	6	30
MWSE	155 1/16	-1/2	1		NITE	156	-1/16	5	34
MASH	155	+0	2	7	BRUT	156	+0	4	22
NITE	154 7/8	+0	2	24	HRZG	156	-3/4	2	9

Downward pressure on YHOO

Now we come to the slow movers (screen shot below). Like a warship in the days of sail, a stock sometimes finds itself motionless and dead in the water. Mariners called this "being in irons." A stock that's stuck in irons may take a while to get going again. Meanwhile, the enemy has ample time to circle its prey and close in for the kill.

Wise traders stay away from stocks such as the one illustrated below, which is stuck and going nowhere. You should note the enormous number of buyers bidding and the equally huge number of sellers selling. How much buying or selling would be necessary to get this stock moving? A lot. Also, if you look at the prints, there are many at the offer and many at the bid. Obviously, this stock is undecided as to which way to go. It is stuck in irons.

The good news in this sort of situation is that you can buy or sell practically all you want. Getting in or out of a position in this type of stock is not difficult because of the sheer amount of stock available. But keep in mind that situations change. Were we to look at this stock again in an hour or two, it could be in play.

DELL COMPUTER CORP

DELL		49 11/16	↓	+1/4		1000		Qt	14:12
High	49 15/16	Low		48 15/16		Acc. Vol.		17890200	
Bid	49 11/16	Ask		49 3/4		Close		49 7/16	

Name	Bid	Chg.	Size	#Best	Name	Ask	Chg.	Size	#Best
ISLD	49 11/1	+0	119	157	ISLD	49 3/4	+0	42	148
INCA	49 11/1	+0	58	119	MASH	49 3/4	-1	31	49
MWSE	49 11/1	+0	14	15	INCA	49 3/4	+0	25	131
BTRD	49 11/1	+0	12	51	NITE	49 3/4	+0	24	53
DLJP	49 11/1	+11/1	10	15	DEAN	49 3/4	-1/8	10	10
BEST	49 11/1	+11/1	10	7	HMQT	49 3/4	-1/8	10	5
SLKC	49 11/1	+1/16	10	34	PWJC	49 3/4	+0	7	15
PRUS	49 11/1	+0	10	20	HRZG	49 3/4	+0	6	30
MLCO	49 11/1	+0	5	24	SHWD	49 3/4	+0	5	29
REDI	49 11/1	+0	5	55	BRUT	49 3/4	+0	4	26
SWST	49 11/1	+0	1	9	SWST	49 3/4	-1/8	1	9
SBSH	49 11/1	+0	1	25	JEFF	49 3/4	-1/16	1	1
JPMS	49 11/1	+1/2	1	7	RAMS	49 3/4	+0	1	15
GSCO	49 5/8	+1/8	10	4	PIPR	49 3/4	-1/16	1	17
MSCO	49 5/8	-1/16	10	31	BRAD	49 3/4	+0	1	3
ARCHIP	49 5/8	+0	9	1	MADF	49 13/1	+0	14	50
ARCA	49 5/8	-1/16	9	59	NFSC	49 13/1	-7/16	10	26
NFSC	49 5/8	+0	7	7	DLJP	49 13/1	+0	10	12

Dell in irons

The L2 screen in the next screen shot shows no massive demand on the bid side and no particularly weak show on the offer. But sometimes you need to read between the lines. There is, in fact, significant interest, if you note the ticker. Look how many trades are printing, and all at the offer price. Within the last few seconds, an awful lot of trades have gone off. If you watch this stock, and you know the participants, you might get ideas. Nobody has conceded yet that this stock is a mover, but this kind of buying, if it continues, can only drive a price up.

RBAK	Last	112		100		12:41		---- 12:41 ----
High	112 7/8	Low	106 13/16	Tot Vol		700500		111 3/4 500
BID ↓	111 11/16	ASK	111 15/16	Close		111		111 3/4 200

NAME	BID	CHG	SIZE	#BEST	NAME	ASK	CHG	SIZE	#BEST
ISLD	111 11/16	+0	1	296	REDI	111 15/16	+0	1	15
RSSF	111 5/8	+0	10	6	ISLD	112	-1 3/8	2	292
MWSE	111 1/4	-1/16	1	11	MWSE	112	+0	1	6
USCT	111 3/8	+3 15/1	1	14	SLKC	112 3/8	+1/2	1	8
					BRUT	112 7/16	+7/16	2	27

Ticker:
111 7/8 100
111 7/8 200
111 7/8 200
777 7/8 100
111 15/16 100
112 100
112 500
111 59/64 100
111 5/8 200
112 100
112 200
112 200
112 100
112 100
112 100
112 100

No great demand for RBAK

Three minutes later, look at the same stock (see the screen capture on page 56). Some sellers are starting to come in, but the stock is 1-1/2 points higher. Still, there is no sizable interest on the buy or sell side. But clearly this stock moves.

Knowing the behaviour of a stock and of the participants involved, you might feel like moving into this sort of trade. But you have to be very careful. In this case, the size of all the prints is very small, and the volatility is great. Everyone seems to be bidding or offering only 100 shares. If a wave of sell orders hit the market at the same time, the price could suddenly plummet.

This is a double-edged sword. Lack of liquidity breeds volatility. By knowing and watching a stock, you will see these sorts of scalps all the time. On the other hand, if you don't know how these stocks behave, you could easily be misled into making a bad decision.

RBAK	Last 113 3/8				12:44
High 113 5/8	Low 106 13/16	Tot Vol 742200			
BID ↓ 113 3/8	ASK 113 1/2	Close 111			

NAME	BID	CHG	SIZE	#BEST	NAME	ASK	CHG	SIZE	#BEST
MASH	113 3/8	+5/16	5	34	NFSC	113 1/2	+0	3	9
ARCA	113 3/8	+3/8	1	23	MWSE	113 1/2	-1/2	3	7
ALKC	113 3/8	+0	1	32	ARCA	113 1/2	+0	1	11
ISLD	113 1/4	+0	6	310	ISLD	113 3/4	-1/8	4	301
NITE	113 1/4	+0	1	43	MASH	113 3/4	+0	1	27
BRUT	113	-3/8	3	26	SELZ	113 7/8	+0	1	0
MWSE	113	+0	2	11	BRUT	114	+0	4	29
BMUR	113	+0	1	0	SBSH	114	+2	1	2
RSSF	112 1/2	+0	10	6					

113 1/2	200
113 1/2	100
113 1/2	100
113 1/2	100
113 1/2	100
113 1/4	100
113 1/2	200
113 3/8	300
113 3/8	200
113 1/2	200
113 1/4	200
113 1/2	200
113 1/2	200
112 7/8	2800
113 1/2	500
113 1/2	100
113 1/2	200
113 1/2	100
113 1/2	200
113 5/8	100
113 5/8	100
113 3/8	100

The same stock, three minutes later

To summarize: We use Level II not only to determine the strength and direction of a stock in the very near term, but also to determine the route we should use to execute. Following are several important concerns in analyzing Level II:

- What is the strength and direction of the stock?

- Is there a sizable buyer or seller causing the move?

- Who is on the bid and offer? Is it the axe? Is it mostly day-trader-driven liquidity? Are there a large number of market makers trading size?

- How many shares are generally bid/offered by non-ECN participants? Do they generally bid/offer the very minimum allowed (100 shares) or do the participants bid/offer a significant number of shares? (In DELL, at time of this writing, for example, market makers often show several thousand shares.)

– How liquid is the stock? Is volume increasing or decreasing?

As we'll see, all of this information, taken directly from Level II, directly influences your choice of execution vehicle. In the next chapters, we'll discuss how all the routes work. Then we'll take a look at what market makers do to enhance your ability to read between the lines of Level II.

12

Going Up: The Next Level

In late April 2000, the NASDAQ and the province of Quebec penned a deal that, over the next couple of years, will bring terminals with the NASDAQ Level III quotes montage to Canada. The details are still a bit sketchy but they are on their way here. As mentioned before, Level III provides similar information to Level II. But it is organized differently. (The shot below shows an example of a Level III screen.)

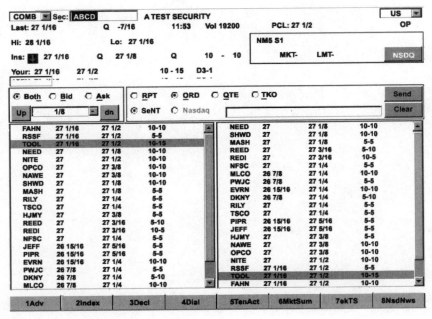

NASDAQ Level III quotes montage

As with Level II screens, the bid appears on the left and the offer on the right. The major difference between the Level II and Level III quotes montage is that Level III shows both sides of the participants' market. In the example above, the best bid is FAHN at 27 1/16, and the best offer is NEED at 27 1/8. You will note that FAHN's offer is at 27 1/2, and that NEED is bid at 27. Why would they arrange the screen in this way?

Well, keep in mind that this was designed in the 1980s. And market authorities are slooooow to change. Note also the box on the left, which allows the market maker to move a bid, an offer, or both at the same time. You can see the up and down buttons, as well as the increment of the move, which is currently 1/8, the default. Note also that there are no routes to select. Typically, market makers have access only to SelectNet and SOES, which I'll discuss in Chapters 13 and 14. And they are prohibited from using SOES for their own accounts.

There is a widespread public misconception that Level III screens provide much more information as well as special, secret information, such as the location of stop and limit orders given to other market makers. Nothing could be further from the truth. At this time, there is no central order book for the NASDAQ. (Compare this with the listed exchanges like the NYSE, where one specialist controls each stock, and the specialist keeps all stop and limit orders in a central order book, which no one is allowed to see.) On the NASDAQ, there is nowhere to keep stop and limit orders. Individual traders on the NASDAQ maintain their own book of orders and are responsible for executing them when they become marketable. At this time, brokerage houses are not even required to accept stop orders. Many do, however, especially those with traders who will take on the responsibility.

What this means for people trading their own accounts is that the traders are responsible for the execution of their own orders. In a sense, all stop orders must be mental stops for those trading their own accounts directly. People who want the services of a full-service brokerage should consider this fact before taking on the responsibility of trading their own accounts.

There is hope on the horizon. Currently, the NASDAQ is developing a central limit book. With any luck, it will be online within the next two years. In the meantime, I hope this illustration of an actual Level III screen ends the misconception about what such screens contain. In fact, in some ways, the Level III workstation offers less information than top-end Level II screens like those offered by RealTick. Level III is easy to understand once you get used to it, but I've been told by several market makers that they prefer their information organized in the RealTick fashion.

The only fundamental difference found on Level III is that a registered market maker can raise or lower the price and size directly on the screen by pointing and clicking. Since day traders are not market makers themselves, they must enter bids and offers through an ECN and broker/dealer, then cancel and enter a new order to change the price or size. They may use the point-and-click method, but their order will still go to the ECN—a registered market participant—and then to the NASDAQ system. Using an Internet-based order execution system, this can happen nearly as quickly as a market maker can change the price/volume, although some execution systems are faster than others, as I'll discuss.

At time of this writing, NASDAQ Level III does not offer #Best and several other important informational items. No wonder market makers are a little jealous.

As I've said before, being familiar with all the items on the Level II market maker screen is an absolute necessity. The Level II screen is the map for your position's entry and exit. A thorough and instant consideration and interpretation of these items will be crucial to the quality of your decisions. Your understanding of the Level II screen will make the difference between exiting your position cleanly, at a profit, and being frustrated or worse and stuck with a loser, wondering why you can't close the position.

13

Big Deals: The Small Order Execution System (SOES)

The Small Order Execution System (SOES) and SelectNet went through a major change in their rules and regulations in May 2000. It was the first major overhaul of the two original day trading systems in over a decade. For further changes and modifications, you should check the NASDAQ Trader Web site at **www.nasdaqtrader.com**.

The Small Order Execution System created the day trading phenomenon and changed the balance of power in the NASDAQ market, and haunting stories of SOES bandits circulate through the bars on Wall Street. SOES is so scary for market makers because it executes, automatically, instantaneously, against a market maker, without the market maker's choice or involvement. If market makers make a market in an SOES-able security, they are accepting the risk that they'll be forced to buy or sell up to 9,999 shares of the stock at their price, at any given time. (I'll discuss this in detail in a moment.) In other words, if they turn their heads for a second, they may find that they own 9,999 Microsoft. At over US$100 per share at time of writing, that's a lot of money. And if they have activated their Auto-Refresh, their displayed size will automatically be refreshed, allowing them to be SOES-ed again and again. That can be one expensive trip to the rest room.

However, that's as much sympathy as I'll give to the market makers, because SOES will execute only at the price that the market maker will buy or sell. Market makers are obligated to buy or sell at that price, but it's still the price of their own choosing. If they don't really intend to buy at that price, then they shouldn't be there. Of course, if the market tanks suddenly, or if the market makers are inexperienced, they can get caught. But they knew that risk when they signed up for the job.

SOES was created as a result of the crash of 1987, when some brokers would not answer their phones. It has been said that the phone lines simply could not handle the volume. It has also been said that brokers, being paid on per-share commission, would take only institutional orders, preferring commissions on, say, a trade of 30,000 shares to one of 100 shares per phone call. Whatever the reason, new regulations were enacted. These give the small investor, defined as someone who trades fewer than 1,000 shares, the same access to the NASDAQ market equal as an institutional investor. SOES was the first product to come out of these new regulations. And though many people now consider SOES useless, it still has value. In fact, most people who call it useless simply don't understand how it works.

SOES provides a point-and-click routing option on most direct-access platforms. It accepts market orders and limit orders placed at the current inside market (also called marketable limit orders). All or none, fill or kill, good till cancel orders are not accepted. And SOES will execute only against market makers. It won't execute against ECNs.

An individual may buy or sell up to 9,999 shares (depending on tier size, which I'll explain in a moment). The individual can buy or sell on either side of the market in a 5-minute period using SOES, placing a limit or market order, simply by designating SOES as the execution route.

Participation in SOES is mandatory for all NASDAQ national market (NNM) securities. For NASDAQ small caps, however, participation in SOES is optional for the market maker, and over-the-counter bulletin board (OTCBB) non-NASDAQ securities are never SOES eligible.

NNM securities are divided into three SOES liability categories—or tier sizes—of 200, 500, and 1,000 shares. That means that SOES transactions in these securities cannot involve more than the maximum allowable number of shares in each tier size.

For example, at the time of writing, Dell is a Tier 1,000 Security. That means you may both buy and sell 1,000 shares of Dell within a 5-minute period. You cannot buy or sell more than that. In other words, you cannot buy 1,000 shares of Dell, then buy an additional 1,000 shares within a 5-minute period.

Obviously, you must know the tier size of the particular stock you are dealing with if you plan to use SOES to exit. I have received calls from traders who've watched in panic as their orders automatically deleted themselves one after the other while the stock tanked. On many occasions the security was a price-inflated small cap in which none of the market makers elected to participate in SOES. And in others, only ECNs were bid or offered, rendering their limit orders useless. (Remember, SOES will not transact against an ECN.) So, in these cases, SOES wasn't even a possibility. (The NASDAQ Trader Web site provides full, up-to-date information on tier size and whether an issue is an NNM or a small cap.)

(Currently, all tier sizes [200, 500, and 1,000], along with the 5-minute period rule, are tentatively set to be abolished in the year 2000. In other words the SOES tier sizes and the 5-minute rule information outlines above will be irrelevant. Again, please check the NASDAQ Trader Web site for up-to-date information concerning SOES rules, at **www.nasdaqtrader.com/trader/whatsnew**.)

PROS & CONS

SOES advantages include:
- instantaneous execution against market makers
- limit or market orders
- odd lots (any number of shares, up to tier size)

SOES disadvantages include:
- small order size (any number of shares, up to tier size)
- inability to execute against ECNs (see electronic communication networks below)
- orders are handled by the NASDAQ in the order in which they are received. In a fast market, SOES market orders may get you out at a price you're not happy with.
- not all securities are SOES-able

If you are in a position that you need to liquidate quickly, and there are market makers on the bid, then SOES is the light-speed alternative. When you are first in line with an SOES limit order, you can be executed before your finger even leaves the keypad. However, if you are in an extremely volatile and active security, keep in mind that the NASDAQ executes trades in the order in which it receives them. If it receives a number of similar SOES orders ahead of yours, your limit order may not be executed, as these prior orders may soak up all available liquidity.

It is vitally important to understand that, when there are very few shares bid in an extremely volatile stock, an SOES limit order may not get executed at all. Someone will likely put an order in ahead of yours that will be executed ahead of yours. Then the market maker will move their position, and your order will be cancelled because the market moved away. (In other words, the price changed, and your limit order automatically was cancelled). Furthermore, because orders are filled in the order they're received, your order may be executed at a price you really don't like. The few shares bid for will be traded automatically, and the market makers, faced with such supply, will lower the price/size of their bids. Just imagine an SOES 1,000-tier security of whose shares only 200 or 300 are bid for at each price level. Suddenly, out comes some bad news, and ten SOES market orders are entered, each for 1,000 shares. The first order may take out the first three price levels!

Just imagine how far down the price could move, in mere seconds, as those SOES orders execute, for 10,000 shares total. The price could spike down dramatically, and you could get the worst print of the day. So you must be careful when using SOES market orders, especially in fast markets characterized by extreme volume and rapid price fluctuation.

However, if volume is just starting to pick up, you think the stock is going to rocket higher, and you are willing to buy at the offer or higher, you might want to place an SOES limit. If you miss it, then you're faced with opportunity cost. Keep in mind that, if you place an SOES market order to buy, and so does everyone else at right about the same time, your order could be executed much higher.

THE BOTTOM LINE: Given normal market conditions, if you need to be out at any cost, the security is SOES-able, you have less than the tier size of shares, and market makers are on the bid, SOES market is one of the fastest ways out. But in a fast market in which there is not much liquidity, your market order could stay live for several moments as the price races away from target and your order is executed far far away from your intention. SOES limit orders are great for an instantaneous trade. But in that fast market, your order may be killed by the exchange (NASDAQ) as the price moves outside your limit. At that point, you might try another SOES limit or get out through one of the ECNs.

The late eighties and early nineties were amazing times for day traders. Spreads were big, display size was 1,000 shares, ECNs were new,

Page Design MarketMaker Window Help

EFNT | 49 ↓ | 300 | Ot t 11:23
High 50 1/4 Low 43 Acc.Vol 2374400
Bid ↓ 49 Ask 49 1/16 Close 0

Name	Bid	Size	#Best	Name	Ask	Size	#Best
DKNY	49	2	8	ARCHIP	49	8	1
ISLD	48 5/8	1	25	ARCHIP	49	5	0
SHWD	48 1/2	2	8	ARCHIP	49	3	0
AGIS	48 1/8	2	2	ARCHIP	49	1	0
SLKC	48 1/8	1	20	ARCHIP	49	1	0
				RAMS	49 1/16	1	12
				ISLD	49 1/16	1	22
				AGIS	49 3/16	1	12
				HRZG	49 3/16	1	13
				REDI	49 1/2	3	2
				FBCO	49 1/2	2	6
ARCHIP	0	0	0	ARCHIP	0	0	0
ARCHIP	0	0	0	ARCHIP	0	0	0
ARCHIP	0	0	0	TNYKD	0	0	0
ARCHIP	0	0	0	BRUT	0	0	0

Right-side price column:
49 100
49 300
49 100
48 3/4 500
49 100
49 3/16 100
49 1/32 100
49 1/16 200
49 1/8 300
49 1/16 200
49 11/16 100
48 5/8 100
49 200
49 3/16 100
49 1/32 800
49 1/16 100
49 100
49 5/8 100
48 1/2 100
49 100
49 200
48 3/4 100
49 1/8 100
49 1/8 200
49 100
49 1/16 200
49 100
49 1/8 200
49 100
49 1/8 200
49 100
49 100
49 1/16 100
49 200
49 100
49 300

Potential spike downward

and market makers didn't bother to protect themselves against the SOES bandits, who prowled the virtual floor of the exchange like alligators, searching for an out-of-line price, an unusually large spread, anything to snatch. New technologies and rules permitted this. Call it retribution for the stranglehold the market makers had kept on the industry prior to the crash of 1987. Traders like Harvey Houtkin, the so-called "SOES Bandit" made fortunes, in months. One didn't need to know much about the stocks traded, or even anything about the market at all. The skills of the day were intense concentration, fast typing, and generally, access to a Level III machine through a local hedge fund or broker dealer willing to let individuals in on the markets. The modern PC-based front-end order entry systems did not yet exist.

It's not so easy anymore. The new order handling rules, which allow market makers to display actual size, with a minimum liability of 100 shares, and the growth in popularity of the ECNs, which are not SOES-able, have again changed the landscape. The playing field now is truly more level, with a balance struck between the "executionability" of SOES and the "vulnerability" of market makers.

This has made it harder to make a buck scalping. Most of the players who move in and out of the markets hundreds of times a day, picking up a 16th, a 32nd, an 8th, are gone. Way too much risk for such a tiny profit? But the opportunity for even greater profit still exists, with the advent of SOES, ECNs, online brokerages and electronic brokerages offering direct access to the securities markets. These factors have created huge new liquidity and volatility. Now the best traders ride the trades for three, five, ten points, and on thousands of shares. The tools they use include most of the tools in the MM's arsenal, SOES, and several other important ones: the modern "active" ECNs.

SOES STORIES

Here's a story a professional broker who had access to DAD terminals told me: "In one recent situation, a client of my firm had been partially filled by some market maker with only 93 shares. Subsequently, when he wanted to sell, he found he could not. He preferenced several market makers with SelectNet (declined), tried offering the stock out on the Island (it would not appear in the montage; less than the minimum number of shares, i.e., 100), Archipelago (won't accept odd lot orders), and finally called in, frustrated beyond belief. Keep in mind that this was a $240 stock that moved 20 percent a day, and he traded only in cash, not on margin, so he had serious risk. After learning that he just wanted out, at the bid, and fast, I entered a limit order on SOES. I saw that there were several market makers on the bid. I knew that the SOES tier size was 500 shares, and each of the market makers was showing at least 500 shares. I felt confident the order would be executed. Sure enough, before my finger left the keyboard, he was filled, for 93 shares. His response was "*@#!! how did you do that?"

THE ANSWER: SOES. If you have an odd lot of shares (less than the SOES tier size), and are willing to sell or buy at the inside market, and market makers are there—as opposed to ECNs (remember, SOES will not execute against an ECN) try SOES. It won't always work, because in a fast-moving stock it's altogether likely stock will trade ahead of you—but SOES is often lightning fast. In the right situation, it's as close to instant gratification as it gets.

A WARNING: Be very careful using SOES market orders. A friend of mine tells me that he bought ONSL at $107 using a SOES market order, entered when the price was $97. You may also remember the day in 1998 when ONSL went from $46 to $108 in one day, only to close the day back down at $56. In an extremely fast market, using a SOES market order is like ... well, it's just plain crazy, in my opinion. Think about it: a huge volume, tremendous demand, little to no supply, and a SOES market order. What a recipe for disaster. When a stock trades like that, consider sitting it out. Better not to engage and miss a potential opportunity than to get the highest print of the day and see the stock tank like a piledriver.

I didn't have the courage to ask what price my friend sold out at. Or if he used an SOES market order to get out. I sense he's glad I haven't asked. He told this to me as a warning, to get the word out: In a ridiculously fast market, beware the SOES market order. Of course, under normal market conditions, SOES market may be just what you need, particularly if there are numerous market makers with huge size, and you just want to be done with the order quickly.

Other proposed SOES rule changes include:

- The 17-second filling rule will be reduced to 5 seconds
- Registered individuals (like in the above story involving the professional broker) will be able to use SOES
- It will remain a forced execution system
- The old SOES rules will still apply to small cap stocks (tier size, forced fills, etc.)

For the current status of these proposed rule changes, check the NASDAQ Web site at **www.nasdaqtrader.com/trader/whatsnew**.

14

SelectNet: The Market Maker's Tool

NOTE: NASDAQ has proposed the following changes to the SelectNet Execution Platform as of May 15, 2000.

- SelectNet will no longer be a liability execution system. This means market makers will no longer be liable to fill trades at their advertised price.

- A day trade can only preference market makers for at least 100 shares more than they are advertising on the Level II montage

- Preferencing ECNs through SelectNet will not change.

More information is available at **www.nasdaqtrader.com/trader/ whatsnew**.

SelectNet is an order-routing option available to all market makers and customers of the better direct access electronic brokerages. Like SOES, it is run by NASDAQ Market Systems. Both SelectNet and SOES are order execution systems, not ECNs. (I'll explain ECNs in the next chapter.)

SelectNet is currently the preferred method of execution for market makers, for a number of reasons. First, it enables market makers to trade stock without picking up the phone, dialling, and holding: it allows for speed. More importantly, it removes any confusion that could arise from telephone conversations. It is a vehicle for swift, decisive, transparent transactions. Another reason SelectNet is used so widely is that market makers generally do not have access to the ECNs available to day traders. In the near future, they probably will have access, but large institutions are slow to change. For the moment, day traders have the edge on market makers when it comes to ease of execution.

A SelectNet order works like an instant message: When an order is entered via SelectNet, the market participant receives notification that some other market participant wishes to buy or sell a certain amount of stock at a particular price.

SelectNet orders take two forms: SelectNet broadcast, and SelectNet preference.

SelectNet broadcast orders are broadcast to all Level III participants who have an interest in the particular stock. Generally, the market makers configure their workstation so that broadcast orders in the stocks they follow appear as a one-line message on the screen. This lets them know that some market participant wishes to buy or sell a specific amount of particular stock at a specific price. Since the order was not directed at them, they are under no legal obligation to respond unless it is at their price/volume. So for traders, this order may or may not generate a response.

SelectNet preference orders are directed to a specific market participant. Many market makers configure their Level III workstations with a pop-up window to let them know when they are being preferenced. During market hours, if the order occurs at the current price and size of the market maker's bid or offer, it will be designated an "incoming liability order." The market maker is legally obligated to respond by accepting, declining, or partially filling the order.

Orders are processed by market makers and ECNs alike on a first-come, first-served basis; that is, if the participant is holding out to the world a firm quote to buy 1,000 shares of ABCD at 38 1/4, the first order to sell the market maker's 1,000 shares at that price will be executed, since that is the market maker's liability. Beyond that number, the market maker can decide to buy more there, change the quote size, or move the market altogether.

If you preference a market maker or an ECN, at their price and volume, and somebody else has preferenced them first, the market makers or ECNs are under no obligation to fill your order because the stock traded ahead of you. Likewise, if they are bidding 1,000 shares, and receive two preferences, one after the other, one selling 300 shares and the other selling 1,000 shares, they are obligated to fill 300 shares on the first order, and only 700 of the next (300 + 700 = 1000, their quote size).

All this may happen so fast that watching Level II won't give an adequate view of the transactions. If you feel that a market participant backed away (the NASD's description of not fulfilling the number of shares they are liable for) one must examine Time of Sales (discussed in Chapter 8) to determine just how many shares traded at that price. Backing away happens, sometimes by plain error and sometimes for other reasons. But it doesn't occur often. The penalties are aggressive for that sort of activity, and any potential gain is remote and far outweighed by the penalties imposed.

Additionally, pre- or post-market SelectNet preferences do not carry the obligation of a response. You may indeed get an execution, but the process resembles pounding on the doors of a bank after hours. Probably, no one will answer.

SelectNet holds one major disadvantage for the trader, especially in high-volume stocks. Market makers are given 30 seconds to respond to a liability order. In a fast market, 30 seconds can seem like an eternity. And after the delay, the transaction can be outright declined ("the stock traded ahead"). In this light, SelectNet loses much of its luster.

However, SelectNet also comes with several redeeming qualities for the trader. First, SelectNet provides a link to the ECNs. When a SelectNet preference is placed to an ECN, it results in nearly automatic, instantaneous execution, up to the size currently available. So if you want to transact with an ECN, SelectNet may be an excellent choice.

A SelectNet preference to a market maker can also help move a large amount of stock in a volatile market. To do this, you have to identify the current axe (discussed in Chapter 9) and preference them with your entire order. For example, say you are long 5,000 ABCD. If you offer 5,000 shares, they might weight the market down, and you might not be able to sell your stock at a good price. Suppose as well that all the market makers are bidding small size, 100 or 200 shares each. If you can locate the axe and offer the stock to them and them alone, as a SelectNet preference, they may buy all of your stock, even, in rare circumstances, if the price is slightly higher than their quote.

They might do this for a variety of reasons, but the most obvious one is that they have proven to be a size buyer on the day. You won't know how much stock they have yet to buy, but one might assume they've got a lot more to buy since they've been buying so heavily so far. Keep in mind that they have to write a ticket for each and every transaction they do. So if they're going to buy 5,000 shares in 100-share lots, they have to write 50 tickets and possibly enter them into the system. It would be in their best interest to pay a little more and write only one ticket, particularly if they've got only 5,000 or 10,000 more shares to buy on the day. In any case, the worst that can happen is they decline you and move their market. The market at large won't be aware that you are trying to sell size, and you are still free to pursue other options.

PROS & CONS

SelectNet advantages include:
- Any size order up to six figures
- Preferencing an ECN can mean near-instantaneous execution

SelectNet disadvantages include:
- Market makers have 30 seconds to respond to preference orders, and a broadcast order may generate no response whatsoever.

SELECTNET STORIES

A client called to sell his stock. The problem was that he had 10,000 shares of an illiquid stock, and the market makers were all bidding small size. Most were bidding only 100 shares. If I offered it on ARCA, the world would see his order and might lower their bids. Selling 10,000 shares into that illiquid market could conceivably hammer the price. But I noticed that one of the market makers, who was priced at 1/16 lower than the inside bid (who was also showing 100 shares bid), had been on the best bid 63 times that day. Consulting #Best further, I saw that the next market maker in line had been there only eight times. A quick glance at the chart suggested there was a buyer of size somewhere in the jungle, and I suggested to the client that it might be the market maker who'd been there 63 times.

The client said he would be more than happy to get out at 1/16 below the current bid (as he'd had a large profit on the position). So I suggested preferencing the market maker who'd been a buyer at least 63 times that day, who was at 1/16 below the best bid, with 5,000 shares. With more than 5,000 shares, we might scare the market maker away and get only a partial fill of 100 shares.

We did this and, several seconds later, received the fill for 5,000 shares.

The market maker stayed bidding where they were, still showing 100 shares (even though they had just bought 5,000). So the broker suggested sending them another preference, for the balance. This time, they took 3,000 shares, and moved their market.

The client just wanted out, and he now had 2,000 shares left. I suggested putting the rest out on ARCA (see Chapter 18 on ARCA for a full description) with a limit at his price. He was executed for the remaining 2,000 shares—1,000 at the same price (and that market maker moved their market) and 1,000 at 1/16 above (at the inside market), and that market maker moved their market as well. I checked on the stock later in the day, and the buyer of size had never re-emerged. In fact, the price dropped approximately 5/16 from where my client sold.

All in all, my client sold 10,000 shares into a fairly illiquid market at a decent price. Had he gone out on the Island (ISLD) showing 10,000 shares, he might never have gotten filled, and probably would even have driven the price down.

15

Going Solo: Electronic Communication Networks

Using an electronic communication network (ECN), you can enter and widely disseminate orders to third parties, which they can execute against, in whole or in part. In the NASDAQ Level II screen montage, ECNs appear just like market makers. In fact, market makers desiring anonymity often place orders in ECNs. For example, market makers may have institutional orders to buy large amounts of stock, but they don't want the rest of the world to know their intentions. (If we all know they're going to buy a huge amount of shares, we'll raise our prices in anticipation.) So they might sit on or near the best offer, to look like a seller, when in fact they're on the inside bid through an ECN, buying everything they can get their hands on.

An ECN allows market participants to both bid and offer stock anonymously. However, ECNs are also available to individuals, through electronic brokerages offering direct access to the markets. The best brokerages offer execution systems with all the major ECNs to individuals as a point-and-click route to use when buying or selling stock. The order-entry system will ask you to specify the route you'd like to use when buying or selling stock. You might choose SOES. But SOES will not allow you to buy at the bid, so you might choose an ECN instead. An ECN allows you to sit on the bid or offer, so you appear (participate) in the NASDAQ Level II quotes montage just like a market maker.

Through ECNs, you can both buy at the bid and sell at the ask. If the stock is bidding 10 by 10 1/4, you can join the bid at 10, and buy the stock at 10. Given the right circumstances, you can offer it out right away, at 10 1/4. If done correctly, you may reap a profit of 1/4 in several minutes or less. That may not sound like much, but 1/4 on 1,000 shares is $250, and the best scalpers are doing just that dozens of times a day.

As I mentioned earlier, scalping as a bread-and-butter technique is rapidly losing appeal. The new order-handling rules instituted by the NASD (National Association of Securities Dealers) in July 1998 have made scalping considerably more risky and generally an uneconomic activity. As a result, scalping for 1/8 or 1/16 has become uneconomical. Several years ago, when spreads were wider and the order-handling rules were different, scalping worked, although even then, with the lower level of risk, it still benefited the brokerages as much as it did the individuals who scalped. But now there are numerous brokerage houses teaching (for an extortionate fee) outdated techniques (scalping) and offering huge "margins."

In fact, these are not really margins at all. Regulation T of the Securities Act of 1934, which governs use of margin, has set the maximum size of a margin account at 50 percent. Brokerages that offer 10-to-1 margin are not offering margin at all, but using sophisticated techniques of equity participation in the firm to lend you the money, as long as you abide by their rules. Usually the rules are (1) scalp only, and (2) hold no positions overnight. These brokerages are really day trading shops, and they are not only designed to separate you from your money, but they may also be operating in violation of the law. But I digress. (More on this later.)

The first ECN was InstiNet. InstiNet appears on your Level II screen as INCA. Among other peculiarities about InstiNet, it does not legally have to show its bid and offer through the NASDAQ Level II quote system except in certain situations. Most of the time, it doesn't. More important, InstiNet is so liquid, and has so much listed and OTC stock trades on it, that it is known as the Fourth Market, after the NYSE and NASDAQ. (The first market is the primary distribution of shares.)

InstiNet trading occurs continuously, 24 hours a day. When you see a Level II screen looking static, but Time of Sales is showing a lot of activity, those trades may be happening on InstiNet. And when you see INCA in the Level II montage, what you see reflects only the very best bid and offer currently available on InstiNet. You never know how many limit orders are in the InstiNet book. What you see reflected in the Level II montage may be only the tip of the iceberg.

InstiNet was once the domain of institutions and traders who wanted to trade large blocks of stock anonymously, without appearing in Level II. Until recently, it was practically unavailable to nonprofessional traders, because INCA will not allow individuals direct access to the

INCA order book. Now, however, that's changing. More—and more savvy—individuals now ask their brokers for quotes on InstiNet, and forward-thinking electronic brokerages have installed InstiNet terminals. Now additional liquidity is appearing from nonprofessional traders.

However, InstiNet has major, crushing competition. Several years ago, some forward-thinking people came up with an idea: Why not create an ECN that is specifically geared toward individual traders and open the order book to them as well? With that concept in mind, the Island was created. Most traders know and love the Island. By its very nature it is designed to provide the electronic trader direct access to the market. At time of writing, the Island (seen in your Level II as ISLD) has such tremendous volume and liquidity that it is considering becoming an exchange unto itself. Recently, total share volume traded on the ISLD exceeded that of InstiNet for the first time. This can only be a harbinger of what will come.

Also, since the coming of ISLD, many new ECNs are opening for business, more and more each year. Some of these ECNs, such as Archipelago (ARCA), offer exciting additional options and new ways of routing orders. ARCA uses artificial intelligence algorithms to actively work your orders for you.

Then there's the OptiMark, created by the man who created InstiNet. Its multifunctional, multidimensional order-execution system may create a whole new trading universe. It's being rolled out online as this book is being written.

LADIES AND GENTLEMEN, THE ECNS

Below is a list of the ECNs currently in use. You should memorize them. Knowing that a market participant is an ECN as opposed to a market maker will influence your choice of route.

In the NASDAQ

The Company	Symbol in the Quotes Montage
InstiNet	(INCA)
The Island	(ISLD)
Archipelago ECN	(ARCA)

The Company	Symbol in the Quotes Montage
NexTrade	(NTRD)
Bloomberg's Trade Book	(BTRD)
Spear Leeds and Kellog	(REDI)
The Brass Utility	(BRUT)
Strike	(STRK)
Attain	(ATTN)
MidWestStockExchange	(MWSE)

Several more ECNs are scheduled to start business soon. In the years to come, many more ECNs will likely appear, as the NASDAQ evolves toward a 24-hour auction system open to anyone who wants to buy or sell stock.

A standard ECN allows you to bid and offer stock anonymously in the NASDAQ market. Additionally, ECNs offer subscribers access to their order books and add liquidity and speed to the traders' arsenal. Most ECNs post in the NASDAQ montage in the same manner as a market maker. This resembles placing an ad in the paper (the NASDAQ montage) displaying your firm intention to buy or sell a specific amount of stock at a specific price.

Keep in mind that, if you want to buy stock and appear at the best bid, someone must sell stock to you. Conversely, if you appear at the best ask, someone must buy stock from you. In a fast-moving market where there are virtually no sellers and numerous buyers, your chance of buying at the best bid is limited, at best. It's like waiting in line for a movie: Eventually the movie will be sold out and no tickets will be left (at your desired price). Conversely, if you are trying to sell at the best offer when there are numerous sellers and virtually no buyers, chances of quick execution are limited. You must remember that the NASDAQ is a real market, where buyers try to buy cheap and sellers try to sell dear. There are occasions (such as those described above) when posting to the best bid or ask may not be the fastest route.

Another disadvantage of going through a standard ECN is that ECNs may not be executed against by SOES. Therefore, ECN users will miss out on the SOES-driven liquidity. But judging by the popularity of ECNs, many traders don't seem to mind.

Not all ECNs are created alike. Though no ECNs are SOES-able, some have terrific features beyond just posting in the NASDAQ montage.

Terra Nova's Archipelago, for example, is a cutting-edge example of an ECN with an attitude. Archipelago acts like a great big dragnet. It will not only post to the best bid/offer, but it will also match stock with all the other ECNs. If your order is still not completely filled, it will then preference market makers individually (using SelectNet) for the remainder of the order. Finally, if your order is still not completely filled, it will post to the best bid/offer and wait for someone to complete it, just like a standard ECN. Additionally, all of the partial fills will be charged only one aggregate commission for the entire order. All of this happens in real time, with one mouse click.

In the next chapters, I'll take a closer look at all of the ECNs currently available, including OptiMark, created by the guy who made InstiNet, which came online in the NASDAQ market in late 1999.

16

Off the Book:
InstiNet (INCA)

InstiNet is still primarily the domain of institutional order flow and is not directly available to individuals. It does not make its order book available to the individual trader, so only brokerage houses and institutions can use the InstiNet order-entry terminal.

However, individual traders can still get access. Some brokerage firms have purchased InstiNet terminals and made them available to individuals by proxy. You can phone these firms and ask for a look at a particular stock, and then place an InstiNet order with your broker.

Some other brokers have an order-entry button for InstiNet on their own order-entry systems, but an InstiNet operator still has to execute the trade, so it still may be faster to use a broker with phone-in service. Phone-in gives you a real sense of what's going on in the stock, as well as the ability to modify your order in real time by speaking with the executing InstiNet trader.

One further logistical detail: InstiNet may appear in Level II as INCA. When INCA appears, it may be preferenced like any ECN.

Here's how InstiNet works: Pre-market, post-market, and during market hours you call the InstiNet trader and ask for a look in a particular stock. For example, let's say you make the call pre-market, at 8:30 a.m. The InstiNet trader may respond to your call with, "300 shares bid for at $128; 1,800 offered at $131." The large spread is typical, since InstiNet is a pure auction system. Nobody makes a market. Individuals just show up, anonymously, with stock to buy or sell. Theoretically, if you believe your shares of INTC are worth $1 million apiece, and you are the only person offering at the time, the quote would be, "INTC is currently offered at $1 million a share on InstiNet."

During market hours, prices on InstiNet will often closely match prices on the NASDAQ or listed exchanges. However, InstiNet provides additional information that's not available anywhere else. The trader in the previous example may also say, "The $131 offer is an accumulating seller. They have sold 161,000 shares in the past two weeks. Additionally, there are several other accumulating sellers of size. There are no accumulating buyers of more than 2,000 shares in the past two weeks." This information, when combined with news of an analyst's downgrade of the stock, which came out after market yesterday at 4:15 p.m., and yesterday's closing price of $133, may give you the idea that the stock is being heavily sold and that it is trading down pre-market. If you have been considering going short the stock, this information might be of serious interest.

```
INSTINET                                                         _ @ X
File   Functions   Orders   Messages   Settings


09:21 ATHM&RSSFp 40/2x41/0 1x10 CL    ATHM&RSSFp 40/2x41/0 1x1 CL
09:21 ATHM&INCA 40a9x41/0 4x10 CL

09:20 ATHM&PERTp 39a15x40/6 10x10 CL    ATHM&PERTp 39/7x40a11 10x10 CL
09:20 ATHM&PERTp 39/7x40a11 1x1 CL    ATHM&SLKCp 40/4x41/6 1x1 CL

GRIN   GRAND TOYS INTL INC            Last&S    100 13/6-      Up 0/3      C
Intr-207  Pres-3   WP 14.218            H&S 14/7   L&S 13/4   V 944,100
Age.E....Bid.3..Ask.3..Size    Buy.................  Sell.............USD
CL    S   13/6' 13a13'  2x5   ▮13/3    500           13/7   4,600 A 09/03
CL USCT  12a13  13a13'  1x1   11/0=    500           14/3   5,000 A 09/03
CL CIBC  13/6'  15a3    2x10  14/3   2,000 A 09/03   14/3   3,000 A 09/02
CL SHWD  13/1  13a13'   5x5   14/2   2,000 T 09/03   15a5   7,100 A 08/31
CL NFSC  13/6'  14/4    1x1   13a15  2,000 A 09/02   15/0   2,500 A 08/31
CL MASH  13/6'  14a5    1x1   15/1   2,000 T 08/31   17a3   4,000 A 08/27
CL NITE  12/2  13a13'   1x1   17/3   5,000 X 08/30   17/5  15,000 A 08/27
CL HRZG  13a11  13/7    1x1   17/0   4,400 A 08/27   15a1   3,600 A 08/27
CL SHRP  13a9   14a1    1x1   17a9  10,100 A 08/27   14/6  22,500 A 08/27
CL REDS  13a9   14/2    1x1   17a15  5,000 A 08/27   14/6   4,000 A 08/27
09:22  DJI 11078.4 +235.2   V&N 666.6m (798.3)  TIC +728    CLOSE  (c) INSTINET
```

InstiNet quotes montage

The screen shot above, for fun and reference, portrays an InstiNet quotes montage. On the left is a current read of the NASDAQ quotes montage. On the right is the InstiNet order book. It is quoted in eighths. You can see that only prices and size are mentioned. Market participants transacting in InstiNet are guaranteed anonymity. The best bid is @ 13 3/8 for 500 shares (quotes are default in eighths. On the INCA screen, the 13 3/8 bid is quoted as 13/3.) There is no current offer.

You should also note the presence of dates (09/03, for example) and the designations "A" and "T." The date refers to the last time that this particular market participant bid or offered, while the A refers to accumulating, and the T refers to timed out—in other words, the order was good until a certain time and is now defunct.

You can see that, as recently as 09/03, someone sold 4,600 shares for 13 7/8, and there are numerous accumulating buyers and sellers. Often, you will see many accumulating buyers in a stock that is up significantly. Obviously, given the laws of supply and demand, continuous buying demand tends to create a rise in price. Basically, this is the information your broker sees when you call for a look at a stock in InstiNet.

You may buy and sell stock pre-, during, or post-market through InstiNet, and the majority of post- or after-market trading currently takes place in InstiNet as well. During market hours, prices generally reflect the current market. In other words, the bids and offers in InstiNet are generally less favourable than in the other exchanges during market hours. If the prices were better on InstiNet than in the other exchanges, there would be a cottage arbitrage industry devoted to scalping InstiNet and other exchanges. No such industry exists, though from time to time a more favourable price may be discovered on InstiNet. Often, these more favourable prices reflect big size and are non-negotiable. You might be able to save substantially on a purchase now and again, but you might have to buy 50,000 shares to do it.

PROS & CONS

InstiNet delivers the following advantages:
- Majority of pre- and post-market trading happens in InstiNet
- Information on accumulating buyers and sellers
- Pre- and post-market indications of a stock's direction
- May be preferenced through SelectNet when quotes appear in the NASDAQ montage (Additional charges may be incurred.)

InstiNet's disadvantages include:
- No direct individual access to order book (though reportedly, at press time, InstiNet is rumbling about giving individuals access to viewing the book, but it would allow viewing only, and individuals could not actually enter trades)
- Extra charge: InstiNet currently charges $.015 per share per trade, which is passed along to the individual

If you want to trade before or after market hours, you can often find buyers and sellers through InstiNet. Additionally, during market hours, INCA is often in the NASDAQ montage and can be preferenced through SelectNet, or Archipelago (another ECN, which utilizes SelectNet). You pay 1 1/2 pennies a share for any stock traded with InstiNet.

Some electronic brokerages have begun to offer an InstiNet Key on their platforms as an alternative to individual access to the InstiNet order book. When you use this INCA key, you are not necessarily placing an order directly to InstiNet. You are sending the order to the brokerage house, where an operator will (you hope) see the order and hand enter it into the InstiNet system. In other words, an intermediary has been added to the transaction, so you give up the ability to get looks into the InstiNet order book. As I mentioned before, some of the better firms offer InstiNet on a phone-in basis only. While on the surface this may seem slower, you should consider the way the InstiNet Key really works and what you give up in the process. The looks you get over the phone into the InstiNet order book can be very valuable indeed.

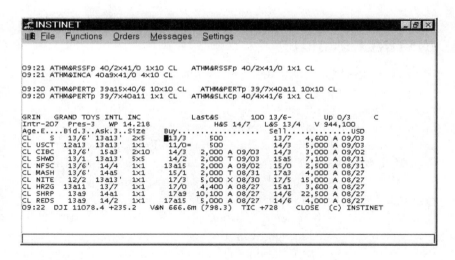

InstiNet terminal

Above is an InstiNet terminal. It is divided into right and left sections. On the left side is a version of the current NASDAQ quotes montage; on the right is the InstiNet bid-and-offer quotation. Note that orders with an A or T are not current quotes—and therein lies the interesting information. T simply stands for timed out. In other words, the order is expired. But A stands for accumulating.

In the example above, at the time the shot was taken, there were a number of accumulating buyers and sellers. During the day this can be of particular interest. For example, let's say you notice that the volume of trades in a particular security seems unusually high, and you wonder if it is simply day-trader-generated liquidity or if an institution is a buyer or seller of size. If you can call your broker and ask for a look at the security, including any accumulating buyers or sellers, you might be surprised at what you hear. Suppose you find that several institutions (you'll never know who they are) have bought 200,000 shares so far on the day and, further, that there are no accumulating sellers. Then, in looking at Level II, you notice one particular market maker, who seems to always show size on the offer but keeps moving away whenever things get close. You might develop the idea that they are really a buyer, not a seller. A look at InstiNet is not necessarily the very best of indicators, but it does help clear the picture.

INSTINET STORIES

More times than I can remember, fellow clients/traders have tried to buy stock on InstiNet pre-market, only to see it gap up several points on open, at which point the client sells it for a handsome profit. I've also seen clients who, upon hearing adverse news shortly after market, sell their stock in InstiNet, beating the selling rush that follows the next day.

BUT BE WARNED: Just because a price trades up on InstiNet pre-market, it doesn't mean the price will keep rising once the NASDAQ or NYSE opens. I've also seen a price trade artificially high as traders bid it up pre-market, only to see the highest print of the day on InstiNet and then watch the price fall right from the open. In my experience, the fact that a stock is up on InstiNet doesn't in itself qualify as a true indication of its eventual price in the markets.

17

No Worries, Mate: The Island (ISLD)

The Island, which appears in the NASDAQ montage as ISLD, is rapidly becoming the most liquid of all ECNs. Because it was designed for use by all, it is readily accessible at any electronic, direct access brokerage worth its salt. So much volume is transacted on ISLD that it is considering becoming its own exchange.

ISLD functions like a standard ECN. It allows you to place limit orders of specific price and quantity in the ISLD order book. When the price of the stock reaches the limit of the order, the order appears in the Level II montage, allowing you to buy at the bid or sell at the ask. Market orders are not accepted, since the ISLD posts to the Level II montage, and someone must either buy or sell stock to you at your specific, firm price.

Another advantage of the ISLD is its order book. You can view the order book for free, in real time, during market hours on the World Wide Web (**www.isld.com**). The Island order book simply lists the orders that individuals and institutions have placed in a particular stock. This is useful because you can see a partial listing of the world's interest in a particular stock. For example, if there are very few orders to buy a stock and a great many orders to sell, it may indicate weakness. In any case, the Island order book tells you where resistance and support lie, at least in the ISLD.

Some less-than-scrupulous electronic brokerages advertise the ISLD order book as part of their software setup, which they charge for. But the ISLD order book is actually available to all, at no cost, at the ISLD Web site.

One of the reasons for the tremendous liquidity of ISLD is its relationship with Datek Securities, a revolutionary online brokerage. Both Island and Datek (**www.Datek.com**) were founded by the same forward-looking people. Datek uses ISLD extensively in its daily brokerage activities, and you can buy at the bid and sell at the ask through Datek, via the Island.

ISLD is available as a point-and-click routing option through most electronic direct access brokerages. The trader simply designates ISLD as the route, enters the limit price and number of shares, and hits enter. The order is immediately placed in the ISLD order book. If the order is executable in the ISLD order book (i.e., if there are enough shares bid/offered at the price), the order is executed instantaneously and is printed to the ticker tape. If the order is not executable in the ISLD order book, it is displayed automatically in the Level II montage. The trader then waits for someone to fill the order.

Like all ECNs, ISLD is not executable via SOES. You must wait and either buy or sell shares from another market participant. (After all, one characteristic of a limit order is that it may never be filled.) Because the NASDAQ is a market, there may be nobody who wants to buy or sell at your limit. If you're trading a fast-moving stock on its way down, and there are many sellers and few buyers, you may not get the order filled by offering out at best ask. Conversely, in a fast-moving stock on its way up, you may not get the order filled by attempting to buy at the best bid. If you absolutely need to be in or out of a particular position, there may be faster routes. However, if a stock is on its way up, offering through ISLD may be just the ticket to get you in or out at your price, because scalpers often exit their positions through ISLD.

In certain situations, ISLD can also be a speedy alternative to SOES. You must choose one or the other, because ISLD is an ECN, so SOES will not transact with it. SOES orders are processed and executed in the NASDAQ system in the order in which they are received. As I mentioned in Chapter 13, they may hang out there for an eternity, especially in a stock with major volume and volatility and on a day when the NASDAQ is experiencing high volume. ISLD, however, has its own order book, separate from the NASDAQ. If there's an ISLD offer or bid already out there at an acceptable price, you can often fill an order almost instantly by choosing ISLD as your route instead of SOES. The order will transact in the ISLD order book, and the transaction will then be printed to the tape.

Transacting in the order book of an ECN often brings faster results, particularly in high-volume stocks. For similar reasons, an ECN execution within the ECNs order book will often transact faster than a SelectNet preference (see Chapter 14).

An ISLD-routed order may result in partial fills. But many brokerages charge only one commission per order, regardless of the number of partial fills. However, if the order partially fills and is then killed by the exchange, the trader can be left holding an odd lot of shares. It is not unusual to be left with five or ten shares of a stock. When this happens, many brokerages require you to place another order and sometimes incur additional commissions. (In such situations, an SOES order may offer a better alternative, since SOES will accept odd lot orders and generally will execute immediately.)

The ISLD also offers a feature called "subscriber-only orders." Some brokerages offer this as an optional feature. A subscriber-only order will fill in the ISLD exchange only and will never post to the NASDAQ quotes montage. If you have access to the ISLD order book, you will see subscriber orders designated by a little "s." If you don't have access to the book, you'll never see them at all.

I see merits and problems with hidden orders. The problems are as follows: You must wait for ISLD-based liquidity to get your order filled. (Nobody can SelectNet pref you, since nobody can even see you there.) On a more philosophical level, subscriber orders hide liquidity from discovery in the open market.

There are also some strong benefits to hidden orders. As some people say, "What the market doesn't see won't hurt it." Placing subscriber orders may even reduce volatility by dampening the effect of additional liquidity. It will be interesting to see if subscriber-only orders gain market share or lose it over time. My bet is they'll lose favour in the long run. However, I'd still like the option available in my software. I like the choice.

PROS & CONS

Here are the advantages of Island:

- Can post to the NASDAQ montage; buy at the bid or sell at the ask

- Tremendous liquidity in the ISLD order book (The ISLD order book may be viewed for free and is open to all who would like to view it.)

- ISLD order-book execution is often faster than routing through the NASDAQ Market (Trades occurring in the ISLD order book are reported instantly to the tape.)

- Any number of shares; keep in mind, however, that if it involves fewer than 100 shares, the order will not post to the NASDAQ quotes montage

- No extra charges for doing business with ISLD (ISLD does charge a fee per order. But in most cases the brokerage firm picks up this cost and doesn't pass it on to the individual.)

- ISLD order book is available to all, at no cost, over the Internet (**www.ISLD.com**)

- ISLD trades after market. Orders stay live on ISLD until 8:00 p.m. EST

- The Island is open for business both pre- and post-market. Orders may be entered starting at 8:00 a.m. EST. Orders will stay live until 8:00 p.m. EST. Orders entered on ISLD pre- and post-market will be visible in the NASDAQ montage.

Island's disadvantages include:

- Only limit orders accepted

- Sometimes pesky partial fills

- ISLD will only post to the montage. It will not actively execute against other market participants. However, other participants may transact with the Island. (That is, they may buy stock from, or sell stock to, the Island).

As I mentioned, the Island order book is freely available in real time on the Internet. However, since it is so useful, many brokerages offer it as part of their software package. The screen capture at the top of the next page shows an example of the ISLD order book. The capture at the bottom of the page shows the Level II montage. Both screen shots were taken at the same time. The ISLD book is elegantly simple in design, with bids, prices, and sizes on the left and offers and prices on the right. As mentioned previously, only the very best of the ISLD bid/offer will show in the Level II quotes montage at any time.

The screen shot below it shows the Level II quotes montage screen shot, taken at the same time as the shot above. Even though there is a fair amount of liquidity to be found on ISLD at 3/8, it simply doesn't show in the NASDAQ Level II quotes montage.

Many traders do much of their trading on the Island. Executions in the ISLD order book are nearly instantaneous. Bidding for or offering stock may take longer, since someone must either sell stock to or buy stock from the Island. This is particularly important in fast markets. As I

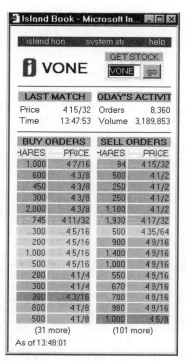

The ISLD order book

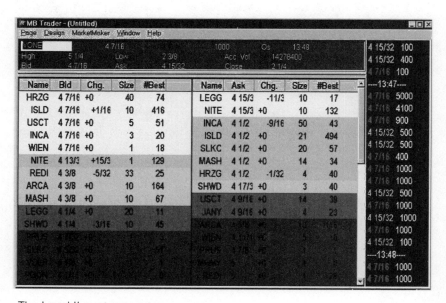

The Level II quotes montage

mentioned earlier, when there are many buyers and few sellers, trying to buy stock by posting to the NASDAQ bid may be slow and ineffective. The same goes for selling when the market is tanking.

One further note on the Island concerns a frequent order-entry error: One of the most common mistakes in placing an ISLD order results in the order being deleted because "it would lock or cross the market." Once the order is deleted from the trading system, it never goes live, and nothing is done. During the half minute or so while you're trying to figure out why the order was deleted, the market can move away from your desired price. The shot below shows a simple illustration of what it means to "lock or cross the market." Note the inside market of 11 by 11 3/8, with ISLD offering 100 shares at 11 3/8.

Placing an order on ISLD

If we were now to place an ISLD order to buy 100 shares at $11, the order would appear after a few seconds in Level II as it does in the next screen shot below.

In placing this order, you are showing to the world your intention to buy 100 shares at $11, not unlike placing an ad in a newspaper. Now you are waiting for someone to sell the stock to you. Note again that ISLD is also on the offer, at the limit price of 11 3/8.

If instead you placed an order to buy 100 shares at 10 3/8 on ISLD, the order would be executed in the ISLD order book (since there is already an order in the ISLD order book to sell 100 shares at 10 3/8).

ODETA	Last	11 3/8					13:55	----13:55----
High	11 3/8	Low	11	Tot Vol	22800			11 3/8 200
BID ↓	11	ASK	11 3/8	Close	11 3/8			

NAME	BID	CHG	SIZE	#BEST	NAME	ASK	CHG	SIZE	#BEST
RILY	11	+1/16	500	1	NITE	11 3/8	+0	500	1
ISLD	11	+0	100	1	ISLD	11 3/8	+0	100	1
NITE	10 7/8	+0	100	0	BRUT	11 1/2	+0	1400	2
SLKC	10 7/8	+0	100	0	BTRD	11 1/2	+0	1000	1
ALLN	10 7/8	+0	100	0	MASH	11 1/2	+0	1000	4
CRUT	10 3/4	+0	100	0	ALLN	11 1/2	+0	100	1
HRZG	10 3/4	+0	100	1	SLKC	11 5/8	+0	100	0
BRUT	10 5/8	+0	100	1	HRZG	11 5/8	+0	100	0

The order appears seconds later in Level II

In a few seconds, you would see a Level II shown in the screen shot below. You would also be the proud owner of 100 shares.

ODETA	Last	11 3/8					13:55	----13:55----
High	11 3/8	Low	11	Tot Vol	22800			11 3/8 200
BID ↓	11	ASK	11 3/8	Close	11 3/8			

NAME	BID	CHG	SIZE	#BEST	NAME	ASK	CHG	SIZE	#BEST
RILY	11	+1/16	500	1	NITE	11 3/8	+0	500	1
NITE	10 7/8	+0	100	0	BRUT	11 1/2	+0	100	1
SLKC	10 7/8	+0	100	0	BTRD	11 1/2	+0	1400	2
ALLN	10 7/8	+0	100	0	MASH	11 1/2	+0	1000	1
CRUT	10 3/4	+0	100	0	ALLN	11 1/2	+0	1000	4
HRZG	10 3/4	+0	100	1	SLKC	11 5/8	+0	100	1
BRUT	10 5/8	+0	100	1	HRZG	11 5/8	+0	100	0
CWCO	10 5/8	+0	100	0	RAJA	11 11/16	-1/16	100	0

The proud owner of 100 shares, as shown in Level II

Now let's say the Level II looks as it does above before you place your order. If you tried now to place an order to buy 100 shares at 11 3/8 on ISLD, the order would be automatically deleted, because it "would lock the market." This means it would cause the best bid to equal the best ask, a condition in which the market is locked. NASDAQ Fair Market Practice rules will not allow a locked market condition to exist. The bid price must be at least 1/32 below the best offer to post on the NASDAQ Level II montage.

Additionally, if you wanted to place an order to buy 1,000 shares at 10 1/2, that is, post to the NASDAQ montage an intention to buy (bid) the stock at 10 1/2, this order would also be deleted, because the bid price is higher than the offer price. This condition is referred to as a "crossed" market. NASDAQ Fair Market Practice rules will not allow a crossed market condition to exist.

LOCKED AND CROSSED

A locked market condition occurs when the bid price is equal to the offer. Locking the market is a violation of NASD Fair Market rules. A crossed market condition occurs when the bid is higher than the offer. It also violates NASD Fair Market rules.

Sometimes you can enter an order that on face value would seem to cross the market and get filled, often to your detriment. Here's how it works.

Remember first that ISLD operates like an exchange unto itself. You can transact in the ISLD book often, and ISLD's speed can be a great benefit. However, let's say stock in ABCD is bidding 10, offered at 10 1/16. Now let's say that you are a seller of 1,000 shares and, further, that ISLD is not bidding or offering at the inside market. Looking at Level II, you see an ISLD bid for 100 shares at 9 3/4. But the current inside bid is 10. If you were to place an order on ISLD to sell at a price *above* 9 3/4 and 10 or less, your order would be cancelled, because it would "lock or cross the market" as we discussed. But if you were to place an order to sell 1,000 shares at 9, you could be done. The reason you could be done is because there may have been liquidity in the ISLD book at a price above your limit of 9.

If there is liquidity in the ISLD book at a price that is better than your low (in this case, $9), your order will be treated as a limit order to sell. The price will be entered as a low, and the order will be executed entirely in the ISLD book regardless of the NASDAQ market.

Let's say that, in the ISLD order book, there were bids at the following prices:

- 100 shares bid at 9 3/4
- 100 shares bid at 9 1/2
- 100 shares bid at 9 1/4, and
- 700 shares bid at 9 1/8

If your sell were treated as a limit order to sell with a low at 9, to be executed in the ISLD book, you would receive the following prints: 100 @ 9 3/4, 100 @ 9 1/2, 100 @ 9 1/4, and 700 @ 9 1/8.

As far as ISLD is concerned, you have just received a price improvement over your order to sell at 9. Lucky you. It's kind of nuts that ISLD will do that, isn't it? Kind of like being hit by a car and then being told that you just got a free ride. But ISLD will do this, and for good reason too.

Here's why. Let's say the same stock ABCD is bid 10, offered at 10 1/8, and ISLD is the only market participant on the bid. ISLD's bidding only 100 shares. At the next lowest price levels, few shares are bid as well. But now you take a look at the ISLD order book. (I will again mention that it is free and available at **www.ISLD.com**.) Now in the ISLD order book, you see a bid for 2,000 shares at 9 15/16. Keep in mind that ISLD will show only its best bid and offer in the NASDAQ Level II montage, so you won't even know that a bid of this size exists unless you have the ISLD order book. But you know what you're doing, and so you have it handy. You also know the time has come to sell. So you enter your order: Sell 1,000 shares ABCD @ 9 15/16 on ISLD. And, whammo, you're done at the following prices: 100 shares @ 10 and 900 shares @ 9 15/16. Now you watch with a grin as everyone else lines up and chases the stock down, more desperate to sell with every moment.

As you can see, the ISLD book can be a good tool. But like all good tools, somebody can get hurt if it's misused. What happens if you accidentally enter an order to sell on ISLD with a ridiculously low price and get filled? Well, the ISLD governors are very fair and will sometimes break trades if clearly erroneous. They base their rulings on such factors as general liquidity, trading patterns, and other relevant information about the stock. If they conclude that a trade occurred at a price so far outside the norm that it must have been done in error, they'll break it. The ISLD governors weigh the facts and base their decision on the market, not on your particular situation. They don't care if your cat died or you drank too much coffee for breakfast. So be careful not to make a mistake.

ISLD STORIES

Many of my clients have faced the following situation: In an extremely fast, overly liquid market, a client has been trying to sell her shares. But the price bounces around so much that, before she can point and click to enter her order, the stock has moved. It moves again and again, up and down, down and up, and all within one or two points. ISLD and many ECNs appear on the bid for a moment, only to disappear as fast as they show up.

In these cases, when the stock is not really going strongly up or down, but just flitters up and down like a hummingbird, I'll ready an order to sell or buy on ISLD. Then I'll wait, finger on the trigger, till ISLD shows up best bid or offer, at the price I have entered. In stocks like these, the wait is usually only several seconds. As soon as I see ISLD there (knowing that it will probably stay there only a fraction of a second) I execute. I call this The Island Magic Trick.

The result? Usually an instantaneous fill. This works because of two factors:

1. Most market makers will preference ISLD using SelectNet. This results in the order routing through the NASDAQ computer first, then going out to ISLD, which takes time. If you have direct access to ISLD, you should use it. You might just beat everyone else by a few milliseconds. And the early bird gets it, every time.

2. I believe that the ISLD computers run a little quicker than those of the NASDAQ. This is probably because a truly unimaginable amount of data is racing around the NASDAQ. In fact, it's a wonder the NASDAQ computers don't fail more often, with such massive burdens placed on them. In any case, if you have direct access to ISLD, and the opportunity to use it strikes, you should.

A NOTE OF CAUTION

ISLD has an infuriating habit of partially filling orders with weird partials, like one share. Try selling one share. One share is the investment equivalent of a hot potato, getting passed from hand to hand, market maker to market maker. Nobody wants the thing. It's damn hard to sell one share.

If you find yourself with one share, or any tiny odd lot for that matter, give it right back on SOES. Obligate somebody to take it off your hands. Why not? After all, they gave it to you (the dirty pranksters!).

There is nothing you can do to avoid the weird lot partial fill, from time to time. And to add injury to insult, every time you place an order, you pay a commission!

Once, very early on in my trading career, in my own account I placed an order to buy 1,000 shares on ISLD, just below the bid. This was a type of scalping play, the unsound economics of which will become clear: I bid for 1,000 shares, hoping to turn right around and sell them immediately at 1/8 profit. The stock traded down to my price, and I watched, as first 53, and then 130 shares traded.... And that was it.

So there I was with 183 shares, and the axe, who had been long gone, entered and appeared on the offer. Other market makers began to shy away immediately, and I knew there was no way I would get my eighth now. All I could think of was retreating. I cancelled the remainder of the order and offered the 183 shares out at the offer.

I got one partial, of one share. And then I noticed that my order was deleted, because it would lock or cross the market. So now I had 182 shares of this stock, which was in the process of falling out of bed, and I had already incurred two commission charges. So (silly, silly, greedy me), I offered out at the best offer again. The stock traded down for a moment, then back up to my price, and I was filled again, this time with six shares. Now, I had 176 shares of a stock I didn't want, and owed three commissions. So (silly, silly, foolish, greedy me), what did I do next? I offered out at the bid, of course!

Five commission charges later, demoralized, humiliated, and with a loss of approximately 3/8 a share, I was done. Well done, burnt, and stuck to the pan, actually. But I had learned a lesson: I didn't know S@#*! about buying or selling stock! This trade began the learning curve.

(In this example, I could have chosen any number of ways of getting out. Given the situation again, I would probably use SOES.)

As with all these systems, it takes some time to learn how to use ISLD. But as the trader on the account, you are responsible for all trades, stupid or not.

18

A New Generation: The Archipelago (ARCA)

The Archipelago ECN is possibly the most controversial routing method available today. Many active traders swear passionately by it, some decry it for its partly institutional ownership, and still others complain of its terribly slow fills. One thing is for sure: ARCA, properly used in the right circumstances, is pure white lightning. Just like all other routing systems, which work well in certain situations and poorly in others, ARCA has its Achilles' heel. But if you know how to use it properly, the Archipelago is one of the most powerful execution tools you can find.

The Archipelago ECN is similar to the Island in that it will allow an individual who has direct access to execute orders within the order book and, additionally, to post to the NASDAQ quotes montage if no liquidity is found elsewhere. However, that is where the similarity ends. Archipelago does several additional things, which make it an amazingly powerful tool. In fact, it's the first of a new generation of ECNs. Because of what they do, I call them the active ECNs. (More on that shortly.)

Like INCA or ISLD, Archipelago has its own order book. Unlike the order book of the Island, however, which is freely available to all over the Internet, Archipelago's order book is available only to those who have access to the Archipelago. A curious and sometimes confusing feature of the Archipelago order book is that, for those who have access to it (and only those who have access to it), the order book is displayed within the NASDAQ Level II quotes montage. If you have access to the Archipelago, your Level II quotes montage might resemble the screen shot at the top of the next page.

There, you can see many ARCHIPs. These ARCHIPs represent the individual orders that comprise the total liquidity available in the Archipelago book. If you have access, it is invaluable to be able to see all the individual orders, since it gives you insight into the thinking of other

Level II with Archipelago

traders. If, suddenly, 25 individual orders to buy appear on Archipelago, then you may safely assume there is increased demand. Additionally, if there are very few shares offered, and you see many chippies bidding at the offered price, you can bet you won't get those shares. You might even be influenced to place a buy order slightly above the inside market. Sacrificing 1/16 here may often be better than chasing the stock and wondering why you aren't getting filled.

You can also notice a lack of ARCHIPs below. The frames in the shots above and below were frozen simultaneously.

What you see if you don't have access to ARCA

The screen shot at the bottom displays what the rest of the world sees, without full ARCA access. They can determine only the aggregate of all individual Archipelago orders. For example, if there were individual orders to buy 100, 500, 400, and 1,000 shares on Archipelago, and you had access to the Archipelago ECN, you would see all the orders displayed individually, along with ARCA at the bottom, reflecting the aggregate size of 2,000 (100 + 500 + 400 + 1,000). If you did not have full access to the Archipelago ECN, you would see only ARCA with a size of 2,000. This feature can be confusing, but once you get used to it, it can be very helpful, since any insight into current market sentiment will always add value when you make buy or sell decisions. You can also see clearer areas of support and resistance this way. If you note, for example, a tremendous amount of liquidity in the ARCA book at say, 30 1/16, when a stock is on its way up, and it's currently at 29 7/8, this might add value to your exit strategy.

Archipelago is available as a point-and-click routing option in the order execution platforms of the better direct-access-oriented electronic brokerages. Archipelago makes use of the SelectNet execution system, run by NASDAQ Market Systems, to facilitate its order handling external to its own order book. When a limit order is entered to buy using Archipelago, the following operations occur almost instantaneously and with the push of one button: ARCA checks its own order book and matches as much stock as is available in-house. ARCA then uses SelectNet to link to all the ECNs like a big dragnet and transacts as much stock as is available. You might recall from Chapter 14 that a SelectNet link to an ECN provides a near-instantaneous execution at electronic speed, provided the stock hasn't traded ahead. Also note that ARCA will attempt to work your order, first tapping the inside market and working toward your limit price and potentially providing price improvement along the way.

Let's say for the sake of explanation that there is no liquidity available in any ECN at the current inside market. ARCA will then preference each market maker individually, taking as much stock as possible. It uses a proprietary algorithm to dynamically identify the market maker to preference first, then sends a preference to them. This process continues repeatedly until the order is filled or until the limit price is reached. This is why you can enter market orders as well as limit orders on ARCA. If a limit order becomes unmarketable or was entered as a limit outside the market to begin with, ARCA will post the order to the NASDAQ quotes montage, just like a standard ECN.

All this happens at a speed faster than your eyes can track and with a single mouse click. So you can see why Archipelago can fill massive orders almost instantly. I have had an order of 10,000 shares fill in less than 10 seconds on Archipelago.

But there is one gaping hole in the armour of Archipelago, and it's big enough to render ARCA almost useless in certain circumstances. That's because its utilization of SelectNet, which makes Archipelago so powerful, is actually a double-edged sword.

You will recall from Chapter 14 that a SelectNet preference against an ECN works at electronic speed. However, you will also recall that when a market maker receives a SelectNet preference, they are obligated to respond immediately, but are also given a grace period of 30 seconds. Thirty seconds in a fast-moving market is a lifetime. A stock can run like a freight train right past you while you wait for your order to be ... to be ... to be ... declined. So you repeat the process, preferencing more market makers, waiting for their replies, and again, 30 seconds later, you're declined. Then, as the stock continues tanking like a piledriver, you repeat the process again and again and again until you fall off your chair or rip your hair out, whichever comes first.

Aware of this chink in its armour, the creators of Archipelago programmed the system to cancel a preference after 30 seconds and move on to the next market maker. But even with this modification, ARCA becomes nearly useless in certain situations. For example, you own 4,000 shares of ABCD stock, which is very active, trading 10 million shares a day. Some major news appears, and you need to sell now. You look on Level II, and you see very few buyers and many sellers queuing up. You can tell this in advance, because you have full access to the ARCA order book. On the bid there are all market makers, showing measly 100-share bids, to boot, and there are no other ECNs in sight. Now the stock starts trading down. Having had many near-instantaneous executions with Archipelago, you enter your order to sell 4,000 shares at market, and then you wait. The stock goes crazy as everyone panics to get out. The price drops like a piledriver, and still you wait for your fill. And wait....

Finally, after an apparent eternity, you get filled, three points below the price when you entered. All this happened because of the extraordinary supply of stock combined with very little demand. Into this market, you preferenced market makers and gave them the ability to decline you. On top of it all, you gave them 30 seconds each to do it.

Selling a large amount of a crazy stock into a tanking market requires finesse. Thankfully, however, most stocks do not behave this way. However, you should still understand the possibilities so you don't get caught unawares. There are better ways to sell into an insane market and to buy into a market that's going ballistic, if you see only market makers and no ECNs.

If you are long a crazy, fast-market stock (which I hope doesn't happen too often), a very effective way to sell your position may be a SelectNet preference to the axe, at a price lower than the current best bid. You may find yourself saving time and money by foregoing 1/16 or 1/8 in these circumstances, and just plain getting out, rather than chasing the stock over hill and dale into the valley of the damned.

But what if you wanted to sell and there were no market makers at the bid? What if on the bid were five or six ECNs instead, a situation that's not atypical. The ECNs show an aggregate total of shares well in excess of your 4,000. You place your order on ARCA, and wham, you're done, practically before you can move your fingers off the keypad.

That's because a SelectNet preference against an ECN fills almost instantaneously, as long as there is available stock. And ARCA goes out to them all, automatically.

There is a second situation that renders Archipelago nearly useless. ARCA will accept only round lot orders placed in multiples of 100. If you have 193 shares of ABCD stock, ARCA simply won't accept your odd-lot order. In this case, SOES, or ISLD offer better alternatives.

What it lacks in particular situations, ARCA gives back when it works. One of the most striking features of ARCA is that it will often improve the price of your order. Say you want to sell a stock, and you enter a limit price of 58 1/8. If the current bid is higher than 58 1/8, ARCA will work the order, hitting bids all the way down to your limit level. This is convenient if you want to sell the stock now, but you don't want to offer it and wait for someone to come along and buy it from you, and you have a limit price you feel comfortable with. Often your order will be price improved, since their buyers will pay prices higher than your limit. This obviously works on the buy side, too.

ARCA accepts market orders too, but I'd advise against using ARCA market orders unless you're sure there is adequate liquidity at the price you like. That's because a sudden onslaught of market orders can whipsaw a price down, only to get filled with a lousy print. The concept here is similar to an SOES market order described in Chapter 13.

Archipelago may be used to buy or sell stock pre- or post-market and on weekends too. Orders entered in Archipelago during market hours expire at 4:02 p.m. EST. However, you can enter orders after 4:02, and they'll stay live, viewable in the Level II quotes montage until they cancel at 5p.m. EST. At 5:01, you can enter the order again, and it will stay live until midnight EST. Additionally, orders may be placed before market, starting at 8:45 a.m. EST. Archipelago intends eventually to become the 24-hour trading vehicle of choice, open round the clock to all who have access.

PROS & CONS

ARCA's advantages include:
- Accepts market and limit orders
- Will actively work the order as well as passively post to the NASDAQ quotes montage; can buy at bid or sell at ask
- Tremendous liquidity in the Archipelago order book
- Order book appears in the Level II montage
- Preferences other ECNs and market makers through SelectNet
- Buy or sell pre- or post-market hours

ARCA's disadvantages include:
- Accepts round lot orders only
- Utilization of SelectNet when only market makers are present can cause slow to no execution, particularly during fast market conditions

Many traders do the majority of their trading through Archipelago. Trades executed in the Archipelago order book are often nearly instantaneous, as are trades executed when ECNs are on the inside bid or offer. You can move large amounts of stock in minimal time through judicious use of Archipelago. Also, you pay only one transaction charge per order on Archipelago, regardless of the number of partial fills. In selling 5,000 shares of stock, for example, you can easily get ten or 20 partial prints as the order is being filled. On Archipelago, you would pay for only one transaction. However, if any of the executions are against ECNs that charge per share for doing business with them, the ECN charges are passed along to you. These charges are not insignificant. (Recall, for example, that InstiNet charges 1 1/2 cents a share). You must weigh this cost against the benefits of holding the position or using alternative routes. However, it is still often beneficial to incur these charges on partial orders with the various ECNs rather than pay additional commissions for additional orders, as often happens with the Island and other routes.

ARCA STORIES

For a full experience of ARCA's potential you must try ARCA when many ECNs are on bid/offer. As I mentioned before, I've had nearly instantaneous fills on ARCA on orders of up to 10,000 shares. But ARCA is not all rosy, and danger lurks in its system as well.

I remember one such non-rosy occasion with crystal-clear vision. I was going to execute an order for 10,000 shares of a very volatile stock. I was a bit nervous because of the size, but I'd decided the moment was now, and for the full amount. I'd been watching carefully with my finger on the trigger. I'd filled out my order-entry screen completely, and my finger was on the mouse button. I was waiting for enough ECN liquidity to appear at the inside price to fill the majority of my order.

In really volatile stocks, you'll often notice a fluttering ECN-driven liquidity that often appears at the inside market. The key is to wait a few seconds until enough ECNs have lined up to fill most of the order.

Suddenly, things resolved: ISLD, INCA, REDI, BRUT, and BTRD all appeared at the inside best. This was an ideal situation. I clicked automatically, without hesitation, instincts primed and honed, milliseconds after recognition.

Within seconds, partial fills started covering my order entry screen. But something was wrong. I wanted to sell, not buy.

I had clicked the wrong button, and partial buys were filling my screen with a vengeance. The hair on the back of my neck stood up and, in slow motion, I saw my entire erroneous order fill, right before my eyes. I drove the cursor over the cancel button, but by the time I clicked it, I had my complete fill: 10,000 shares of a stock I not only didn't want, but I also wanted to sell.

Let's just say I learned my lesson. Meanwhile, if you're truly a masochist, you should try selling 20,000 shares of a ridiculous, volatile stock into a tanking market.

The lesson is this: ARCA truly is a fast vehicle, and will fill your order given proper circumstances and use. Use it wisely, and it will do what you ask.

19

Quiet, Unassuming, and Effective: Attain (ATTN)

Attain (ATTN) is a lesser-known ECN owned and operated by the electronic brokerage All Tech Securities. It is part of a complete trading platform offered by the brokerage of the same name. Founded by electronic trading revolutionary Harvey Houtkin, author of the seminal book *The SOES Bandit*, ATTN tries to match stock in its own order book. Then if it hasn't completed the order, it uses SelectNet to link all ECNs at the price specified. Still not having filled the order completely, it will preference market makers at the inside market. If it still hasn't transacted, it will post to the NASDAQ quotes montage.

Similar to Archipelago, during fast-market situations or when no market makers are on the bid, ATTN's efficiency is greatly reduced, making it especially susceptible to partially filled or cancelled orders. Unfortunately, ATTN is not enabled to show its order book, even if you have direct access.

The system also offers point-and-click order changes. In using other ECNs, you must first click on the live order to cancel it, wait for the cancel to be confirmed, then re-enter the order at a new price. ATTN has a nifty feature that will cancel the order for you and automatically re-enter it. It works in the following way: You click the order, then click on a little arrow button to raise or lower the price. Then you hit enter. The old order will be cancelled and the new order entered. I have been told that this saves time and aggravation when changing an order. In reality, the order will still be cancelled by the NASDAQ just as if you'd pressed cancel. But in a fast-moving stock, seconds count, which makes this a very useful feature.

ATTN has another interesting feature that the others don't. It's called Hit the Street. This preferences all market makers at the inside market with the full size of the order. Obviously, this results in a more complete fill, since all market makers have an incoming liability order and must respond by either accepting in full, partialling, or declining. This function is available only to the better traders, and for good reason. If all market makers accept, you may wind up owning more shares than you know what to do with. However, if there are only one or two market makers at the bid/offer, and the combined size is much less than you've got to transact, a fast and favourable fill can be achieved with minimal effort. The risk, of course, is that you will overfill. However, if your experience and observation tell you that the market makers at the inside market are not size buyers on the day, then you might just get a great fill with minimal effort.

Much like the other ECNs, ATTN will accept orders and post them in the NASDAQ montage after hours.

PROS & CONS

The advantages of ATTN include:
- Accepts market and limit orders
- Will actively work the order as well as post to the NASDAQ quotes montage; can buy at bid or sell at ask
- Preferences other ECNs and market makers through SelectNet
- Buy or sell pre- or post-market hours
- No extra charges for doing business with ATTN
- Point-and-click raise/lower price
- Hit the Street function
- After-market trading

ATTN's disadvantages include:
- Accepts round lot orders only
- No visible order book
- Utilization of SelectNet when only market makers are present can cause slow to no execution, particularly during fast-market conditions
- Hit the Street can cause overfills
- Lack of comparative liquidity

ATTN has suffered lately from a comparative lack of liquidity. Total volumes of ISLD and ARCA have surpassed ATTN by huge leaps and bounds. It's hard to say why. Perhaps ATTN's competitors have developed more effective marketing plans. Nevertheless, users of ATTN swear by it. Clearly, it is a good system, created by a true market reformer. When Harvey Houtkin says he's changed the markets, I believe him. His influence on day trading is truly unique, and it will be interesting to see how his company continues to evolve after the revolution is accomplished.

20

Other Systems You'll Meet: OptiMark, SuperDot, Bloombergs et al.

BLOOMBERG TRADE BOOK (BTRD)

The Bloomberg Trade Book (BTRD) is used by mainly institutions and individuals associated with institutions, such as money managers. It is run by Bloomberg, the news/analysis/research provider. Bloomberg terminals are expensive, but they deliver high-quality information, which institutional clients can afford and appreciate. As a result, mainly institutional trades are originated through BTRD. However, you can often see BTRD bidding or offering in the NASDAQ montage, ready to be executed against. Likewise, you can transact with BTRD through SelectNet and therefore Archipelago as well. At the time of this writing, BTRD charges a fee of 1 1/2 cents a share to those who do business with it on both buys and sells.

BRASS UTILITY (BRUT)

Also used mainly by brokerage houses and institutions, the Brass Utility (BRUT) is more than an ECN. It is a full-featured, position-minding front-end-order execution system. However, for the time being, Brass Utility confines itself to institution-originated business. In the near future, rumour has it that it may open its doors to individual traders. After all, a market can only be ignored for so long. For now, the cost of transacting with BRUT is 1 1/2 cents a share, both buy side and sell side. One may do so through SelectNet, and therefore Archipelago as well. BRUT will not transact with odd lot orders.

SPEER, LEEDS, AND KELLOG (REDI)

REDI is also a front-end order-execution system used by institutions and the individuals associated with them. Transacting with the REDI ECN costs 1 1/2 cents a share, buy or sell, and may be done via SelectNet and therefore Archipelago. REDI will not transact with odd lot orders.

NITE SECURITIES (NITE)

I've included NITE here since there seems to be some confusion as to whether NITE is an ECN or not. NITE is reportedly the largest market maker in the NASDAQ. It trades staggering volume and is gaining in volume daily. NITE runs an internal ECN of sorts. It uses Brass Utility as a front-end order-matching and -entry system. If you were an institutional client, it's possible that you would be filled within NITE's book. If not, NITE would bid or offer in the NASDAQ as NITE (market maker) or BRUT (ECN) or through any of the other available ECNs. NITE's internal order book is not open to individuals. It can be accessed through SelectNet and therefore through ARCA, ATTN, and BTRD.

OPTIMARK

OptiMark, which began operating in the second half of 1999, is the call market of the NASDAQ, functioning like its central order book. In addition to providing the NASDAQ market with a central limit book, OptiMark also provides access to all the listed exchanges.

OptiMark is not an ECN or a broker/dealer. It is a facility of the NASDAQ. This means that, since it is not an ECN, it is not subject to the ECN display rules. In other words, bids and offers in the OptiMark system will not show up in the NASDAQ montage. Orders entered in OptiMark will simply execute once they become marketable, and nobody will have the ability to view any kind of order book for it. OptiMark takes pride in this feature: Buyers and sellers are guaranteed anonymity. In fact, the anonymity of buyers and sellers in OptiMark is so completely protected that individuals and institutions alike will be able not only to enter simple orders, but also to enter entire order profiles, encompassing trading strategy and discretionary choices.

For example, if you were an institution and you wanted to buy 700,000 shares of ABCD, currently priced at 30 by 30 1/8, you might choose to work into the order, buying right here, at 30 1/8. But if you knew that, once you'd bought a lot of this stock, the price might start to rise due to simple laws of supply and demand, you'd have developed a complex trading strategy to get the stock as economically as possible. As part of your strategy, you'd be willing to pay up to 30 7/16 if you could buy the entire 700,000 shares in one shot. But if anyone got wind of your plan to buy 700,000 shares, you'd be screwed.

Using OptiMark, you could enter an order profile with these stipulations, and nobody would ever know that you were a buyer. No one would even know that this order existed.

You could go even further. To control ticket costs (which I describe in more detail in Chapter 25), for example, you can execute orders in minimum blocks of 10,000 or 20,000 or more. You can set minimum block sizes at different price levels, and you can enter your preference (on a scale of 1 to 10) for transacting at different price/size levels. Obviously, many of these features will not be of interest to individual traders just trading their own account, but OptiMark provides a glimpse of the future regarding automated execution systems.

OptiMark has another revolutionary aspect: its graphical user interface. Orders placed in OptiMark are represented by a grid composed of multicoloured blocks. The order itself can be changed by point-and-click methods of dragging blocks, lines, and colours around. A picture is

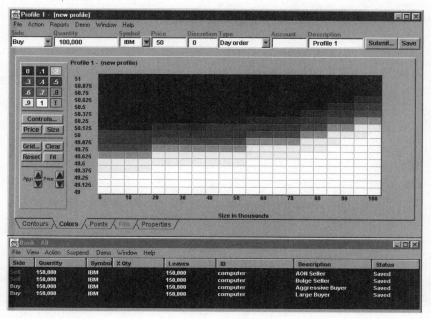

OptiMark order profile

worth a thousand words. The screen shot on the previous page shows a picture of an order in OptiMark.

Though representation of the order as a grid of coloured blocks may seem exotic, it is simple to understand once you know how the thing works.

And the system operates at truly amazing capacities. One five-minute entry of an order into OptiMark will do the work of a human trader watching the market full time and working the order for days. It will even encompass all the trader's discretionary choices, automatically, without the trader even being there.

OptiMark is, in my opinion, one of the most revolutionary developments in the equities markets. If it becomes widely accepted by institutions, it will change the very nature of the markets. Needless to say, there may be some resistance amongst the trading community. In particular, market makers may be facing a predicament similar to the one that faced the autoworkers in the 1970s and 1980s.

TRADING THE NYSE WITH SUPERDOT

The NASDAQ is an auction system in which many market participants bid and offer competitively, thereby theoretically creating a more fair and efficient market. Unlike the NASDAQ, the listed exchanges utilize the specialist system with a centralized order book. The order book contains all the buy-and-sell limit orders placed in the particular stock, as well as all the market-on-close/market-on-open orders. The orders drive the market. It follows the laws of supply and demand with an administrator in between called a specialist.

The specialist controls the order book and sets the prices according to supply and demand. When America Online (AOL) traded nearly 100 million shares in a single day recently, one person oversaw the entire staggering volume of shares. The specialist alone knows where all the future orders are (i.e., many sellers at 30, many buys at 28 1/2). As a result, that person is in a unique position to manipulate the market to his advantage, which he does.

Being a specialist is special indeed. It is a licence to make nearly risk-free money, and gobs of it. A specialist might receive a huge order to buy 100,000 GE from a floor broker representing a large mutual fund, and would say, "What a coincidence. I'm a buyer too." The specialist then participates along with the buy, maybe even selling shares back to the buyer as the price rises.

To be fair, a specialist faces the real risk of a downturn or crash, in which an inordinate amount of sell orders come in. When this happens, the specialists have to make a market and take the other side, all the way down "to the mats," as they say. In such a case, the specialists quickly run through all their capital, then have to mortgage everything they have and borrow from all of the investment houses to the max. During the crash of 1929 and again in 1987, the markets came precipitously close to closing because the banks (which were contractually obligated to back the specialists) refused to come up with the necessary cash.

None of this, of course, concerns the day trader. But the SuperDot does. The SuperDot is the proprietary, electronic link to the order book of the specialist. It is available as a point-and-click routing option on all the better trading platforms. Orders entered and executed through it are said to go through "the machine"; as opposed to a floor broker who also brings the specialist orders. Many times, large institutional players prefer to engage the services of a floor broker, as that person is in a unique position to see what's going on in a stock (even though nobody but the specialist gets to view the order book).

The order book for each stock on the NYSE is centralized. There is only one. (On the NASDAQ, many market makers possess various orders.) So market and limit as well as stop orders and stop limit orders are accepted, as are "good till cancelled" (GTC), and they all may be entered via SuperDot.

If they involve more than 1,000 shares, these orders may be automatically matched and executed by the machine. However, it's important to note that there is only one true market participant, the specialist, and the price the specialist sets is the price where the stock trades. Unmarketable orders will sit in the order book until the stock trades to a marketable level. However, you can bid or offer stock, and the specialist is required to display your size along with their own.

Several traders I know who like to scalp often find NYSE stocks with little to no volatility that trade within a certain established range. They'll buy at the bid and turn around and sell at the offer. One trader I know employs this as a regular strategy, scalping 1/8 or 3/16 a dozen times a day on 900 shares. This is an odd strategy, for which the specialists are relatively unprepared, when compared with market makers on the NASDAQ. It is not, however, an approach that I would seriously consider.

Nevertheless, specialists get paid by the exchange on a per-share basis for the number of shares they transact, and they'll often fill a small order if they stare at it long enough. Furthermore, studies have been done regarding price improvement on the exchanges. They have found that small orders of less than 300 shares done on the NYSE tend to receive price improvements a small majority of the time.

Regional exchanges generally follow the NYSE's pricing cues. However, if you can execute on the regionals in a timely manner, you'll find arbitrage opportunities from time to time. A listed exchange may be slow to update its price, and you may be able to profit from an offer that's lower than the current NYSE bid. But these are few and far between.

Below is a screen shot of AOL, a listed security.

AOL	Last	95 3/8	- 1 7/16		12:58		95 5/16	500
High	96 11/16	Low	94 1/4	Tot Vol	5640700		95 1/4	100
BID ↓	95 1/4	ASK	95 3/8	Close	96 13/16		95 5/16	1000
							95 3/8	200
							95 3/8	200
							95 3/8	100

NAME	BID	SIZE		NAME	ASK	SIZE		---- 12:58 ----	
NYS	95 1/4	30		NYS	95 3/8	40		95 1/4	500
CSE	95 3/16	8		NAS	95 3/8	1		95 1/4	100
NAS	95 3/16	1		BSE	95 1/2	10		95 5/16	200
CIN	95 1/8	1		CIN	95 1/2	1		95 3/8	100
BSE	95	9		CSE	95 1/2	1			
				PHS	95 3/4	1			

Shot of AOL, listed on the NYSE

In early 2000, Datek Securities sent a message to its clients stating that it was the first brokerage to offer after-hours trading. That may be so for the full-service brokerages, but day traders have had access to the after-hours markets since 1998. In both pre- and post-market, the vast majority of market participants are absent. However, the ECNs that bid and offer in the aftermarket still participate actively. Subject to their individual policies outlined earlier, you can bid and offer on the ECNs around the clock. Yes, liquidity is limited, and yes, not all ECNs post their bids/offers to the NASDAQ data feed after hours—InstiNet comes to mind—but all this is changing.

Below is a screen shot for the after-hours market. Note the active ISLD, ARCA, and MWSE bids and offers.

RED HAT INC									
RHAT	R	108	↓	+23 1/16	200		Ot		16:01
High	109 7/8	Low		83 3/8		Acc. Vol.		8215800	
Bid ↑	108	Ask		108		Close		84 15/16	

Name Bid	Chg.	Size	#Best	Name Ask	Chg.	Size	#Best
MWSE 107 1/16	-7/16	1	34	ISLD 108 1/4	+0	2	1253
ISLD 107	+0	11	1640	ARCA 108 5/16	+1/16	1	111
ARCA 0	+0	0	122	MWSE 108 15/1	+0	1	45
DKNY 107 15/1	+0	2	56	NITE 108	+0	1	209
SHWD 107 15/1	+0	2	56	RAMS 108 1/16	+0	2	77
SLKC 107 15/1	+0	1	101	USCT 108 1/8	+0	1	11
MONT 107 7/8	+0	1	31	GSCO 108 3/8	+0	2	5
INCA 107 3/4	+0	10	163	INCA 108 3/8	+0	2	169
MASH 107 11/1	+0	10	64	MASH 108 1/2	+0	10	35
HRZG 107 5/8	+0	1	33	PFSI 108 1/2	+0	1	1
MLCO 107 1/2	+0	2	41	NFSC 108 9/16	+0	1	61
SUSQ 107 1/2	+0	1	15	PERT 108 3/4	+0	1	14
NITE 107 1/4	+0	1	239	EVRN 108 13/1	+0	1	19
AGIS 106 15/1	+0	2	10	HMQT 108 15/1	+0	1	7
BEST 106	+0	1	15	SHWD 108 15/1	+0	1	28
GSCO 105 5/8	+0	2	29	HRZG 109	+0	4	30

The after-hours market

Note the live orders on MWSE, ARCA, and ISLD. All of these may be executed against if you have access to the ECN.

At the moment, the issue of online trading seems overblown. There is so little liquidity after hours that you cannot seriously trade. But when the Chicago Board of Options opened, there was no liquidity there either. Now it is one of the most vibrant, active exchanges in the world. Recently, eight of the major ECNs reached an agreement in principle to link all their order books for seamless transparent price discovery and execution. And Datek's announcement has stirred great interest in after-hours trading. In the near future, trading after hours may be ubiquitous.

21

Fast and Crazy: Market Profiles

For ease of discussion, I've divided the market into several conditions that will affect your trading. You should use the information in this chapter for reference only. Remember, the nature of the negotiated markets is constantly changing, and there is no sure-fire route to executing a trade. You must analyze all relevant factors and make the best choice based on your knowledge and interpretation of the situation. The following charts do not represent the be-all and end-all to routing. That depends entirely on your comprehension of the situation at hand.

FAST MARKET CONDITIONS

Fast market conditions (FMCs) exist when NASDAQ advises all participants of FMCs. But they also exist at all times in certain stocks. If you are trading a stock with an average daily volume of several millions, and the volume available at the inside market usually amounts to several thousand shares as opposed to the multi-thousand share size that tends to limit volatility, you are trading a stock which I call a "fast market stock." These stocks are much more difficult to trade, given their general volatility and lack of volume at the inside market. Often, the price/size of participants will change before you can even enter an order.

In trading these stocks, consider strategy first. It may be necessary to accept the loss of an eighth right away (and just get out) rather than offer stock out repeatedly, chase the stock down, and finally lose because of plain old greed. Likewise, if you get stuck trying to liquidate an odd lot (say 932 shares), it's often better to sell the round lot number of shares first (in this case 900 shares) because a round lot opens you up to many more order routing possibilities. Of course you will incur an extra commission doing this, and I don't like that sort of slippage. But consider this: $25 extra commission, plus the loss you will incur when you SOES

Fast Market Routing

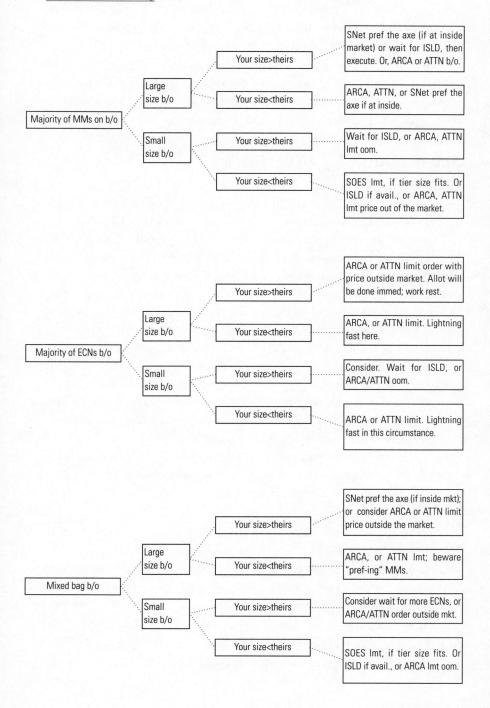

out of your 32 remaining shares (say $1 on 32 shares, or $32) for a total "charge" of $57 vs. the potential one-point loss on the entire 932 shares ($932!). Common sense will tell you: Get out of the majority of your shares the quickest way possible, then pick up the pieces.

Review the chart on the previous page, a diagram of a common sense approach to fast market conditions. Try to stay away from these stocks until you are confident of your knowledge and on-your-feet thinking. Buying or selling in fast market conditions always requires finesse.

SLOW MARKET CONDITIONS

These are the most straightforward conditions in which to trade. Since many slow stocks also trade in low average volumes, several unique situations may be present. One situation is that the axe in the stock may show several thousand shares on the b/o at any given time. This happens because these slow-moving stocks (that nobody cares about) are not often traded actively by day traders and the like. Consequently, the market makers feel a little more free to show the world what they are doing. When there is not a lot of stock actually traded, sometimes they wish to attract buyers or sellers by showing size. But beware. Stocks with the smallest float and the smallest average daily volume are often the most volatile ones if there is sudden tremendous interest. So if you've just found out about a stock (because it's launching a new Web site or something) and it normally trades 60,000 shares a day, but today, it's already traded 4 million, throw all slow market ideas out the window.

You may also find few shares shown at the b/o. If so, it is of real importance to identify the axe. In these sorts of stocks, the axe often controls a truly disproportionate amount of liquidity. Watch for them and try to do business with them. They'll have the orders or inventory to facilitate your trade.

If the stock doesn't trade many shares (relatively speaking) beware offering out large size. In a stock that trades 20,000 shares daily, with market makers showing small size (100–500 shares), an offer of 5,000 shares can really affect the market. Market makers may lower their bids, and you may get stuck with nothing done.

Often in slow-moving low-volume stocks, there are few ECNs to be found. This is another good reason to know the axe. I've discussed how to find the axe in a stock that doesn't trade (see Chapter 9). Since no shares

Slow Market Routing

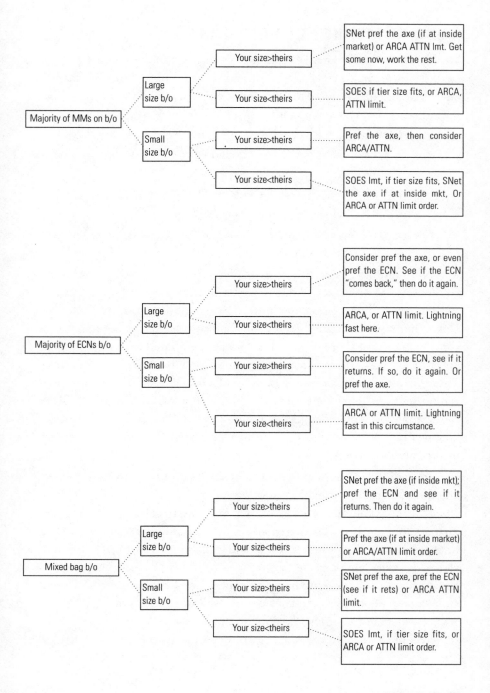

may have traded today, Level II information like #best or hammer may be useless.

NORMAL MARKET CONDITIONS

We experience normal market conditions every day, in the vast majority of stocks. Unfortunately, we often find ourselves trading crazy stocks, in crazy market conditions. If you're wondering if the stock you are trading falls into the normal category, ask yourself the following questions:

– Is the stock an IPO?

– Has major news with huge consequences for this stock just hit the market?

– Is this a thinly traded security on an average day?

– Is this stock a high-flying Internet stock?

If you answered yes to any of these questions, chances are you are not trading a normal market condition stock.

Normal market conditions exist when a stock is trading in typical volumes based on its month-over-month performance and the events of today carry no major news concerning the stock. Perhaps, for example, Dell Computers has traded 10 million shares today. This is normal. It is a volatile stock, but there is almost always enough liquidity in this stock to enter or exit a position of small size (under 1,000 shares) at one price. There are almost always several thousand Dell shares bid or offered at any given time. This is in contrast to the high-flying Internet stocks (UBID, for example), which often have so few shares bid/offered that the price changes before you can even type in your order. (Thank goodness for macros and hot keys.)

In trading normal market condition stocks, you need to consider the amount of liquidity available before entering an order. For example, in a stock with big volume, offering out when trying to sell might be a great idea, as long as 100,000 shares aren't offered alongside yours. With a huge amount of volume trading and relatively few shares offered alongside yours, chances are that your inside market offer may get taken. But if the stock is tanking hard, and there are 100,000 shares offered already, you might want to reconsider and sell your stock now. ARCA and ATTN will work the order for you if you place the order at a price below the current market. In the language of chess, you must always consider

Normal Market Routing

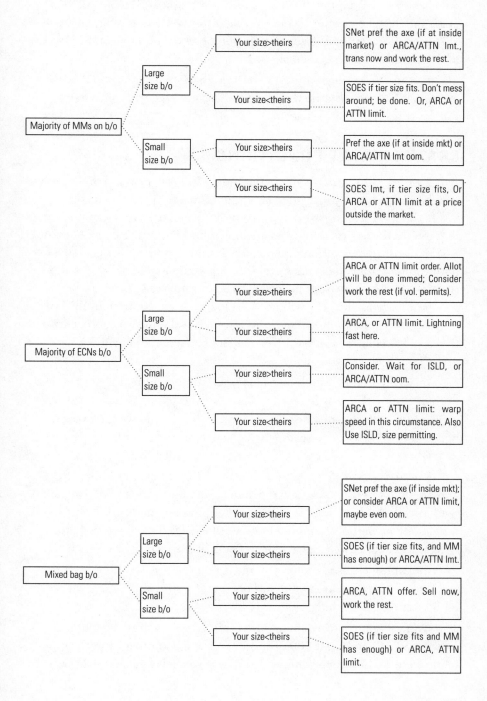

the efficacy of sacrificing your pawn (the 1/16 more you might make or not lose) to save your king. In other words, when you need to be out, don't make the mistake of offering out over and over while watching the stock plummet. Bottom line: If you decide you need to sell now, do it. Don't mess around and put yourself at risk for a 16th.

The previous page shows a routing chart that you should try to understand, along with the reasoning behind it. Once you understand it, you won't need to look at it again.

CRAZY MARKET CONDITIONS

No chart exists for crazy market conditions. In crazy market conditions, which occur everyday, the price and field of market participants change faster than you can possibly type an order. Finesse with a capital F is required in these situations, and a simple chart just won't do it. A chart would just distract you from the market. Try not to trade in this condition until you have fully mastered Level II interpretation and all the execution systems. To do otherwise is to accept huge, crushing risk.

In a crazy market you will need crystal-clear concentration. You will need to anticipate the local move in advance and enter your order with the next 30 seconds in mind. If you get stuck in a preference order, those 30 seconds will cost you dearly.

You will need to watch and plan your strategy in real time, maybe even sitting with an order ready, finger on the trigger, waiting for the screen to resolve into one favourable for the sort of order you are placing, before executing it. Once again, it may be necessary to sacrifice a pawn to save a king.

Countless times I've heard from traders who have, because of ego and greed, chased a stock down, placing order after order—offering out—in a stock that was dropping like a rocket-powered piledriver, only to be repeatedly passed over and declined until they sold at the very bottom (when buyers finally came back in and bought the stock at the very low.)

In trading crazy markets, you must be pound wise and remember your size. On 99 shares, the loss of one point isn't really significant. On 6,000 shares, it's crushing.

Don't sweat the tiny shares. If you have 932 shares, do yourself a favour and sell 900 first. 900 is a round lot and you open yourself up to many more routing opportunities this way. If you sell your 900 right away, you won't really sweat a loss of one point on the 32 remaining shares. Get out of the majority of your position, then consider SOES for the rest and just be done with it.

In crazy market situations, market maker size will almost always be smaller than you've got, and it requires skill and finesse to sell even 100 shares into a crazy, tanking market. In these periods, you must function like an athlete. Your response must be automatic and conditioned.

In a crazy market, market maker size is irrelevant, unless the market maker is at the inside market or you have very few shares (100, for example). Why? Because there is so much volume and confusion in the fray that you will be declined in all likelihood.

Likewise, ECN size in a crazy market disappears right before your eyes. Consider the ISLD trick of getting an order ready and keeping your finger on the trigger until ISLD appears, then executing. Your execution, routed through the ISLD system, will trade ahead of all the others trying to link to ISLD through SelectNet (and therefore ARCA and ATTN, too). Or wait for the field to resolve into many ECNs gathered there at the same time, then hit the ARCA or ATTN button and be done.

If you hold odd lots in a crazy market, transact the majority of your shares first. Always keep a calculator with big numbers beside you to keep your positions clear in your head. Then use SOES or the ISLD trick to get out of your shares.

Understand Level II, and review the routing system explanations in this section. You should know what they do and the best situations in which to use them. Use the diagrams as a handy reference. But please don't use the diagrams too much. You really have to learn how the tools work, as every situation is different. In the end, your own knowledge, judgment, and experience will make the day.

PART THREE

Swift Trading

swift ('swift) adj

1. Moving or capable of moving with great speed
2. Occurring suddenly or within a very short time
3. Quick to respond

synonym see FAST

22

Home Truths: Day Trading & Margin Accounts for Canadians

In Part One, I discussed the differences between direct access day trading (DAD) and online day trading. As I mentioned then, there is no such thing as a Canadian DAD account. Companies like Swift Trade Securities Inc., which have the proper regulatory licences and exemptions, have laid the groundwork to allow Canadian residents to open U.S.–cleared DAD accounts. All direct access trades are cleared through U.S. corporations like Southwest Securities in Dallas, Texas, or Spear, Leeds, Kellogg in New York. Currently, there are no clearing companies in Canada.

If you decide to open a DAD account and have already found the firm you'd like to deal with, you will be handed a new account-opening package by the customer service/accounts department. The package will include such forms as a U.S. W8 for non–U.S. residents, a risk-management form, disclaimers, an account-opening information sheet, and other material. You should read every last word on each sheet before you initial and sign your name to it.

I have met many DAD traders who often lament afterwards that they didn't understand what could happen. Often the first words out of their mouths after losing a significant amount of capital (after the customary expletives) is a version of "I didn't know that could happen."

The three most important elements among the account-opening forms for Canadians are as follows:

1. The W8 form, which allows you to open a U.S. account. Without that, your account will be delayed.

2. The acknowledgment-of-risk statement, stating that you accept all responsibility for trades done by you or on your account whether intentional or accidental.

3. The boxes on the account-opening sheet asking for your net worth and a statement about the type of trader you are. The net-worth box is important. If your net worth is a negative number or under $50,000, the firm may not open an account for you, for obvious reasons. The type-of-trader box is also important, because you have to describe yourself as a speculator or high-risk trader. If you say instead that you're an investor, the firm will turn down your application to open a DAD account. This is because DAD accounts and DAD terminals are used by high-risk speculators only for short-term trades.

In both Canada and the U.S., federal agencies protect the banking, investment, and insurance accounts of their citizens against losses arising from the failure of a financial institution, as long as the organization you deal with is registered with the proper authorities.

In Canada, the Canada Deposit Insurance Corporation (CDIC) protects all registered Canadian bank accounts for up to $60,000 against the failure of the deposit-taking organization. If the Royal Bank, for instance, were to close its doors and all the cash deposited were to vanish, the CDIC would pay out any claims made against the bank up to $60,000.

For accounts held at broker/dealers, the Canadian Investor Protection Fund (CIPF) covers its members' accounts for amounts up to $1 million for losses arising from the failure of a broker/dealer. (You can get more information on the CIPF at **www.cipf.ca**.

If you open a DAD account, however, you will not be covered by a Canadian agency, because your account is maintained in the U.S. Instead, it will be protected by the U.S. Securities Investor Protection Corporation (SIPC). Established in 1970 under the U.S. Securities Investor Protection Act, SIPC protects clients of its member broker/dealers such as Swift Trade Securities Inc. for up to US$500,000. If the broker/dealer or the clearing firm goes under, SIPC will reimburse each account holder for losses, providing the first US$100,000 in cash and the remaining US$400,000 in securities.

You can find more extensive information on SIPC and how it protects your DAD account at **www.sipc.org**.

All this brings us to the concept of margin. (Please note that the U.S. Federal Reserve has proposed several important regulatory changes that could affect margin rules. You should always consult your broker to get the specific rules and regulations that apply to your own account. The information in this chapter is no substitute for your own due diligence.)

Day traders must account for their money and securities on a daily basis.

Day traders all agree that this is important. Yet many traders rarely examine their Daily Margin Report. The only reason I can find is that most margin reports look scary enough to spook a professional accountant.

However, you need to understand margin to succeed as a day trader and make a profit. At Swift Trade Securities Inc., for example, 30 percent of your examination focuses on margin and margin reports. By understanding margin, you can avoid unexpected and unnecessary calls, which brokerages issue when they want you to give them more money, immediately, to cover your account or lose the account altogether. Unfortunately, the concept of margin looks complicated, and many people don't get beyond that first look. In fact, it's not so complicated at all. And it's very important.

It's more important to understand the general concept of margin than it is to know the specific minutiae of the regulations. So when you encounter terms in this chapter that seem vague or incomprehensible, I'll try to provide you with an exact definition. If a term still seems confusing, talk to your broker or refer to a Wall Street dictionary.

The first concept of margin is easy: Brokers may lend you money toward the purchase of stock. In the U.S., the lending of money toward the purchase of stock is covered by Regulation T of the Securities Exchange Act of 1934. This regulation covers purchases of stock in a margin account, short sales of stock, and day trading, all of which I'll discuss.

As I'll also discuss, special regulations cover pattern day trading accounts. These regulations differ substantially from "standard Reg T" in several ways. You have to determine whether your account will be coded "pattern day trading."

Any brokerage account in which you borrow money or stock is called a margin account. All margin accounts are regulated by Reg T.

When you open a margin account, you are giving your brokerage certain rights, in consideration of which you are getting certain things in return. What the broker gives you in return is the ability to borrow money to purchase marginable stock. The U.S. Federal Reserve Board (the Fed) initially determines the stocks that are eligible for borrowing against. Then your clearing house makes its own decision about lending specific securities.

For example, the Fed may determine that ABCD stock meets its requirements and is therefore eligible for lending. However, your clearing house may feel that, despite the Fed's determination, ABCD is still too volatile or risky to justify issuing loans against. It may allow purchases of the stock only if the buyer pays cash. Remember, if you purchase on margin, you are borrowing funds (i.e., getting a loan) to pay for the stock. The stock is held by the brokerage to secure the loan.

When you open a margin account, you get the ability to borrow money towards the purchase (or short sale) of securities. You also agree to several binding conditions, including the following:

1. You will pay interest charges on borrowed money.

2. You will allow the brokerage to lend your stock to secure your loan—and for this you will not receive interest, but you will be free to sell your stock at any time.

3. You agree that if the equity (cash value) in your account drops to less than 25 percent of the current market value of your margined positions (positions purchased with some of your own cash and some of the money lent to you by the brokerage), you will be called (required) to deposit more money to your account or liquidate enough stock to cover the maintenance within a certain period.

4. You further agree that, if you don't cover the maintenance, the brokerage or clearing house will liquidate your account.

5. You further agree to abide by the regulations set forth in Regulation T, as well as any additional "house rules" of your brokerage/clearing house.

The Federal Reserve specifies a maximum margin that a brokerage can lend toward purchases of stock. The amount is calculated as a percentage of the total purchase price for the stock, and the percentage varies. Currently the rate is 50 percent. That means your broker may lend you 50 percent of the total initial value of your position. Your own purchasing capacity or buying power is therefore always double your excess equity in a standard Reg T margin account.

To determine how much stock you may purchase, ask your broker to give you your current buying power, then divide that amount by the current price of the stock you want to buy. For example, let's say you have no positions and $10,000 in cash. All $10,000 is excess equity, since you have no positions, and it represents 50 percent of your buying power. To get your full buying power, multiply $10,000 by 2. Then, to find out how much ABCD stock you can currently buy for $20,000, you divide your buying power of $20,000 by the current market price of the stock.

Let's say for example that ABCD stock is marginable and is currently offered at 10 1/2. At that price you could buy 1,904.76 shares ($20,000 divided by the current price 10 1/2 = 1,904.7619). Since you can't buy partial shares, you'd end up with 1,904 shares. Generally speaking, any purchase you make in a margin account will consist of 50 percent your cash and 50 percent borrowed money.

But what if you have $100,000 in cash, and you decide to buy only $10,000 of stock in your margin account? The same principle applies. The first $5,000 (50 percent) of the purchase cost comes from your pocket, and the next $5,000 (the other 50 percent) is lent to you through your margin account. That leaves you with $95,000 cash (and twice as much buying power: $190,000). If you close the position by the end of the day, generally you pay no interest on the loan of $5,000 at all. But if you hold overnight, then the interest begins to accumulate. This is one way brokerages and clearing houses make money.

Many people mistakenly think that as long as they don't spend more than they have in cash, they are not buying on margin. On the contrary, every purchase in a margin account is made on margin, unless your clearing house has different rules or you specified "cash only" at time of purchase. To avoid using credit, you must tell your broker to purchase the securities outright with 100 percent cash. The better electronic trading platforms even carry a little box that you can check to specify 100 percent cash only. Of course, this reduces your buying power, because you won't have access to any money on margin.

If you purchase a nonmarginable security in your margin account you'll automatically pay 100 percent cash, since your brokerage cannot or will not lend money toward the purchase. Remember, clearing houses may be more restrictive than standard Reg T. For example, many brokerages require you to pay 100 percent cash to purchase some of the more volatile Internet stocks. Even though the Fed allows clearing houses to lend against these stocks, some clearing houses believe they are still too risky to make loans on. Their own rules prevent clients from purchasing these stocks on margin. This serves two purposes: to protect the consumer and to protect the clearing house.

It's not uncommon for one brokerage to allow the purchase of a stock on margin, while others will not. Some brokerages also have standard policies requiring the trader to put up, say, 75 percent of the cost of any volatile Internet stock.

Let's say you've been trading with a brokerage that allows you to purchase volatile marginable stocks with only 50 percent cash (standard Reg T). You switch to an account that requires you to put up 75 percent cash, but you don't know this because you haven't bothered to read the fine print. After you purchase the stock, the brokerage asks you to deposit cash to cover 75 percent of the purchase. If you don't, your account will be liquidated and closed.

The reasons why you might buy on margin are obvious: You can double your returns. You can, of course, double your losses, as well. So is buying on margin more risky? Yes. You are increasing your exposure to profit and loss. (I'll discuss risk and money management further in Chapter 24.)

What happens when you make a $10,000 purchase in a standard Reg T margin account? First, you are subject to the initial call for money. You must deposit cash in your account to cover 50 percent of the total initial cost of your position. In this case, your required deposit amounts to $5,000. The other $5,000 is a loan. The value of this loan never changes, though the price of the securities likely will.

For example, the stock appreciates in value to $20,000, and you decide to sell. With the proceeds, you pay $5,000 to the brokerage house, along with any interest charges if you held your position overnight. The rest of the money is yours. You paid $5,000 for the initial purchase. The other $10,000 is your profit.

Now let's suppose you held the stock for a year to achieve this appreciation. You'll have to pay interest on the $5,000 loan for each day you held the stock. Interest charges are usually relatively small, but significant. They fluctuate with the prime rate, which is called the "broker's call." Ask your broker for the rate. Usually the broker will respond with something like "1/4 point above broker's call; currently 8 1/4 percent annually." If you hold a stock for a year, and you pay 8 1/4 percent interest on the money you borrowed to buy it, you must generate a total return of at least 4 1/8 percent on the position just to break even.

Now let's say you made the same purchase, but this time, you have only $4,000 cash (and no positions) to begin with in your account, not $10,000. Your buying power is going to be $8,000 on the day ($4,000 × 2 = $8,000). Another way of putting it is that your $4,000 cash equals 50 percent (half) of your buying power. You have a good relationship with your broker, and so you go ahead and purchase $10,000 worth of stock.

How can you do this when you have only $8,000 in buying power? By regulation, you have three days to bring in your payment for a purchase. The broker knows you are responsible, because you read, initialled, and signed all the small print on your margin account agreement signifying that you had understood it. The broker knows that you intend to pay for any purchases you make. The initial call for a purchase in a margin account is 50 percent and, in any case, the broker may never lend more than 50 percent toward a purchase. This means that, for a $10,000 purchase of a marginable stock in a standard Reg T account, you will need to contribute $5,000 as the initial call. You have $4,000 already in the account, so you will need to send in an additional $1,000 to cover the initial call of $5,000.

What if you buy stock on margin and then sell it before the end of the day? Do you still have to send money to the brokerage? Yes. You bought the stock, and you'll need to have money in your account to cover the initial call. Even if you made a million dollars in intraday trading, you'll still need to send in that initial call, under Regulation T. There's no getting around it.

If you fail to submit the initial call, the brokerage has to liquidate your purchase and freeze your account for 90 days. In fact, many clearing houses will simply declare you a risk and close your account altogether. This means you'll be unable to open an account with any of the brokerages that clear through that clearing house.

This situation occurs more often than you might think. Imagine if you grossly exceed your buying power, erroneously thinking that you'll sell all your positions before the close, so you won't have to submit an initial call. You make a killing and immediately go on vacation. Upon your return several days later, you find that you must send $100,000 today to your broker or your account will be closed. You might not have access to $100,000. Even if you have the cash readily available, you might have missed your bank's wire deadline. This happens all the time, to highly intelligent, educated people. That's why you have to understand how margin works.

Always keep in mind the initial call requirement. Calculate your intraday buying power at the start of every day, and never exceed it. That way, you will never have this nasty kind of surprise.

You should, as a day trader, calculate your intraday buying power daily to avoid problems. The procedure is fairly simple. Once you've done it for a few days in a row, it will become second nature. You should ask your broker for details about calculating your buying power. Most top-end trading software will also provide you with this information.

Alternatively, a full-service brokerage always calculates your buying power for you, as part of its service. But at many direct access firms, you have to keep tabs on it yourself, using the information available on your margin report.

Suppose you decide to hold $10,000 of ABCD, a fictitious NASDAQ NM stock, overnight. You will need 50 percent of the value of the position in equity to hold it overnight. If you have less, you will have to send money to your brokerage. In this case, you will need at least $5,000 (50% of $10,000 = $5,000) in equity. The current market value of the stock ($10,000) minus the loan value ($5,000) equals your equity: $5,000.

Let's say that you ignore all your best intentions to cut your losses and decide to hold a terrible position overnight. News comes out today that ABCD will re-state its earnings for the previous quarter, and they are terrible.

ABCD Corp. has even fired its accountant. During the day the stock trades down so much that your total position is now worth only $7,000. Remember: The loan value never changes, but your equity does. To calculate your equity, take the current market value of your position and subtract the loan value (which never changes).

You can also figure it this way: your original equity +/– the change in the value of the position. Your original equity was $5,000. If you keep less than 50 percent equity, but more than 25 percent equity in a long position, you will not receive a maintenance call, but your account will be frozen. If your equity dips below 25 percent, you will be required to send in money or liquidate enough stock to bring your equity up to 50 percent.

Now for the dreaded maintenance call. If you get through this, you're well on your way to trading with complete confidence and fewer nasty surprises in a standard margin account.

To hold overnight you must maintain 50 percent of the value of your position in equity. In this example, your position is now worth $7,000, and you have at this point $2,000 in equity—clearly not a good situation. But you will not be required to send in money yet, because your equity still amounts to 28.6 percent of the value of your position.

If ABCD continues its downward descent, you will eventually be required to send in money or suffer your account being liquidated. The point of no return occurs when the equity in your account equals 25 percent (or less) of the total value of the position. If you ever let it get to that point, you will receive a maintenance call. You will have to deposit enough money to bring the equity in your account up to at least 50 percent of the value of the position. If you do not send the money, the brokerage will be required, under Regulation T, to liquidate stock in your account to bring your equity up to at least 50 percent of the market value of the position.

Until it gets that bad, you don't have to deposit more money. However, your account will be frozen. This means you can sell at any time. But to buy, you will have to pay in advance.

If you really like to be in control, and you wish to calculate in advance the point at which you will receive a maintenance call, consult your broker.

All this becomes more complex as the number of your positions increases. But the idea is the same: The total value of all your positions, minus your total loan value, equals your equity. And your equity, minus your minimum maintenance requirement—the minimum amount of equity you must maintain in your account to hold your current positions—equals your overnight buying power.

Minimum maintenance requirements (MMRs) differ from one type of account to another. If you're holding overnight, your MMR is 50 percent, as discussed above. In pattern day trading accounts, MMRs depend on several other factors, which I'll discuss soon. And when you hold short positions, even in a standard margin account, the requirements are different again from the long position requirements.

MARGIN AND SHORT POSITIONS

When you sell stock short, you borrow the security and sell it immediately, with the intention of buying the security back at a lower price and returning it to the lender at some later date. The difference is your profit. (See Chapter 23 for more specifics on short selling.) Because you borrow securities when you sell short, the transaction must take place in a margin account.

Regulation T governs the extension of credit, including lending stock, toward the purchase or sale of securities. But there are several important differences with regard to margin when shorting stock. The first difference is that you are selling stock and receiving cash in return for the sale. You will not have use of this cash; the brokerage house holds it, in a sort of escrow. You also have to pledge 50 percent of the value of your position in equity. Your initial call of 50 percent is held by the clearing firm, again in a sort of escrow. The brokerage house puts up the other 50 percent. However, it is not considered a debit, as when you purchase equities. It is a credit. The loan value of this credit never changes, although the price of the security likely will. The rules that apply to purchases regarding initial margin and maintenance also apply to short positions, except that you calculate them based on a credit loan balance rather than a debit loan balance.

However, the maintenance threshold is different. In a long position, when your equity drops below 25 percent, you receive a margin call. In a short position, the threshold is 30 percent.

In a short position, if your equity falls below 50 percent, but not below 30 percent, you will not receive a call, but your account will be frozen. If it dips below 30 percent, you will be required to send in money or liquidate positions to bring your equity up to 50 percent of the value of the position(s).

Let's say you have $4,000 cash in your account and no positions. You see terrible news about ABCD Corp. ABCD is going to restate its earnings for the previous quarter, and the earnings are going to be really bad. Having access to real-time news and being a practised observer of this stock, you short $10,000 worth of it immediately, expecting a harsh drop in price.

But if you have $4,000 in your account, you have only $8,000 in shorting power. You intend to cover the position later today, but you realize you will still need to send in $1,000 in initial margin anyway. (Remember, the initial margin requirement is 50 percent; total value of the position is $10,000, and the brokerage house can lend you only 50 percent of the value of the position. Fifty percent of $10,000 is $5,000—the loan (credit) value. You must also contribute $5,000 as initial call, and you have only $4,000 in your account, so you write a cheque immediately for $1,000 and send it overnight mail.) It is worth it to you, since you think ABCD will fall to zero, and you'll make a killing.

You are now short ABCD stock, and you're pleased to see it drop quickly as the news spreads and sellers emerge. At the end of the day, your position is worth only $7,000. You have indeed made your killing, on paper at least. Were you to cover the position now, you would make a profit of $3,000. (You borrowed the stock when it was worth $10,000. You can give it back by paying only $7,000 for the same amount of stock.) Presently the stock is marked to market at its current replacement value (CRV).

Now here's the interesting part. This paper increase in equity (whether gained from a short sell as in this example or from the purchase of a security that appreciates in value) is only theoretical until you close the position. However, you may still use the paper profit. Your brokerage house will lend it to you by sending you a cheque for the amount (minus withholding), or allowing you to put it toward the purchase or sale of additional securities, as long as use/removal of this money doesn't cause you to drop below your MMR. The paper increase in equity is recorded in the special memorandum account (SMA) on your margin report. (Whenever you have a paper increase in equity, it is recorded as a journal entry to your SMA.)

In this example, you have a $3,000 increase in SMA, which the brokerage house can send to you or allow you to use subject to Regulation T. Remember, under Reg T, the brokerage house can lend up to 50 percent of the value of a position. Your position has increased in value by $3,000, so the brokerage house can lend you $1,500 (50 percent of $3,000) right away. You can use this money in any way you see fit. Keep in mind that, since the profit is for now on paper, it has not been realized. Only by closing the position will you have a real profit. In the meantime, any money withdrawn is a loan, backed by your position. And you pay interest on loans held overnight.

What happens when the stock goes against you? If you are short, and the stock appreciates in value to the point where your equity falls below 50 percent of the value of your position, your account will be frozen. You will be able to cover your position at any time, but to initiate any new positions, you will be required to send in cash up-front. If your position keeps increasing in value until your equity is 30 percent or less of the total value, you will have to send in money to maintain your position. If you don't, you will be subject to liquidation to bring your account back to at least 40 percent equity. The process is the same as I discussed earlier for long positions, but with one significant difference: the 30 percent threshold, as opposed to 25 percent.

The higher maintenance requirement reflects the added risk associated with short positions. Remember, in a long position, your loss is limited to 100 percent of the value of the position. If you are short, the stock may rise against you to a potentially unlimited loss. Imagine, for example, that you had shorted a ridiculous online bookseller that didn't even have a store or any inventory in the salad days of Internet commerce just three short years ago. At the time, Amazon.com was trading at $8, with little hope of earnings in the near future. If you'd shorted it, you would have watched your liability soar past $100 a share before it dropped to its current level around $55.

(If you wish to calculate in advance the price that a short position would have to reach to generate a maintenance call, you should call your broker.)

You may, of course, elect to purchase stock with 100 percent cash, using no margin at all. At the better direct access electronic brokerages, you can click somewhere on your screen to designate your purchase as 100 percent cash only. Obviously, if you purchase a nonmarginable security, for which your clearing house won't lend money, you must pay cash. So what happens if, say, you have $50,000 in cash and no open positions, and you purchase $40,000 worth of a nonmarginable security?

Your buying power on margin will then be reduced to $20,000 ($10,000 in equity, $10,000 in borrowed money). Alternatively, you have $10,000 in cash to purchase more securities.

As a rule of thumb, new issues and securities that generally trade at prices under $5 are not marginable, and you will have to buy them with cash only. Generally speaking, securities that are well established and trade in good volumes and at prices well above $5 will usually be marginable, and so you may often purchase them with a combination of your equity and funds borrowed from your brokerage. However, despite the security's designation as marginable, a brokerage house may prohibit purchases on margin or may lend a smaller amount toward its purchase.

Sometimes, a security with a longstanding marginable history falls on hard times and trades for less than $5. Such a security may in fact still be marginable because its new status hasn't yet been reviewed. You should always check with your broker to determine the status of a desired stock before trading it.

SPECIAL EFFECTS: PATTERN DAY TRADING ACCOUNTS

A day trading account is any account in which there is a pattern of day trading—i.e., opening positions intraday and closing them intraday, therefore ending the day flat with no positions. In the old days, maybe four short years ago, day trading was largely limited to professional traders. These professionals were given a special type of account, coded pattern day trading account (PDT). Now, new technologies allow individual traders everywhere to participate and trade actively, and PDT accounts are being utilized by many more traders. But many more use standard margin accounts and are not aware of the special effects that come with a PDT account.

In addition to being subject to Regulation T, PDT accounts come with some advantages as well as some additional restrictions for the active trader. The current regulations are not very user-friendly, and have led to confusion. An acute lack of understanding of the special conditions of a PDT account often leads to the painful and sudden closure of the account.

If you have an account at a full-service or an online brokerage like TD Waterhouse or E*TRADE, chances are the account is regulated only by Regulation T or even more restrictive house rules, even though you trade actively. That's because the accounts at full-service brokerages are often designed for individual nonprofessional investors. They may often be actively traded, although for reasons enumerated in Chapter 1, they may not be suitable or desirable for active intraday trading. If you have an account with a direct access firm, however, it will likely be coded pattern day trading and be subject to different methods of accounting.

Keep in mind that Reg T and related rules are American. We do not yet have PDT or direct access trading accounts in Canada.

There are several differences between a standard margin account and a PDT. A PDT carries different requirements covering intraday and overnight buying power. One of the advantages is that, intraday, a PDT comes with a maintenance withholding on positions of only 25 percent as opposed to 50 percent, so you'll have more money to play with.

For the purposes of day trading, in a PDT account, you have to maintain only 25 percent rather than 50 percent of your positions intraday. Therefore, your intraday buying power is greater in a PDT account than in one regulated by Regulation T alone. However, there is a price to pay. Unless you understand it, you may encounter a brutal lesson that summarily finishes your trading career.

At the end of the day, when calculating equity and margin calls and the like in a PDT account, only the trades made intraday are considered. A PDT calculation assumes you've held no positions overnight. It looks only at buys and sells made during the day and matches them.

Ideally, you start the day flat and end the day flat. But if you hold a stock overnight today, this will go unnoticed for the PDT part of the calculation.

What's this mean? Let's say you have a full-service brokerage account or an online discount account. Let's say also that you maxed out your buying power, bought 1,000 Yahoo (YHOO) yesterday and held your position overnight for the gap-up. It gaps, and today, at market open, you sell all 1,000 shares. Then you buy 1,000 shares again, and sell the 1,000 shares, at a profit, and then buy the 1,000 shares and sell them again, again for a profit.

In a standard account, you would end the day flat, having sold your overnight position and then traded YHOO intraday, finally going flat into the close. Provided you didn't exceed your buying power, you'd be fine: no calls.

Things are different in a PDT account, which subjects you to both the Regulation T calculation and the PDT calculation. Remember, the

PDT side of the calculation doesn't look at what you held overnight, but only at what you traded intraday. In this example, you sold your 1,000 shares that you held overnight. Since the PDT calculation doesn't take into account your overnight position and looks only at trades made intraday, it sees the first thing you did as a sell short.

Then you bought again, which the PDT calculation interprets as covering the short. Then you sold again. PDT says you went short again. You then bought and sold again. According to the PDT calculation, you finished the day short. This may sound nuts, but this is the way things work currently, under securities regulations that have evolved over time.

Now it gets really weird. Remember, you're still subject to Regulation T in a PDT, and the PDT calculation says you have a short position. So now you get a Reg T call on your short position. But the fun isn't over. What about the stock you held overnight, which the PDT calculation didn't notice? You still hold that too, at least according to the calculations, so you'll have a maintenance requirement on it too. For the purposes of this example, you had a substantial position in Yahoo, which you held overnight. It's easy to see how the calls generated by this additional PDT calculation could run into the hundreds of thousands of dollars.

YHOO currently trades at $320 a share, and you held 1,000 shares. The 50 percent initial call would be $160,000. And you'd be required to send in this amount or have your account closed. This is seen as an initial call on the short position, and there is no way of getting around it. Once the call is generated, it must be satisfied, or the account will be closed.

This scenario is typical, generated by nothing other than the arguably outdated rules. Of course, had you managed your risk properly, you would get no such call. But this example is predicated on the assumption that you maxed-out your buying power with each purchase.

Calculating where you stand on a moment-to-moment basis can be difficult in a PDT account, especially if you have made many trades intraday. But it's worth it, as the following discussion will show.

The Handy Dandy Rule About Overnight Positions in a PDT Account

The following rule of thumb will serve you well in a PDT account. It's designed for simplicity, to keep you safe without having to make tedious calculations. You don't even have to understand the scenarios I've just described. If you stick to it, you'll have fewer surprises.

In a PDT account:

– If you hold a stock overnight, do not day trade it the next day.

In other words, if you hold a stock overnight, do not day trade it the next day.

And furthermore, if you hold a stock overnight, do not day trade it the next day.

So now you know that, if you hold a stock overnight, do not day trade it the next day. Repeat after me: If I hold a stock overnight, I must not day trade it the next day. And again: If I hold a stock overnight, I must not day trade it the next day. I recommend writing this phrase 100 times. I am absolutely serious. As I said earlier, making a day trade with stock held overnight in a PDT account has caused more frustration and anguish than you'll ever know.

With a PDT account, you are subject to all the conditions of Regulation T. So you will need to put up 50 percent of the purchase price of any stock you buy. In addition, you are subject to the additional calculation specific to a PDT, which looks at all trades you have made intraday and matches them. It also allows you to use 25 percent of the Reg T hold as well, as discussed earlier.

But again, things get weird. It looks at the trades you've made today. In other words, if I come into the day with 200 AOL—that is, I bought AOL yesterday and held it overnight—and I sell it at market open, PDT looks upon the sell as my opening trade of the day. The calculation doesn't take into account prior positions held overnight.

So now I've sold my AOL at a nice profit, and I'm flat AOL. In a Reg T account, that's all there is to it. Likewise, in a PDT account, as long as I don't trade AOL again intraday.

What if I do? Let's say I trade 100 shares of AOL five times today. Buy, sell, buy, sell, buy, sell, buy, sell, buy, sell. I should still end the day flat, right? But not in a PDT.

Remember, the PDT calculation looks at actual trades done today, regardless of positions coming into the day. So you take the first trade, a sell, which will be seen as a short, since it doesn't look at the overnight hold; and then, the first buy, which will be seen as a cover buy. Now you run down the trades, and guess what? The PDT calculation sees you as short. If this isn't convoluted enough, you will then be required to send in a Reg T 50 percent cash deposit for the new position that, according to this calculation, you have.

And what about your old position, the one you held overnight and sold first thing in the morning? Accounting doesn't see it, but Reg T does. It thinks you still own it, and so you will be required to keep 50 percent in equity to hold the position overnight. You can see how, if you were caught unawares, this could lead to an unmanageable call for cash, which on such short notice you might have no hope of meeting. Nor can the rules be bent or broken. You will be required to send in any funds necessary, or suffer your account being closed.

This error is almost always made unawares, in ignorance of the regulations governing your account, even though you said you read them, understood them, and have agreed to abide and be bound by them. And it triggers the mother of all margin calls. It can mean the end of the game, because the call generated by this event is often insurmountable. Many otherwise good traders, who know how to pick a stock, how to buy and sell, and how to manage risk, fall short in this one fatal regard: not knowing this simple little killer.

Now you know.

THE LAST WORD ON MARGIN

This chapter does not relieve you of the obligation of talking with your broker and finding out the specifics of margin and house rules that govern your account. But it gives you some general principles so you will have a better idea of the questions you should be asking. For example, you should determine before opening the account whether it will be a regular margin account or one coded pattern day trading.

Once you grasp the general rules and regulations in margin accounts, and once you have done your due diligence to determine whether your account is standard Regulation T or a more restrictive PDT account, and once you have identified any particular house rules, you can always know where you stand. It will be up to you to monitor your account, to make sure you are always exactly where you ought to be in terms of risk.

You will need to make a practice of monitoring your account on a daily basis, just as if you were running any commodity-driven business. You will need to know always where you stand and accept the fact that the responsibility rests with you. If you don't do your due diligence, you have nobody to blame but yourself.

Always understand your overall position. Print out your margin report every day. Monitor your positions and make sure you are never ever over-extended. Plan accordingly. Run your business like a business should be run. And suffer no surprises.

If you'd like more information on the NASD explanation of Reg T and the calculations specific to a pattern day trading account, check out the NASD Web page at **http://investor.nasd.com/notices/98102ntm.txt**.

23

One for the Shorts:
Short Selling

Short selling is the opposite of buying long. When you buy a stock (go long), you hope for appreciation in price. At some point you will sell the stock and keep the profit—the difference between the cost (purchase price) and the sell price.

The phrase "buy low, sell high" applies to going long. But buying low and selling high is only half the story. Suppose you find a stock that's a real loser and that's going to go down (depreciate) in price. It's possible to take a bet on this too, by selling high, then buying low, and keeping the profit—the difference between the price for which you sell the stock and the price at which you purchased it to cover and close your position.

In a nutshell, it works like this: First, you borrow the stock from a willing lender and sell the stock immediately, for cash. Later, when the price drops, you buy the stock back and return it to the lender, keeping the profit—the difference between the sale price and your purchase price.

Selling short is basically the same as selling stock you own. The key difference is that you do not own the stock to begin with, you borrow it. The word "short" simply refers to this fact. When you sell a stock you own, it's called a long sale. When you sell a stock you've borrowed, it's called a short sale. The two approaches enable you to profit not only when the price of a stock goes up, but also when the price goes down.

For example, the stock of a global communications service provider traded as high as $57 last year. Fantastic ads showed a picture of planet earth with the words, "Welcome to your new calling zone." Being a techno-gadget nut, I had to have one of these phones. I checked on the company and found that it had incurred mind-boggling debt to finance the launch of its many satellites, and it had tremendously optimistic goals for new subscribers. But again, being the techno-gadget nut that I am, I still had to have one of these phones, even though the $3,000 cost of the phone was admittedly steep. And that didn't even include airtime—at an amazingly high price, as well.

I figured, "Okay, so the phone's extortionate, and the airtime is just as bad, but it's a global phone. People will eat this up!" And then I tried to buy the phone. And tried. And tried. I could never, not once, get an account rep on the phone—the regular old $25 version I keep at home. Nor could I reach the company by email. I sent literally dozens of emails, and received only one response, from an account rep in Indonesia. My opinion of this company began to change.

"Okay," I said to myself, "this is an expensive product with a limited potential subscribership. And the company could conceivably go bankrupt if it misses its skyscraper-high debt payments. But what a product." Of course, I'd never seen one, because apparently the company didn't want my money.

Then I talked with friends. They had received exactly the same response from the company as I had. In other words, none. We talked jokingly about how we should "short this piece of crap company that doesn't want our business!" But because we were still in love with the idea, none of us did.

I have found it invariably bad to let emotions motivate my business decisions. Add this one to the list of missed opportunities, because one year later, the company has missed all its subscription targets. Wonder why. The company has also missed its debt payments, and it has filed for bankruptcy. The stock recently halted trading, at about $4 a share.

Here's what we all could have done, if we wanted to sell this or any other company short. First, you must find stock that's available for borrowing. Not all stocks are available for this purpose. Your brokerage house keeps an updated list of the stocks that you can borrow. If the brokerage house is doing its job, it will have a list that updates frequently, maybe even daily. The best brokerages employ a person in charge of aggressively pursuing shares of otherwise unavailable stocks. At some brokerages, you can even call in and request a stock for borrowing, and the brokerage will try to locate some shares for you.

What makes a stock borrowable? First, all stocks available for borrowing are marginable. (See Chapter 22 for a longer discussion of margin.) When a stock is marginable, it means the U.S. Federal Reserve has decided that banks may make loans toward the purchase of these stocks through a special kind of account called a margin account. In the process, the Fed has in no way passed upon the merits of these securities. It has simply given banks permission to make loans toward the purchase of these stocks subject to Regulation T.

Clearing houses—the institutions that facilitate the settling of accounts between banks and brokerages—determine which stocks they will lend for the purposes of short selling. Clearing houses often sell their lists of borrowable stocks to other banks and brokerages. This is why it is so important to use a brokerage that aggressively pursues short inventory. As a rule of thumb, new issues and securities that generally trade at prices under $5 are not marginable, and you will have to buy them with cash only. Generally speaking, securities that are well established and trade in good volumes and at prices well above $5 will usually be marginable, and so you may often purchase them with a combination of your equity and funds borrowed from your brokerage. However, despite the security's designation as marginable, a brokerage house may prohibit purchases on margin or may lend only a small amount toward its purchase.

All short sales must take place in a margin account. When you attempt to borrow stock, someone must lend it to you. Therefore, non-marginable stocks may not be sold short. (Chapter 22 provides a more detailed explanation of this .)

ONE MORE VERY IMPORTANT RULE: Short sales must be effected on upticks.

This makes the game a little more difficult, since you can't simply wait till the stock is tanking and then place an order to sell short. Also, shorting OTC (NASDAQ) stocks is different from shorting exchange-traded stocks on the NYSE, AMEX, and other exchanges.

You may short stocks on the NASDAQ only subject to the bid test rule. This rule asks, "Is the current bid higher than the last bid?" If so, then you can sell short. You can also offer stock out short at a price at least 1/16 higher than the current bid. If the stock is bought from you, you have legally effected your short sale.

For example, say the fictional NASDAQ NM stock ABCD is currently bid $10, offered 10 1/8. And it is on a downtick. You can offer out stock short for sale at 10 1/16 or 10 1/8 or any price higher. If someone buys it from you, you have effected your short sale. You cannot legally sell the stock short at 10, since it is on a downtick.

You may short a stock on the listed exchanges subject to the zero-plus tick rule. This states that you may short a stock on an uptick or a zero-plus tick. The stock is on an uptick if the current bid is higher than the last bid. A zero-plus tick means that the stock was at an uptick, but has since traded at the current offer, without the bid having moved. In other words, the stock was on a plus tick and since then has traded but not moved in price. Keep in mind that, just like a long position, a short position can be held indefinitely. You have no more obligation to close a short position than a long one, except under extremely unusual conditions. (I discuss closing a short position at greater length in Chapter 24.)

On the best order-execution platforms, you can designate a short sale using a button or a box on the screen. Basically, you are telling the brokerage house that you don't own the stock, but you're going to borrow it. Once you check the box, you simply sell the stock. The clearing house takes care of the borrowing automatically. Keep in mind that selling borrowed stock is the same as selling stock you own, except you are subject to the short sale rules I described earlier, and you must designate the sale as short. To make things easier, the better day trading platforms usually include an error window, which will pop up if the stock is not borrowable. It will say something like "order deleted—for the reason: the security is not borrowable."

Let's say this stock is a borrowable one. You check the short box on your order-entry screen and place a sell short order on the Island 1/16 above the bid. Several moments later, you receive the confirmation: sold short 1,000 ABCD shares. Several minutes after the sale, more sellers come in. Presently, the stock's price starts tanking, as fewer market participants are willing to pay top dollar to purchase it.

The price continues its drop. After a few moments, it falls below its 50- and 200-day moving averages, where it's been hovering and testing for the last several days. Now the mutual fund managers see what's happening and they begin to liquidate their holdings. Volume suddenly spikes up, and massive trades print to the tape. The price plummets with a vengeance as panic sellers come in, liquidating to avoid margin calls or to preserve what little gain they've got left. Volume skyrockets, ten times higher than average.

Finally, after many pullbacks, toward the end of the day, the price begins consolidating. Not many more sellers emerge. The volume evaporates. Several minutes go by in which not a single trade occurs. Market makers jockey now, trying to put over headfakes and trying to suss out what's going to happen next. Goldman Sachs offers 10,000 shares at the best offer, trying to scare the few that haven't yet sold out of their stock. But no more sellers emerge. Smith Barney bids 5,000 shares, but nobody sells. Goldman lowers its price to within a 1/16 of Smith Barney's bid but doesn't sell any stock to them; nor does Salomon Smith Barney buy any from Goldman. Several more moments go by, with no more trades. Sensing a tidal change, you decide to cover your position, right here, right now.

To close your position, you simply buy the stock without designating anything special at all. Your brokerage house, aware of your short position, automatically closes your borrowed (short) position out. In fact, you buy from Goldman Sachs, ignoring all the rules that say never buy from the axe while the axe is selling. You do this because you gather the axe is not really selling anymore. You believe it's just fading the trend (see Chapter 25, "Games People Play.") Your guess was right, because, after selling a thousand shares to you, Goldman Sachs disappears from the offer.

A moment of silence goes by, as the market digests what's just happened. Then, suddenly, your Time of Sales ticker literally explodes with trades. Buyers rush in, taking all the offers, driving the price right back up. You notice Goldman Sachs on the bid with every pullback, and you smile because you know they're covering their shorts too.

You are now out of the market. All in all, a great day. Things went as well as they could. You didn't sell the high, and you didn't buy the very low. And you got out with a 14-point gain on a thousand shares. You could have gone long and bought the stock as well as covered your short and rode it up again, but you decided not to get too greedy. You go for a walk instead.

At the local coffee shop you hear people talking about their 3 percent return per annum Wilshire 5000 index funds and how 95 percent of mutual fund managers can't beat the S&P 500. Others say why they "just can't play those high-flying Internet stocks. Why ABCD dropped 21 points in a day!" You don't engage. They wouldn't believe you anyway, and at best they'd label you a gambler who got lucky.

Meanwhile, at $3.75, that coffee is a bargain.

The risk of short selling is, of course, that the stock goes up in value. Keep in mind that, if it goes against you, eventually you will need to cover the short position. If you shorted Yahoo at $27 or Amazon.com at $8, you'd have been killed if you didn't stick to strict money-management skills and close the position at a small loss right away.

Theoretically, there is no limit to how high a price can go, but there is a limit to how far it can fall: zero. If you go long, your maximum loss would occur if the stock went to zero. You would lose everything you had in it. However, if you are short, the potential loss is unlimited, since the price can climb indefinitely.

Occasionally, a company's stock will suddenly, for various reasons, become nonmarginable. Any outstanding short positions will be required to cover by a specific date. The danger here is that this can lead to a short squeeze, as people try to cover. If you're at a loss in a short position and the stock is called (that is, all borrowed stock is required to be returned to the owner) take the loss. Remember, all great losses started small.

There are also advantages to short selling. People often sell positions out of panic, and buy only after careful consideration. In other words, stocks often drop much more quickly than they rise. Many times a stock will tumble several points in several minutes, only to rise slowly throughout the day to a high above the open.

Stocks tend not to close at their high or at their low. I've seen statistics that say eight out of ten times a stock will close lower than its high or higher than its low. I believe the actual figure should be seven out of eight. The fact remains that, more often than not, stocks tend to close higher than their daily low and lower than their daily high. Selling short is simply taking advantage of the other side of the "buy low, sell high" mentality. If you are in the market and playing only half the game, you may be missing some opportunities.

Another interesting point is that most investors and even most traders don't have a firm understanding of short selling. It is still perceived as some mystical devil's alchemy that requires special knowledge and ability. Nothing could be further from the truth.

Of course, there are pitfalls. The so-called short squeeze is one, and it is a killer. Beware the short squeeze. A short squeeze occurs when there are a very large number of short positions in a stock relative to the number of long positions and the number of shares outstanding. If and when the price goes up, many shorts will try to cover their positions. This increased buying drives the price up higher, attracting more buyers.

As more buyers buy, the price shoots up higher, fuelling more interest, and driving the price even higher. All the while, the shorts are losing money at accelerating speed. Eventually, the shorts must cover at any price. The results can be dramatic.

Some stock, like K-Tel Records, is widely considered to be a joke. For months, maybe years, people have been taking short positions in this stock every time it trades up a little. In February 1998, K-Tel Records (KTEL) had a huge portion of its stock in short positions. The consensus was that the record was played out and the music was over. People figured this company was going to zero. And so they shorted it whenever they could.

This was dangerous, because KTEL had a very small float of only 700,000 shares outstanding. (By comparison, Dell Computer has 34 billion shares outstanding.) With such a tiny float, and supply so very limited, you can only imagine what would happen to the price if someone decided to buy 100,000 shares.

Well, that's what happened. Rumours of KTEL's demise had been greatly exaggerated. The company issued a news release that it would sell its records over the Internet. Gossip had it that KTEL would become the Amazon.com of the record industry. Day traders and people savvy to Internet stocks jumped in immediately and bought. The price of KTEL, which had started the day near $7, began to shoot upwards.

But there was no supply. There were no more sellers of this stock.

Everyone who was short KTEL got word of the news and checked on the price. I can only imagine the utter astonishment of people calling their brokers for a quote and hearing "KTEL is 15 1/8 by 15 1/4." Many hesitated in astonishment. "15 and 1/8?! Well....What is it now?"

"KTEL is 17 5/8 by 3/4."

"WHAT!??"

You can imagine what followed: several failed attempts at limit orders, followed by abject desperation and finally, market orders to cover, at any price. "Just get me out!" screamed the shorts. "Just cover!" By mid-day, KTEL hit $40 a share. Misery prevailed among the short sellers.

If you ever encounter this situation, when there is no float and everyone in the world is short, don't you short it too.

How do you find the float? And how do you find the short interest? Go to your broker's section of fundamental analysis information. Or if your brokerage doesn't have such a section, go to Yahoo Finance or a similar page and look at the number of shares outstanding, then look at the float. (Shares outstanding refers to the number of shares the company has issued; the float refers to how many are actually in the market. Note that by regulation, stock owned by the corporation or controlling shareholders cannot be liquidated readily. The float refers to the actual number of shares available that can be readily bought or sold without restriction.)

The company may own the majority of its shares or controlling shareholders may own a majority of the shares, and the law limits the number of shares they may sell at a given time. For short-term trading, you need to look toward the float to see how many shares are actually available. The fewer shares available, the less supply and the more potential volatility.

In addition, you need to look at the short interest relative to other companies in the same industry. Brokerages are required to report quarterly the number of shares customers hold short in every stock. Since this is only a quarterly indication, and a lot can happen in a quarter, it isn't a fail-safe indicator. But it is one of the best available, and certainly bears looking into, especially before shorting a company that's relatively unknown to you.

Of course, if you find a KTEL situation or a SIEB (Muriel Siebert Inc., a short-squeeze-initiated rise that occurred in February 1999, when shares rose from $7 to $30 with a float of only 600,000 shares) or a JBOH (J.B. Oxford Inc, $5 to $25, March 1999, 700,000 share float), or any of the many others, you might consider a buy-and-hold approach.

Yahoo (YHOO) was trading at $27 dollars a share in November 1997. I used to trade it daily for 1/2 to one-point profit everyday. I didn't pay any attention to the fact that, at that time, the float was only about 700,000 shares. Shame on me. Never again. (Split-adjusted, YHOO is about $1,000 a share now.)

You can also short all the way to zero. Since I am not a licensed broker, however, I am unable to recommend the following situation. But since many people abuse this loophole in the law, I am allowed to discuss it here as a warning.

Successful day traders in Canada will pay a lot of taxes. I pay the least I can under the law, but I am proud to be a Canadian and I consider myself to be fortunate and blessed to be able to contribute my fair share to this wonderful country I call home. I am the son of first generation immigrants, who came here for many reasons, among them the desire to pay lower taxes on their earnings than they did in the old country. We Canadians have few tax loopholes as day traders (so my wife, the Chartered Accountant says!). As far as Revenue Canada is concerned, day trading is *not* capital gains, for instance. However, for my American readers, here is a loophole I learned while living and trading in the States (a loophole the Internal Revenue Service has been trying to close for the last 60 years):

HERE IT IS: If, in your margin account, you short a stock and it depreciates in value, your account equity will increase. But until you close the position, that is, until you buy it back to cover your short, you have no actual taxable profit. If you were to close the short position at a profit you would obviously be subject to short-term capital gains taxes.

Yet, before you close the position, you do have increased equity in your account (See Chapter 22) that can be withdrawn in cash as a loan, lowering your equity and increasing your debt balance. This equity, held in your special memorandum account (SMA), may also be used toward the purchase or the short sale of additional securities.

Suppose you shorted a listed stock that slowly but surely went to zero. But you never closed the position. Instead, you used the equity created in your SMA to short other stocks that went to zero, as well. Now you have a lot more equity than you started with, and it is withdrawable as cash or useable for purchase or short sales of other securities. But let's say you never closed those positions. Instead you used the created equity in your SMA to short more stocks that also went to zero.

As I mentioned, the IRS has been trying to close this loophole for the last 60 years, and the IRS will eventually get its way.

Finally, one more warning about shorting. You should always make sure to designate a stock you intend to sell short as "short." Many software programs will allow you to sell a stock not in your portfolio by simply selling it (without designating it "short"). You may have the stock long in another account, and you are in the process of transferring it in. If you do this with a stock that is not shortable (not borrowable) you will have created an illegal short position. You will have sold the stock without owning it, and without borrowing it either. The important point is that, while you probably will not be criminally prosecuted for this, the NASD and listed exchanges reserve the right to break bad trades.

Here's how it could happen. You sell a stock short illegally and buy the stock back, covering your position. Later on, who knows when, the NASD realizes what you did and breaks the illegal short sale. Since the sale never happened, but the buy to cover did, you'll find yourself long the stock. Suppose the stock has dropped significantly since then. You own it, and the accompanying loss is yours, as well. So always be sure to designate a short sale as such, and you won't have trouble.

If you are long stock and you accidentally designate the sale as short, don't worry. Since you cannot be both long and short in any stock in an account at the same time, your clearing firm will notice that you are actually long the stock and will sell out your long position to cover the sale. In the end you will wind up flat, that is you will own zero shares after the sale, provided you sold the same number of shares as you owned. However, accidentally doing this will create a journal entry error in your account: long and short positions are segregated from each other. If you buy long, then sell short, the clearing house's system will think you are long in your long account and short in your short account. In the end, for reasons previously discussed, you will be flat, but you will probably have to spend some time on the phone with your brokerage to clear up the confusion.

If you bend the rules, you can also go short from being long in one transaction and go long from being short in another transaction. Keep in mind that you must designate a short sale as such before executing the trade. If you do not, you may violate the uptick rule and create an illegal short position. You will also circumvent your trading platform's short function. You may even sell stock that is not marginable (and therefore not borrowable) without owning it. Many platforms will allow you to do this, since you may actually be long this stock in another account and be in the process of transferring it in, anticipating its arrival before settlement. Obviously your trading platform will have no way of knowing this and in many cases will allow you to execute the trade.

What happens if you create an illegal short position? For starters, the regulatory organizations governing the exchanges reserve the right to break erroneous and illegal trades. That means that at some time in the future (who knows when?) the NASD may call and tell you that your short sale never happened.

If you later covered the position, you would now be long the stock from whatever price you bought it at.

That's not a good situation, especially if you were right regarding the future of this stock and it continued its downward descent. So you should always designate a short sale as such, and you won't have any problems.

What about going long from being short? You can do this too, but not without problems at most brokerages. Short sales are segregated in a special part of your margin account. When you buy stock to cover, it automatically goes into that type of margin account. Eventually, you wind up being long in your short account.

This sort of situation can often be resolved with a phone call to your broker. But it will probably be a hassle, and some brokerages are difficult to get on the phone. Better to plan ahead and sell your stock. Then sell short, by the rules. And then cover the sale and go long in a separate transaction. Of course, you might then have another commission to deal with, but that's just the cost of playing by the rules.

Finally, selling stock short inherently contains more risk than going long, since your potential loss is unlimited. But if you practise sound risk/money management techniques, you would never ride a stock you hold long all the way to zero and lose everything. Likewise, if you exercise sound money management, you would also close out a short position if you were wrong. Read Chapter 24 on risk management, tune out the ego, and preserve your capital to fight another day. Abide by the rules of selling short and do your research to avoid being caught in a short squeeze. If you do all this, selling short can be another profitable tool in the financial toolbox.

24

Cover Your Assets: Risk Management

In the hall of Great Traders Past, the spirits of the old traders of yore sat in a circle, heads bowed, chanting a quiet mantra. If you listened closely, you could hear "when-in-doubt-sell-it-out, when-in-doubt-sell-it-out...."

Money management is the least talked about and perhaps the most important aspect of trading. It makes the difference between gambling and speculating and distinguishes the winners from the losers. Two traders, trading the same stocks at the same time, with the same amount of capital, can have diametrically opposed outcomes. One wins consistently, on balance, whereas the other loses consistently until all the chips are lost.

The comparison to gambling is often inaccurate but still useful. You have a certain amount of money (chips) with which to play. You buy and sell in the great casino called Wall Street. Fortunes will be made, fortunes will be lost, and the same psychology present at the casino assaults the trader at every turn.

But successful traders take precautions to avoid the gambler mentality and remain unaffected by chance. They structure their plays to remove as much risk as possible. Risk is always present, and good traders recognize it and plan for it in advance. They never roll the dice indiscriminately, never risk too much on one position, and always stack the odds in their favour by studying and finding as many indicating factors as possible. To survive bad trades, they utilize strict, often painful money-management techniques. And they remain in the game for the infrequent, fortune-making, elusive home-run trade.

It is possible to make many bad decisions and be crippled by them. It is also possible, with a little planning, to ensure that those bad decisions (which everyone, and I mean everyone, makes) are merely instructive experiences rather than debilitating, crushing losses.

In this chapter, I'll deal first with the mechanical aspects of risk management and then take a look at some of the psychological ramifications of trading. Trading is a harsh game. It is not to be played simply for the thrill of excitement. Often it is a relatively boring, psychologically gruelling endeavour. You must take care to remove the emotional highs and lows from the game and develop a plan of attack that doesn't allow for emotion-based trading. Decisions based on reason, coupled with sound risk-management principles, will save the day.

Risk management as it applies to trading consists of placing trades to stack the odds towards on-balance, long-term wins while minimizing short-term losses, therefore preserving capital.

If you are actively trading your account, or thinking about it, please pay careful attention to the following: Do not speculate with money you can't afford to lose. Do not speculate with a large fraction of your total portfolio. Limit your trading activities so that you never risk more than 1 percent of your trading capital on a single position. If you currently don't possess enough assets to speculate profitably with only a small percentage of your total portfolio, then don't do it. Speculation is a very risky activity. It requires patience, practice, dedication, and skill. To speculate with your retirement fund or other money that you need for other purposes is plain stupid.

"Watch the pennies and the dollars will take care of themselves," the saying goes. All things being equal, a stock is either going to go up or down intraday. (If you're trading stocks that do neither, you're not making money.) However, these odds aren't the most important ones. The most important ones are your odds of winning on a consistent, long-term basis. In other words, trade not only to win but also to preserve capital.

Start small. Say you've got $100,000 and you want to trade. Should you buy 1,000 (or 2,000 on margin) shares of a $100 stock like Microsoft (MSFT)? If it goes up two points, that's $4,000 profit. If it goes down, however, you've lost $4,000, and tomorrow, your buying power is down by $8,000. (See Chapter 22 for an explanation of buying power.) It's easy to get pulled in by the get-rich-quick mentality and trade big whenever possible. But it may be much wiser to start well below your capacity. Your profits on an average everyday small trade may be smaller, but you might still be in the game for the once-in-a-while windfall grand-slam trade. Everybody knows the windfall grand-slam trade (WGST): It's the one that went up 20 points yesterday, while you were busy losing half a point in

Microsoft. Being in the game for the WGST is arguably the most important thing you can do. That trade will skyrocket your portfolio, eclipsing all the consistent small on-balance profits of the preceding quarter. Preserve capital. Stay in the game.

Instead of buying 2,000 shares of MSFT, suppose you bought 100. 100?? Yes, let's say 100 measly little shares. Now, if MSFT goes down two points, you've lost $200 plus commissions. If it goes up, you've made $200 minus commissions. Just as obviously, it's not worth your time. However, that's just the beginning.

Now increase the size as your stock rises. What if, every time you trade, you start small and, as soon as you find you are wrong, you get out. Your losses on bad trades would be very small. On seeing that your thesis is right, however, and the stock goes in the direction you bet on, you could increase size by buying with every half-point increment in your direction. You might buy 100 additional shares, then 200 additional shares, then 500, then 1,000, and so on, up to a size that feels comfortable. Then, when the stock is up two points and you figure the party is over, you sell out for a profit on all shares. (By then, you might even have 2,000 of them.) Over time, accounting for profits and losses, you can see quickly how much larger your gains will be than your losses.

Of course your commissions will also be comparatively huge too. So let's look at the previous situation again. Say you made five commissionable trades to buy the entire size. Let's say each commission is $25, for a total of $125. This is clearly a sizable amount. But compare $125 with the $4,000 loss you'd have sustained if you'd bought the entire position outright and it moved the wrong way. Keep in mind, the larger commissions come out of profits, not losses. Buying in slowly and increasing size at an average price (cost basis) well below the market keeps your losses under control.

You should also know when to stop your losses. A stop loss is the price at which you will liquidate your position, having decided your thesis was wrong or that factors have changed.

The practice of starting small and increasing size also serves another function. Since your average price is going to be below the current market, you will also have some built-in down-side protection if things turn sour.

But what if your position goes the wrong direction right away? Some traders use extremely tight stop losses, say 1/8 or 1/4. In the trading of extremely volatile stocks, a 1/4 point stop loss may keep you on the edge of your seat all the time, and will probably get you whipsawed out of your position.

Everyone who uses stop losses has at one time or another been whipsawed out of a position only to see the stock go ballistic from there. So, how much is adequate? In extremely volatile stocks, a larger stop loss is warranted. (You rarely buy the very low or sell the very high.) But on how many shares? A large stop loss on a big position can not only take you out of your position if things go wrong, it can also take you out of the game for good.

However, if your plan involves moving into a trade incrementally, opening the position with small size and increasing size only if you are right, then a larger stop loss may be warranted. Ultimately, though, a good stop loss depends on your own comfort level.

Remember, a day trade is a day trade and must be liquidated by the end of the day. Many traders make the gambler's mistake of holding a losing position overnight in the ego-driven hope that the price will go up the next day. It may, but it might also tank. Stocks bought for the purpose of a day trade are probably not the same as the stocks you own in your swing-trading or long-term investment portfolio. Remember the reason you bought in the first place. Don't justify a losing situation because ego won't let you accept failure. If you bought the stock for an intraday bounce, then that's what you own it for. If you were wrong and the stock doesn't bounce, but just tanks, admit your mistake quickly and liquidate the trade at a loss.

Above all, don't average down a losing position. If you've exercised a strict risk/money-management plan, your loss will be small, relatively speaking. You will not have a large position at this time, since you moved in slowly, in anticipation of just this sort of circumstance.

Keep in mind that "All great losses started small." As I'll discuss in more detail, small losses are easier to accept than big losses. It's hard enough to liquidate when you're wrong, so keep your starting position small. You will be either right or wrong about your thesis. If wrong, the best you can do is accept it, get out, and keep enough chips to play again.

If right, you can only be more emphatically right, increase size, and stay in the race all the way to the finish. But be ruthless with your stop loss. If the trade goes bad, close it and move on.

This is one of the hardest and most important rules in the trading jungle. If you lose it all today, you won't be around tomorrow to catch the big one. You will incur many, many small losses, and many, many small gains. Approaching your trading from the perspective of preservation of capital will keep you in the game for the WGSTs. After all, these are the trades that brought you to the game in the first place. They make all the tedium and admissions of failure worthwhile.

Meanwhile, resist gambler's mentality. Buy low and sell high is a great strategy. Unfortunately, human nature often prevents this from happening. Many gamblers who are down big recklessly hope their luck will turn. They gamble with their losses by doing nothing or worse by increasing size on a losing position. This can lead to massive, debilitating losses.

Most curiously, these same gamblers will often close a winning position at a small profit, overjoyed to finally get a bone, only to watch, sickened, as the stock they just sold goes through the roof.

Recognize the scenario? If not, you must be from a different planet, because this happens to everyone at some point. In the words of the great trader Jesse Livermore, author of an excellent autobiography called *Reminiscences of a Stock Operator*, "I sold the wheat, which showed me a profit, and bought the cotton." As Livermore would say, Don't sell the wheat.

The mentality of a successful trader is the exact opposite of a gambler's. You need to cut losses immediately and ruthlessly and gamble only with winners,

Here's why. Let's say the stock you just bought for the anticipated intraday bounce off its low doesn't bounce. Instead, after hovering for a moment near your purchase price, it tanks. In a moment, it drops below your stop loss. You face a choice: Do nothing, get out, or buy more.

Now, in struts your ego, tempting you to justify the loss and supporting your original thesis, in spite of apparent reality staring you in the face.

At this point, you may be tempted to resort to conventional investment advice (often sound for long-term, fundamentally backed investing) and double or average down. You buy more shares to lower the average per-share cost. This misplaced optimism, really just a form of ego-driven denial, will inevitably lead to disaster.

Remember the plan. Remember the reason for placing the trade. If the reason is no longer valid, consider liquidating, and stick to your stop loss. You will make many, many bad decisions. All you have to do is recognize them and call them what they are. Accept reality, and keep your losses contained. Trading is a humbling experience. You will do well to accept it. Ego is the enemy, and worse yet, it's already in your head.

I recently spoke with one of the best traders I've ever known, a man whose trading account has increased from several thousand dollars to over eight figures. I will probably never approach him in terms of game. Even with his track record, he still makes plenty of bad decisions. But he always adheres to strict, ruthless, highly developed risk-management techniques. And he is brutally honest regarding his trading decisions. He calls 'em as he sees 'em, with no ego-induced denials of reality. Still, over time, even with his stellar track record, he insists (with humility) that he has lost much more than he has kept.

Gambling with wins makes sense. One trader I know keeps a trailing stop loss of 50 percent of her gain. In other words, as her winning position increases, she'll move her stop-loss target up, always preserving 50 percent of her gains. I believe this is an excellent starting strategy, and here's why:

Suppose you stick rigorously to stop losses, especially when painful, and keep your losses contained. And suppose, with a small profit in hand, you gambled with it instead of closing the position. Now, instead of closing the position (whoopee, 3/8!), you did nothing. Indeed, you might even buy more, following the upward price with a trailing stop loss. If it turns around, you execute the stop. If it continues upward, you're in the game for the ever-elusive WGST.

Now we come to the psychology of speculating. Trading can be a thrilling, emotional high when you're right. It can also be a debilitating, crushing, depressant when you're wrong, especially when you're wrong several times in a row.

But trading is a business, not a ride in an amusement park. Just as you wouldn't go to an important meeting when you were depressed and unable to make decisions, you shouldn't make serious trading decisions when you're feeling giddy, invincible, and careless.

Many of the biggest losses endured by once hugely successful traders have occurred directly after the biggest gains they've ever made. Keep in mind that you can easily justify a small loss as a lesson. A major loss can make you question your very right to live.

Adhere to strict money-management practices and never let things get out of hand, either financially or emotionally. Understand that being wrong a lot of the time is simply a condition that all traders must deal with.

STRATEGIES FOR EMOTIONAL STABILITY

Many books deal with stress management. Read as many as you can and practise the techniques they recommend. It is of vital importance to your health as well as your trading success that you avoid emotional turmoil. If you're in a constant state of chronic shame-fear-panic-elation, you should consult a mental-health professional for information. Emotional turmoil will do you no good as a trader.

Studies show that physical health affects mental health. If you are in good physical shape, you have a greater capacity to deal with stress. And trading can be highly stressful. However, it doesn't need to be. There are simple things you can do to increase your health and mental stability so you can weather the most gruelling situations.

Simple physical exercise, for example, reduces stress. A physician can advise you before you embark on an exercise regimen, and I'm not qualified to make many recommendations. But when you're physically fit, you can greatly enhance your capacity to deal with difficult situations.

You should also know enough to quit when you're behind. Take a break after numerous losses. Maybe for a day or even a few days. Take as long as you need to clear your mind. If you can take a walk, take one if it gets your mind off trading.

Also, do something nice for yourself. This is very important, especially after a series of bad trades. These can really make you feel desperate and worthless, which can corrupt your judgment and cloud your thinking. You will make desperate choices and suffer for them. So quit for a while. Re-evaluate your strategy. It is not the end of the world.

Re-evaluate your plan later, when you feel calmer. Keep in mind that a penny may turn up heads 50 percent of the time, but it will turn up tails a few times before it turns up heads again. And every time it turns up tails, the odds increase in your favour.

Losses can be instructional. Wins seldom help you to improve. A win just teaches you to do the same thing. A loss offers a chance to grow and improve.

Finally, quit when you're far ahead. A long string of winners will cloud your judgment. It will fill you with feelings of certainty and invincibility, both inappropriate emotions for trading. Ego will enter the equation, and you may make bad decisions. Ego will tell you in a calm reassuring voice to "average down. You know you're right." Many tremendously successful traders have blown not only all their recent gains, but all of their savings, too, because of their insidious belief that they could do no wrong. Better to take a break, take a walk, and do something nice for yourself. Don't continue until you clear your head. Re-read the section on combating the gamblers mentality, and always use strict risk-management techniques. Never put too much capital at risk. Great traders blow up too. No one is immune.

25

Games People Play:
How Market Makers
Do What They Do

This chapter is all about the game. In any forum where traders chat, you'll hear comments like, "This market maker screwed me! Every time I try to sell, he drives the price down. Every time! Why won't he just let me sell my 300 shares!?"

Everyone who has ever been in a day traders' chat room has heard words like these. The sad reality is that these ogres, these beasts, to whom we ascribe so many tricks and treacherous ploys, are really just like you and me, except that, in their case, more money is on the table, and the stakes are higher. Some of what you hear is true, but much of it is not. So let's examine what market makers do and all the myths and fallacies surrounding them. Then we can examine what it really means to "make a market" in this day and age and build an understanding of the gamesmanship that inevitably arises from putting everything on the line day after day.

We'll examine the tricks and decoys market makers use to accomplish their goals. This chapter is not going to endear the old-school trading community to me, but that's okay, because it's a rapidly changing world. I'm not going to say anything outrageous here. In fact, I think it's a shame that some in the trading community view such an exploration of what they do and how they do it as "letting the cat out of the bag."

The proverbial cat has been out for some time. If you want to play on the same field as the market makers and win by taking control and responsibility, rather than by guessing, gambling, and blaming, you should understand these tricks of the trade.

Myth #1: Market Makers Have Access to Much More Information on Level III NASDAQ Workstations Than Anyone Else

If you've read Chapter 12, you will already understand how wrong that is. Market makers have fundamentally the same information as any trader who goes through a top-flight direct-access-oriented brokerage. The only difference is that they may be working an order, so they know the size that they are currently working. Market makers do not have any special access to or special view of limit orders per se.

The situation is of course different on the NYSE, as I've discussed. There, the specialist acts as a dealer. Each stock on the NYSE has only one specialist, and that specialist's job includes maintaining the order book of the particular stock. However, specialists are under strict legal control with regard to sharing the contents of their order books. Nobody but the specialist is allowed to see it. I constantly read usenet posts in which people say market makers can see each other's orders. Ridiculous! There is no such thing!

What OTC (NASDAQ) market makers do have is a whole bunch of orders, which they'd like to execute for third parties (order flow). If they have a whole bunch of orders, or one order to sell 50,000 shares today in a stock that regularly trades a million shares, then they are happy and would certainly hope the stock trades at a price where they can complete the order. If they don't trade, they don't make any risk-free capital at all.

In any case, market makers cannot share the nature of their orders with anyone. To do so would be a gross violation of the client's interest (as well as the law). Someone with that specific knowledge could front run the customer. Front running, an illegal version of "getting in front of size," refers to the practice of an individual with material inside information (such as the fact that George Soros is going to buy 700,000 shares of ABCD stock by Friday) buying or selling the stock short before the customer can effect the trade, in expectation that the price will run as the large order is filled.

Institutions aren't stupid. They are aware of the fact that their intentions can leak out. And since they always stand to lose big, they go to elaborate means to disguise their intentions and share their information with only a selected few. In fact, the trader/market makers executing the trades are often unaware of the totality of the order. They may know only that they are selling 30,000 shares for the client. The client may have

800,000 behind that, but won't let the trader know. The clients would be compromising their own positions if they did.

As I mentioned, there are strict laws covering disclosure of this sort of information. Licensed equity traders must pass a test, which emphasizes the harsh punishments for divulging this sort of information to anyone. Meanwhile, market makers' trading activity is carefully monitored by StockWatch, the police of the cyber jungle. Some well-traded stocks (DELL, for instance) often have upwards of 60 market participants. It would be nigh impossible for all those participants to collude and share specific knowledge of each other's orders on an ongoing daily basis while their phones are recorded and StockWatch is watching.

Myth #2: Market Makers Back Away Constantly

Not so. Sure, it happens, sometimes from bad intentions and sometimes out of plain ignorance. Some neophyte assistant traders incorrectly add how many shares the traders transacted, and the traders, thinking they've traded their liability, decline a legitimate liability order. But this doesn't happen constantly. Yet everyone has a story of how this person and that person are sleaze-bags, that they just back away constantly. Given my background and experience as a market maker, and having been the axe in a dozen or so stocks, I have experienced it too.

When I was Head Trader at MB Trading, a retail direct access electronic brokerage, I heard countless complaints over time. As a licensed equity trader, when this complaint was justified, I'd call the market maker in question or the NASDAQ and get satisfaction. The NASDAQ takes the prospect of backing away so seriously that it monitors not only the trades, but also the bids and offers of every market participant in real time.

A trader can call a special number to request that the regulatory body of the exchange check the records (all time-coded). The regulators can determine, often in a matter of seconds, whether the accused market maker has indeed backed away.

The penalties for backing away are severe, because the practice erodes the very fabric of a fair and stable market, and regulators aggressively pursue such transgressions.

As a former market maker and institutional sales trader, I've had my share of back-aways. I've called the special number on several occasions, and I was wrong on all but one. In the vast majority of cases when a customer complains of this, a simple examination of Time of Sales reports reveals the customer's error. (See Chapter 8 for an explanation of Time of Sales and how to use it).

Many traders don't realize the importance of Time of Sales in determining the quality of their execution. Especially if you trade through a full-service brokerage house, if you enter an order and receive a crappy print, examine Time of Sales. It is altogether possible that your order was executed poorly.

Time of Sales is an irrefutable record of what actually happened, regardless of what you think you saw. I'm not taking the old-school party line here. Backing away does happen, but not that often. In the vast majority of cases, the individual can't close a position because of poor trading. This happened so frequently in my experience that I realized many individuals who are engaged in active trading simply don't have a firm grasp of the tools. In fact, countless hours of conversations (I was recently told that my phone conversations at work, which are recorded, take up almost ten times as much space as the other traders on a daily basis) finally led me to write this book. Anyone who cares to read this book will understand the way things work, and what it really means to take on the responsibility of trading one's own account.

Myth #3: Market Makers Can Short All They Want, Stopping a Rally and Beating the Stock into the Ground

Well, not quite. There are stringent rules and regulations concerning short-selling securities in which you make a market. While it is true that market makers are not subject to some of the same rules as individuals selling short for their own account, they cannot indiscriminately short sell a stock and beat it into the ground. If you make a market in a stock, you may sell short for the firm account only in connection with bona fide market-making activity. Keep in mind that, as a market maker, you are required to keep a two-sided market at all times. You must stand ready to buy and sell as necessary to create a liquid market. And you will need to put firm capital to use in this endeavour. However, you may not just sell and sell, beating a stock into the ground because it pleases you.

You may, for instance, sell short in anticipation of customer sell orders.

You may also work large customer sell orders, which in many illiquid stocks may look as if you are nailing the stock to the ground. Of course, as a market maker, you are usually subject to short-selling rules specific to market makers.

You may, however, sell short for the firm account in a similar manner to an individual if you do not make a market in the stock.

Another myth says that major firms will come out with strong recommendations so that they can sell huge orders (received before the recommendation) into the increased demand or with downgrades for the converse situation.

There is no denying this sort of activity seems to occur. However, there is something called the Chinese Wall doctrine, which says the brokerage house must separate the analysts from the trading department with an impenetrable barrier.

Any trader who trades with advance information concerning a report not yet available to the public would be guilty of insider trading by definition. And StockWatch is not blind to the trading activity of the big firms. Similarly, an analyst who was aware of a pending client order would be in possession of material inside information as well. To issue a report under these circumstances is absolutely illegal. You don't just lose your career for these sorts of crimes, you go to jail.

Nevertheless, I've often wondered if it happens when I watch various stocks. I've seen major buying, followed by an upgrade, and I've seen major selling by one market maker for days, followed only then by a downgrade. So this is certainly an area that bears watching. Much of this could simply be common sense. A company is coming out with earnings. Several major stockholders think the report is going to be bad, so they divest themselves in advance of the report. But seeing what I've seen leaves me with questions rather than answers. With trading violations, there is an irrefutable record (Time of Sales), so proof is positive. The Chinese Wall doctrine is more difficult to enforce. One thing is sure. You can bet these sorts of situations are investigated aggressively.

Prior to the Securities Act of 1934, and particularly in the 1920s, this sort of activity was not only legal, it was rampant. Just read *Reminiscences of a Stock Operator* by James Livermore, and you'll get a feel for the Wild West nature of the markets during that time. Manipulations of the kind described in the book had a lot to do with the crash of 1929. The result, several years later, was the Securities Act of 1933 and 1934, which outlawed most of these practices.

The public, having read the seminal stories from that time and having seen movies like *Wall Street* (but not having read the securities legislation, which is sterile and deadly boring) is often under the impression that these same shenanigans still exist. They don't. But other, more sophisticated ones must.

Maybe I'm a cynic, but I believe it's in human nature to try to cheat. Maybe there are real tricks perpetrated by the majors. But given that they would be so complex as to fool the aggressive investigations of the authorities, I can't possibly speculate on what they would be. I doubt they would be targeted at individual trades, even if they did exist. Believe me, the market makers don't really care about a 16th on our 1,000 shares. They've got much bigger fish to fry.

Many people are under the impression that the stock market is a zero-sum game, that for somebody to win, somebody must lose. Despite what I said on page 25, this is not quite the case. You really never know the position of the contra to your trade. You may think you got over by selling stock to somebody at the high, but you don't know if the other side isn't purchasing additional shares at an average price well below the current market or buying the last shares to cover an on-balance profitable short position. Don't engage in the "this person's a sleaze-bag, and always screws me" mentality. At best, it's usually just a waste of time.

Having said all this, what does it really mean to make a market? The term market maker refers to the OTC NASDAQ market. There are no market makers on the listed exchanges; there are specialists.

Market makers are dealers of stock. They buy for appreciation in value, just like you and me, and they buy so they have an inventory, which may then be resold to natural customers. They buy the stock at a dealer price and mark it up a little.

Market makers must stand ready to buy or sell a minimum number of shares, as determined in the NASD order-handling rules from any market participant, anytime, at their quoted price. This price must be fair in relation to current market. In other words, if you make a market, you're required to both buy and sell stock as the situation warrants, and you are liable to sell it at fair market value, regardless of its cost to you. You cannot take the cost of the inventory into account when filling customer orders. You cannot withdraw your market during bad times and enter your market when things are more favourable to you. In fact, there are punishments for withdrawal. You, as a market maker, are required to be open for business and ready for liability orders during all market hours. You don't go out for lunch. You don't leave your desk. Your bladder develops superhuman capacity.

And that's on a slow day, when you don't have any big orders to work. When you have big orders to work, or when you are the axe, you are focused, like a fighter, an air traffic controller, or a kid playing a video game. But now it's your money on the line. Missed opportunities, little accounting mistakes, add up remorselessly. After all, this is money, and it is your legal fiduciary responsibility to see that it is handled correctly. Everyone is watching. StockWatch on one side to keep you honest, and the customer on the other, whose very financial life you hold in your hands.

To make matters more interesting, the average market maker keeps markets in a dozen or more securities. At smaller firms with fewer traders, market makers make markets in 40 or more securities. They are required to respond to any liability orders within 30 seconds, or they are in violation of the regulations. And there are no excuses. The mutual fund managers aren't going to care if your bladder was about to burst, which caused them to miss the sale of 5,000 shares at $3 more than current prices. That's a $15,000 loss, and they're not going to accept anything but satisfaction, bladder or no bladder.

Nor will they care that you had numerous simultaneous liability orders in several securities, that news just came out on two stocks and you simply couldn't digest the information and click the buttons at the speed it was coming at you. That's your problem. How many shares did you sell of ABCD? How many shares did you buy of ABCD? (You have buy orders too.) And what is your current (the firm's) position? And what about the other two dozen stocks? What about the Dow tanking and the Fed meeting and the earnings reports? And what about SOES? How many shares have you transacted there while looking after your other stocks? (Remember, SOES executes against you automatically as a market maker. You simply receive notification that you've just bought or sold stock.) How many shares do you now own that you didn't want to, now that the Dow is down 75 points and the tick is just ugly? What is your average price in any of these stocks?

Now don't get me wrong. The traders are making money on every share they transact correctly. But not like the old days. In the old days (two short years ago), spreads were positively luxurious. But now, with volatility and the liquidity of day traders, there is, generally speaking, no spread at all. No margin for error. The first-class luxury coach has been traded for a crowded New York subway at rush hour.

It is not an easy job. It's hard enough to trade your own account well, without any of the legal requirements and fiduciary responsibilities of making a market. But that's the career they chose. (You don't just fall into it. The level of responsibility and the emotional demands are too high, not to mention all the licences required.) These people are a breed apart. And the world still needs it's market makers, at least for now.

So what do market makers want? Three things:

1. To trade as many shares as possible for others (order flow); they get paid a commission or a markup on every share.

2. To trade for the firm account and create as much value as possible in inventory (buy stocks low and sell them high).

3. To disguise their intentions so nobody knows what they're doing. If they tip their hands, they'll lose big. Guaranteed.

To these ends they will employ several techniques discussed below. Watch for them next time you are watching a stock.

CLANDESTINE OPERATIONS: REGARDING ORDER FLOW & TRADING THE COMPANY ACCOUNT

Clandestine activity is normally hidden from view, but if witnessed, is clearly recognizable. There is no trickery involved. You just have to look for it, and there it is.

Market makers don't want you to know what they're doing, and they will frequently go to clever lengths to disguise what they do. But the vast majority of the time, their intentions are clear. So, seek and ye shall find.

You may notice market makers on the bid, off the bid, on the offer, off the offer, intermittently, at all different prices during the day. This is normal activity. They probably have nothing major to do on the day, and they're simply fulfilling their role as a market maker. If they are the axe, you may notice they're on the bid or offer more than anyone else. (See #Best in Chapter 9.) But it won't be by a massive amount. They've been there ten times today, and many of the others have been there three, four, or five times. This is normal. They're the axe, and people come to them first with their orders, because, generally speaking, they'll have the liquidity to facilitate an order quickly. It makes sense that they would do more business on the day than many others.

This situation reflects the market makers' first desire: to trade as many risk-free shares as possible. Remember, they get paid a markup or commission for every share they transact. As market makers, they generally get a salary plus a percentage of profits (commissions or markup) as bonus, so the more profitable their business, the bigger their bonuses.

In the days when spreads were huge, it was easier for market makers to make a great deal of money. Nowadays, with spreads smaller (virtually non-existent, many times), it is much more difficult to be profitable. Being profitable now involves more risk because, to really make money, you need inventory purchased at a cheaper price that you can sell to natural buyers as they arrive. With the increased volatility in the marketplace, this inventory is difficult to obtain.

Some of the more volatile Internet stocks will drop $30 a share on a bad day. Can you imagine if you were loaded to the gills with one of these stocks, and the price dropped 20 percent in one day? What would that do to your profitability? And if you were loaded to the gills when the price started to drop, and your clients (probably large institutions) called in and wanted to unload all their huge positions, you couldn't just put them on hold and sell your own stock out so you didn't lose your money. You would have to sell their positions first, regardless of what was happening to your own inventory. In other words, if you were inexperienced as a market maker, you would lose your money and often the firm's, as well.

You might have heard about Nick Leeson, a trader at Barings, which was formerly one of the oldest and richest merchant banks in the world. Leeson was a young, unsupervised trader, operating in the Asian markets in 1995. Trading financial instruments on margin, he singlehandedly bankrupted the entire company, which had existed for 200 years. True, this was not NASDAQ market making, but the risk is the same, and so is the lesson from Barings's failure: Since only a small margin is needed to establish a position, a firm could face rapidly mounting financial obligations that are way beyond its means. These days, particularly in crazy high-tech and Internet stocks, firms carry less inventory. This can make it more difficult to enter and exit positions, because nobody has much of the stock lying around in inventory. To sell your 5,000 shares, for example, may drive the market down a point or two (for a moment or two) as market makers, who don't want to lose money, buy the minimum legally required from you—maybe fewer than 100 shares, depending on current liability requirements—and readjust their market.

Ideally, a firm will acquire a lot of stock in a company that nobody is interested in. As the company's story becomes known, the firm will trade around their position as the stock goes up, making boatloads of money for the firm in the process.

This means if you see market makers on the bid/offer, off the bid/offer, as I've described, and in line with the orders they're filling, they may be buying or selling for their own inventory. This is normal activity.

But trading the company inventory is a challenging job, with the heaviest of responsibilities, both legal and ethical. There is so much risk involved that, if the market makers commit an error, they will lose the firm's money for good. As you can imagine, this has created a conflict between the new directions of today's market makers and the old-school ways. It's a conflict between risk-free capital vs. capital gains.

In a volatile market, holding inventory for capital gains involves substantial risk. On the other hand, risk-free capital in the form of simple order flow may produce less profit.

In the midst of all this, we have the fast rise of the ECNs, which generally charge $.015 a share whether you buy or sell. This means that, for each share the ECN matches, it receives $.03, and it's totally free of risk. Unlike market makers and their employers, ECNs operate automatically and electronically, and they carry no inventory whatsoever. So the demise of the market-maker system as it now stands seems imminent.

This probably explains why Goldman Sachs recently took a 25 percent interest in Archipelago (ARCA), the ECN run by Terra Nova Trading. Clearly, with so much at stake and margins so thin, market makers with a size position or a client order will do what they can to disguise their intentions.

Disguised intentions or covert operations appear to be something other than what they truly are. Ideally, they are conducted in full public view, with the viewers hoodwinked into thinking they are watching one thing, when in actuality, they are watching something very different.

These operations are the most fun to watch, and the most difficult to figure out.

Since we'll never know with certainty exactly what the market maker is doing, we must use common sense, intuition, a feel for the markets, and careful observation of the market makers and ECNs involved to see the reality that market makers try to hide.

Typical tricks involve headfakes and fading the trend, as well as sudden rash selling or buying to drive the price one way or another, panicking the weak hands into taking or closing positions. The reasons for these manoeuvers are many, but they all come down to one thing: profit.

THE HEADFAKE

Headfakes are probably one of the most common manoeuvers that market makers will do to trick you into thinking the market is going one way or another. Many so-called experts say that, when market makers, and especially the axe, sit on or near the offer, they're a seller on the day.

I'll bet that every trader has seen a stock that bears all the traditional attributes of an imminent tank. By conventional Level II interpretation, such a stock is on its way down. The axe is on the offer, few bids are in sight, heavy selling starts, and so you sell short. Moments later, the stock rockets up.

What few of the so-called experts mention is that the axes know exactly how the public perceives them, so they disguise their intentions to fool you. Here's an example: The axe in a stock you are watching suddenly goes on the inside offer showing 10,000 shares offered. You may also notice, depending how devious the market maker is, several other large ECN offers at or near the best offer. Were they there before? It seems that suddenly, there is a lot of liquidity on the sell side. It would take a lot of buying pressure to break through that much stock.

Then, on the bid side, the same market maker lowers the price substantially. Seconds later, the move is followed by InstiNet (INCA), which, seeing the added liquidity, lowers its bid slightly. (Was that really why INCA lowered its bid?) Several trades go off at the offer price, but the axe still offers 10,000 shares and doesn't reduce the size. The axe seems to be saying to the market at large: "I have a huge sell order. Nobody can buy as much stock as I've got for sale."

As soon as everyone has noticed that the market maker's size hasn't lowered, the size changes to 12,000 shares offered. Now the market maker who was buying at the best bid disappears, sensing in a few moments that there might be a better price and leaving a large spread. Suddenly, other market participants, seeing what looks like an imminent drop in price, jump in to sell inside the spread. They hope to sell first, before the axe chops the price down. Other market makers at or near the bid change their size to 100 or lower, with their prices far out of the way. The stage is set. The spring is compressed.

Suddenly, a market participant who can't take the anticipation sells to INCA at its bid price. INCA drops its price by 1/16 and lowers its size to 100. Other market participants hop on the best offer, hoping to sell. If you have access to the ISLD or ARCA order book, you may see many individual sell orders lining up. A few more trades go off at the offer, with the non-axe market participants being the sellers. They play into the axe's hands perfectly, taking the risk upon themselves. (They may be selling short here.)

A moment goes by as the market digests what's happening. Suddenly the axe lowers the offer to the inside. One more moment passes. The tension is palpable. Traders everywhere moisten their keyboards. Then, bong! They're off. Everyone sells. The ticker fills with trades. INCA sucks up all the liquidity, lowering its bid all the while. Then INCA disappears altogether for a moment, spiking the price downward since nobody in their right mind will buy in front of such selling pressure.

Then INCA reappears back on the bid, buying everything in sight. Many, many trades go off, volume spikes up dramatically. Huge prints hit the tape: 10,000 shares, 25,000 shares. These are, in fact, aggregate prints out to the client, whose real order, given to the axe, was "Buy 40,000 shares."

And now for the finish. The axe disappears from the offer and appears on the best bid. Suddenly, the tape goes wild with buys, as the axe takes all the offers, right up to the price at which the stock traded before the axe offered. Only this time, the offer is nowhere near the inside. And all those ECNs who were offering? They're gone too. There is no supply now in this stock.

But now, in comes the demand. The market sees the axe buying, and traders, many of whom are short, realize what just happened. They hop on the bandwagon, bidding the price higher and higher. Now scalpers come in, and they bid the price even higher. The axe, simply using their reputation and the services of an ECN, has managed to acquire a substantial number of shares, at an average price well below current market, with just a headfake.

For better or worse, all those who were tricked into shorting upon seeing the axe's size now buy back, creating a micro-short squeeze. The axe's client is happy, because somehow, that client bought 40,000 shares of this stock for $1 cheaper than it is right now. The fund manager can rest happy because, at least for now, they're up $40,000. (Now we can see one of the advantages of using the axe.)

This is an ideal scenario (at least for the axe). If the stock came right back up to where it was, and no further, the axe's headfake would have been perfect. The extent to which market makers can accomplish their goals without affecting the market is the extent of their success. The axe had 40,000 shares to buy, and did so at a price very favourable to the client.

Situations like this happen all the time. However, they're often a little less dramatic. That's because the market makers may not know the full extent of the client's needs. If the client needs 100,000 shares on the day, for example, and the market makers now have to buy the remaining 60,000 shares at a higher price because the world discovered they're a buyer of size, then their games will have backfired, and they'll be the losers.

What about the risk? The market makers were offering some good size. If other market participants were buyers of size and bought all 10,000 or 12,000 shares, the market maker that was offering would be legally obligated to sell. And then the market maker would be short this stock, in the presence of a buyer of size. The market maker would have to fill its client's order first, without regard for its own position, and would wind up in a bidding war to get the shares back.

What about the client's order? A game like this one can easily end in tears. If it backfires, the market makers' reputations would be greatly diminished and, at the very least, they'd lose bread-and-butter clients.

The ethics of this sort of behaviour are obviously questionable. If the market maker was discovered manipulating the tape, it could result in disaster. However, if you watch the 800-pound gorillas of the market-making world, you'll see stuff like this happen on a daily basis.

So beware the headfake. A misinterpretation of the axe's behaviour will separate you from your money. With practice, you can easily identify this sort of trick.

FADING THE TREND

Now we come to fading the trend. This happens just before an intraday reversal in price and influences the next few minutes or hours. The market makers have finished with their orders or they are in preliminary exercises to set up a headfake. So they try to induce the maximum number of buyers or sellers to exhaust liquidity and prime the market for a price reversal. Keep in mind the market makers may have client sell orders or client short sell orders (or the converse), or they may be buying or selling for their own inventory.

Here's an example: INCA, some other ECN, or even a market maker has been buying up the stock, driving the price ever higher. The axe has been on and off the offer, and there are very few offers of size out there. To many, it looks like there is a lot of support and very little supply. Volume, which was active before, has largely dried up. The axe, however, keeps raising the price on almost every sale, inducing those few last traders who are convinced the price will continue up.

As soon as there are no buyers left at the offer for a moment or two, the axe may lower the offer a little bit. But as soon as someone buys stock from the axe, the axe raises the offer again.

As you can see, the axe is hoping somebody else will buy from them. At this point, it's important to realize that the axe may be selling short here or selling the last shares of a client's order; trying to reel in the last buyers at a higher price by seeming unwilling to sell; hoping all the buyers will disappear, and selling will begin again, at which point the axe may run a headfake or otherwise just buy the short shares back. Sooner or later, someone will get tired of waiting for the expected run-up (while, disappointingly, the price just hovers). And the more people drawn in at that high price, the harder the price will fall when they all decide they were wrong and try to liquidate.

Meanwhile, the market maker, by creating the impression that the stock is going up and luring greedy buyers, has cleverly sold all of the client's order at a very favourable price.

The market makers might also be working a large sell order at a specific price throughout the day. This can be surmised using #Best and a chart, which will have clearly erratic and normal lows, on normal volume, and a flat top price beyond which the stock seems unable to pass. The market makers may get on and off the offer price, but every time the price hits that level, they're sellers.

When you identify market makers who are fading the trend, take a good look at what's happening and be wary of taking an opposing position. Consider that they have unlimited capital to support whatever they're up to. If you can't tell what they're up to, don't put yourself at risk.

Finally, you might notice a stock whose price usually moves but now doesn't move at all and has an uncharacteristically static, narrow spread, with good volume. Check #Best, and you will probably identify two market makers, currently both axes, at least intraday, who both have large buy and sell orders on the day. Supply and demand meet on equal terms. It is a war of the axes. And though the stock doesn't move, it trades.

There are at least a couple of ways to play this:

1. Getting in Front of Size

Wait till one of the axes really disappears from either the bid or the offer. When either the supply or the demand has gone, the stock may move strongly one way or the other.

Last year I noticed one market maker in a particular stock bidding all the time and another on the offer all the time. They did this for a couple of days in a row in a stock that usually moved 10 percent intraday. By my figuring, the two of them had transacted at least 100,000 shares each, and the float on the stock was less than 800,000 shares. While I was eating lunch one day, I noticed the market maker on the offer disappear and reappear, trying to fade the trend. But the bidder wouldn't pay higher. A little while later, I saw two large prints hit the tape at the bid price. (One market maker was printing the aggregate sale or buy to the client.) The market maker on the offer raised the offer way, way out of the way, indicating, at least for the moment, that selling was done, then hopped on the bid.

I assumed the market maker was greedily trying to get ahead of the other market maker's size. And I wasn't the only one watching. Soon, people started taking all the offers. The stock had been trading steadily at 14 by 14 1/16. By the time I bought in, it was 14 1/8–5/16. The stock saw $22 that day, on massive volume. I was out at 18 and change.

Getting in front of size is an excellent way of lowering risk. The difficulty lies in two places. First, you have to determine after close study of the stock and the market participants that the market maker is a size participant on the day. Second, you are never going to know when the liquidity you are getting in front of will dry up. When the market maker's order is filled completely, it's time to consider closing the position. Only with knowledge of the stock and careful observation of the market maker's activity can you make a determination. Keep in mind that your best determination is still, at best, an educated guess.

2. Participating in Line

This is the only time I would consider scalping. Another way to exploit a static market, if there is a large enough spread, is to try to participate at the bid price and sell at the offer. In March 1999, I had just that luck for the first time with Iomega (IOM). It was bidding 4 7/8–5 for what seemed days. Finally, I thought I might as well place an order and see if I could participate in line. So I placed an order to buy 900 shares at 4 7/8. (I knew the specialist would process the odd-lot order.) I figured the specialist would want to execute as many orders as possible.

About 20 minutes later, I got a fill. So I put the order out, to sell at 5. Sure enough, about half an hour later, I was filled. At about $90 profit after commissions, I figured this wasn't bad. If I could do it again, even if the price dropped, I'd have at least 1/16 (1/8 × 900 shares minus commission) downside protection after commission. So I placed the order again, with identical results.

I did this eight or nine times a day, every day, for a few weeks, until, miraculously, my orders wouldn't fill. Opportunities like this abound every day, if you find stocks that fit the criteria. However, I still question the economics and ethics of scalping, and I don't do it much anymore. I think commissions and risk are far too high to make scalping for an eighth or a 16th worthwhile. Nevertheless, there are many day trading brokerages that offer courses in trading when they're really teaching people how to scalp. They offer huge leverage to the trader who agrees to scalp and close all positions by the end of the day.

Unscrupulous would be a flattering way to describe such firms. In today's market, which has changed dramatically from two years ago when many of these courses were written, scalping is an uneconomic activity, benefiting only the sleazy brokerages that insist upon and recommend the activity. If you encounter one of these brokerages, it is in your best interest not to listen to the get-rich talk and steer clear. Remember, brokerages get paid whether you win or lose. Whether or not you break even on the day by scalping, the brokerage gets paid its commissions on the 90 or so trades you've made. So who are you really working for?

RASH SELLING/BUYING

Sometimes, particularly after a news release, a sudden flurry of trades will occur on the bid or offer. This will cause a momentary spike in price. If these trades were executed by parties in collusion or by a single market maker intending to create a spike, it would constitute painting the tape, which is strictly illegal. Only StockWatch knows for certain. But whether they're executed by single parties desiring this effect or multiple parties with natural orders, these few trades will often spark a momentary rally in price.

Watch out for these spikes. Many times, the price returns right to where it was before the momentary spike. The rash of trades just serves to shake out the weak hands.

It is easy to be whipsawed out of a position when your stop is hit this way. Observe these spikes carefully. They may be headfakes, even if unintentionally induced, and they'll shake you out of a position at a loss, when success was close at hand.

The realities of a very volatile market make it arguably much easier to be whipsawed out of a position now than in the recent past. You must pay close attention to money management to plan for and mitigate this sort of occurrence.

STOCKWATCH: POLICE OF THE CYBERTRADER REALM

It never fails to amaze me that some people assume, fancifully and wrongly, that the markets are a Wild West environment where anything goes. Nothing could be further from the truth. A large part of our national livelihood is at stake in our markets, and the assurance of a fair and orderly market is a national imperative. Equity traders are subject to many laws, and they're watched carefully.

The staff at StockWatch watches every security traded on the NASDAQ. They record every bid that is raised, every size that is changed, all shares that are bought/sold, and they record every trader's phone conversations. To that end, they recently pumped approximately $100 million into their surveillance program.

As an example of StockWatch's vigilance, here's a story about my friend Joe. Before he was a day trader, Joe was making markets. "The particular stock I was trading," he told me, "in which I was the axe, was trading near its high, at $8 a share. A young fund manager who was 24 years old was running over $100 million and owned nearly half a million shares of this stock."

The manager had obtained the stock as a spinoff dividend. In other words, his cost was near zero.

"Over the previous month," Joe said, "I had been liquidating his entire position, and was almost done. I could sell only a little bit of the stock at a time, since the daily volume was under 60,000 shares, and there were few market makers who made this stock. If I sold a whole bunch at once, it would hammer the price."

Joe got down to the last 22,000 or so shares. "Then this manager called to ask what would happen if I just sold out the rest, right here, right now. I told him what would happen is we would hammer the price and he'd get nowhere near what the stock was worth. Better to sell slowly into the day and be done whenever we could."

He said: "Sell it right now. Take it to where it trades."

Joe said "But..."

He said, "Sell the stock right now. I'm curious what'll happen. Hit the bids."

There was no news. The guy just wanted to be done with the stock so he could buy another one. He'd already profited enormously from this stock, and he didn't care about price. "So, I did what he said," Joe recalled.

Joe was watching Level II and had a small laugh as all the market makers in the stock panicked and lowered their prices as fast as they could. All the way down to $4 1/2, in about two minutes. "And then we were done, so I hung up the phone. About one minute later, my private phone rings, and there is an unfamiliar, goofy sounding young voice."

"Hey, yeah, is this the trader in ——?" said the voice.

"Yes," said Joe.

"Wow, I mean, what's going on, is there some news, or what?"

"Not that I know of. Why?"

"Wow, man, you're ... um. You just sold so much stock. I just wanted to know what you know."

As I've explained before, nobody can see who's selling stock. That's a confidential matter. A person can surmise, but Joe wasn't even offering the stock. "I just preferenced all the market makers on SelectNet," he said. (The market makers with whom Joe transacted would obviously know that he had sold stock to them, but he had not sold a large block to anyone. It probably took 25 or more trades to sell that stock .)

"I was mad," Joe said, "and the guy sounded like an idiot, not at all like a trader. (There are a great many traders who are idiots, but something told me he was not of this variety.) So I said, 'Who the heck is this, and what makes you think I'm selling stock?' "

The voice on the line became clear and serious. "This is John X at StockWatch," he said. "I noticed you just sold 22,000 shares, at a price that doesn't seem reasonable. I'd like to know why."

Joe established the fellow's legitimacy by phoning him back at StockWatch and told him it was a natural client order. The fellow repeated that it didn't sound reasonable that a client would sell all that stock in that way.

"I explained the whole situation," Joe said, "with every detail, and he said he'd look into it. And furthermore, he'd look into every trade I'd made for the last six months. I was to provide promptly any and all information he needed, when he needed it, and failure to comply immediately would result...."

Thank goodness the money manager was just cocky and young and not trading with any inside knowledge. Thank Big Brother for recorded phone lines. The situation was obviously uncomfortable, but Joe hadn't done anything wrong, and he gained some knowledge from the experience. StockWatch is out there, and it does its job, even in the little stocks that nobody pays attention to. They are aggressive and thorough in their surveillance.

Earlier, I said that market makers play far fewer games than you would imagine if you listen in on the chat rooms. There are people out there who are simply unsuited to take on the responsibility of trading their own accounts. These are the ones who are reckless and who won't take time to learn, even when their very savings are at stake. (We've discussed this too. Common sense tells you to trade actively only a very small part of your portfolio, not your life's savings.) These are the people who are desperate to blame someone else for their mistakes rather than learn and do whatever is necessary to get educated.

Day trading is not easy. There are very few real overnight zero to zillions stories. But there are plenty of success stories. Otherwise the speculative markets would not exist. You can make an extremely handsome living at it, but the point is, it's not easy. If it were, this book wouldn't be necessary.

Keep in mind that market makers generally have been in the business several years before they're allowed to sit near a desk. They are professionals, skilled at a craft they practise every day. Trading profitably alongside them requires knowledge, cunning, ability, and experience. For these requirements, there is no substitute.

26

The Technician's Basic Tool: The Price Chart

I'm neither a technical nor fundamental trader. I day trade, which involves many of the theories you've read in previous chapters. There are a great number of books on the topic of successful technical trading, using charts to predict stock-price patterns. But here's a brief description of technical trading for day traders. Although he didn't want his name used, I will thank one of my students for putting together this very simple primer on how to read stock charts.

Whether you trade short term or long term, discretionary or systematic, your goal as a technician is always the same: to find profitable patterns in price behaviour.

To accomplish this, technicians use a number of methods to identify the prevailing price trend or to identify points at which a trend is about to reverse. (The time scale, of course, can vary). The basis for these techniques can be roughly divided in two categories: chart analysis and technical indicators.

Because basic chart analysis is the backbone of technical trading, I'll explain the most popular chart types, what they tell you, and where chart analysis fits into an overall trading plan.

ELEMENTS OF A PRICE CHART

Price charts can depict price action in any number of time frames or styles. In almost all cases, though, the horizontal x-axis of the chart represents time and the vertical y-axis represents price. Before discussing the different types of charts, though, here are a few simple, but important concepts you need to understand:

- **High**. The highest price of a given trading period, be it an hour, day, week, or month.

- **Low.** The lowest price of a given trading period.

- **Opening price (or open).** The price at the beginning of a trading period (usually a day). For stocks, the open is the price of the first trade that is recorded after the market opens; for futures, the opening price represents the average price (approximately) of the first minute of the trading session.

- **Closing price (or close).** The last price of the trading session (for stocks) or the representative trading price of the last minute of the trading session for futures. The closing price takes on special importance, because it functions as a representative price for a particular trading session—the price the market arrived at after a day of trading. The closing price is most commonly used in technical indicator calculations.

- **Range.** The difference between two specific price levels, most commonly the high and low of a given period. For example, the daily range is the difference between the high and low prices of the day, the weekly range is the difference between the high and low prices of the week, etc.

- **Volume.** The number of shares or contracts traded in a particular market in a given period (usually a day).

- **Open interest.** The number of open trades in a particular market. Both volume and open interest provide measures of liquidity, i.e., the amount of trading activity in a market. This indicates the ease with which you can get in and out of a stock. Liquid markets are generally less risky and easier to trade than illiquid markets because they are less prone to wild swings or gaps between prices. (However, some traders use strategies specifically designed to profit from the volatility in illiquid markets.)

THE BAR CHART

The most popular type of price chart is the daily bar chart, which summarizes the price action of a trading session as a vertical line, or bar, ranging from the high price to the low price. The closing price appears as a horizontal hash mark extending out from the right of the bar. The opening price appears as a horizontal hash mark extending out from the left of the bar. (Sometimes the opening price is omitted.)

The illustration at the top of the next page depicts a typical price bar. A daily bar chart, for example, would represent each day's trading with an individual bar. The high of the bar would be the high price of the day. The low of the bar would be the low price of day. And the left and right hash

Price bar from a daily bar chart

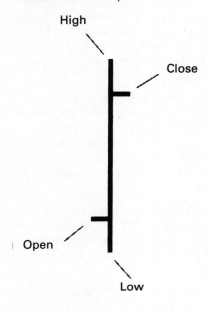

Daily bar chart

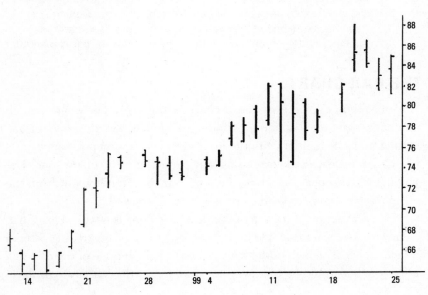

marks would be the opening and closing prices of the day, respectively. The price bar succinctly summarizes the day's trading activity: the daily range (from high to low), where the market opened, and where it closed. The illustration at the bottom of the previous page shows a daily bar chart for Dell Computer.

TIME FRAMES

Price charts can be constructed in virtually any time frame: minutes, hours, days, weeks, months, quarters, years, etc. A weekly bar chart, for example, would be constructed in exactly the same way as the daily bar chart except that it would use the high and low prices of the week rather than the high and low prices of a day.

The opening and closing prices for a weekly chart are simply the opening price for the first trading day of the week (usually Monday, unless there is a holiday) and the closing price of the last day of the week (usually Friday, unless there is a holiday).

Similarly, each bar on a monthly bar chart would use the opening price of the first day of the trading month and the closing price of the last day of the trading month. The figure below shows a monthly bar chart for the same stock.

Monthly bar chart

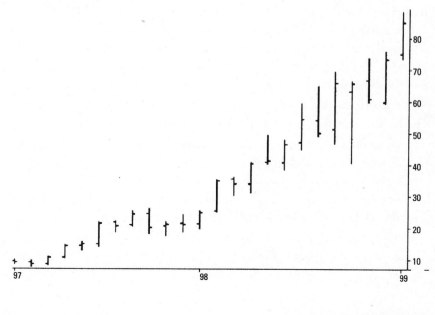

An hourly chart, by comparison, uses the high and low prices of each hour of a trading session to define price bars, and a five-minute chart uses the high and low prices of each five-minute period. For such intraday charts, opening and closing prices are often omitted (since, obviously, there are no official opens or closes reported). Alternatively, the first recorded price of a particular period might be used as the opening price and the last recorded price of the period as the closing price.

The smallest time frame chart that can be constructed is a tick chart, which creates a data point for every trade reported in a market. (Tick refers to the minimum price move in any market.)

Looking at price charts of varying time frames allows you to focus on as short or long a period as you want. Longer-term price charts also provide a context for the price action on shorter-term charts. A trade signal generated from a pattern on a short-term chart may be supported or negated by the activity on the long-term chart. A short-term buy signal might be ignored, for example, if the long-term chart shows that a strong downtrend is in force.

Bar charts are the most widely used chart type, but they are not your only choice as a technician. Other chart styles give you different perspectives on price action.

Line (close-only) charts plot only the closing prices from each trading session, essentially creating a simplified version of the standard bar chart. The line chart on the next page shows a close-only version of the price data from the example at the bottom of page 182. Some charting software will allow you to create line charts using the high price, low price, or average price from a particular bar instead of the closing price. But the closing price is most commonly used in technical analysis.

Candlestick charts originated in Japan and are similar to bar charts, although they pre-date them by a number of years.

Instead of a bar for each day (or week or month, etc.), the candlestick chart uses rectangles that range from the opening price to the closing price of each trading session. The rectangle is dark (usually black) if the closing price is lower than the opening price (a down day), or light (usually white) if the close is higher than the open (an up day).

The high and low price extremes extend as vertical lines above or below these rectangles, forming wicks to the bodies of the candles

Line chart, Dell Computer

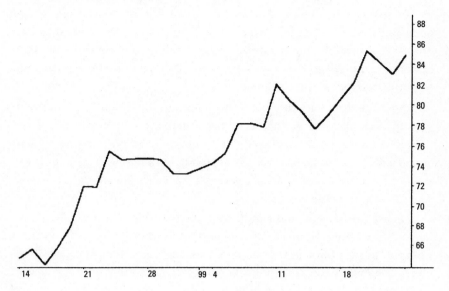

Daily candlestick chart

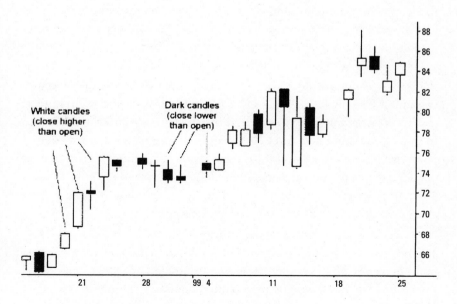

White candles
(close higher
than open)

Dark candles
(close lower
than open)

represented by the rectangles. Of course, if the high and low of the day are identical to the open and close, no wicks will exist. Conversely, if the open and close are the same price, no rectangle (body) will exist. Like bar charts, candlestick charts can be constructed on any time frame. The bottom chart on page 185 shows the candlestick version of the price data from the example at the bottom of page 182.

Some technicians think candlestick charts highlight certain price patterns that standard bar charts do not. There are numerous elaborately named candlestick patterns, ranging from one candle to several, which supposedly portend price reversals or trend continuations, depending on their context. (Most tests of such patterns, however, show little success in the way of systematic application.)

There are also several candlestick chart variations, like renko and kagi charts, but an in-depth discussion of these charts and their interpretation is outside the scope of this chapter. Because candlestick charts use exactly the same price data in exactly the same time frame as a corresponding bar chart, the preference for one chart over another can only be considered a matter of taste.

Point-and-figure charts differ from other price charts in that the time axis is not constant. Prices are not plotted day by day or week by week, etc. Instead, point-and-figure charts use columns of ascending Xs and descending Os to portray up moves and down moves (of a certain magnitude), respectively, in a market.

For example, every X might represent a 0.5-point rise (referred to as the "box size") in the stock's price. Price declines would be denoted by a column of Os only if price fell, say, 1.5 points (three boxes, referred to as the "reversal amount"). In this case, if the stock rose from 25 to 25.5 to 26 to 26.5, you would add three Xs to your column of Xs, one for each .5 point rise from 25 to 26.5. If it rose only a quarter point or a half point, or declined only a point, you would do nothing. Only when price dropped by 1.5 points or more would you stop adding ascending Xs and start a column of descending Os immediately to the right.

The larger the box size and reversal amount you use, the less sensitive your chart will be to smaller price fluctuations. Because a one-point move (or whatever increment you use for your box size) may occur in one hour or two days, the price action depicted in a point-and-figure chart is independent of time. Point-and-figure practitioners feel these charts provide a clearer picture of the tug-of-war between supply and demand in a market. The illustration below shows a point-and-figure chart of the same price data shown in the example at the bottom of page 182, using a box size of .5 points and a reversal size of 1.5 points.

Regardless of the type you use, all price charts communicate the same information: where prices have been, a clear picture of market trends, significant historical high and low prices, and an idea of the volatility in a market. Such information can suggest both the kind of trading approach that might be appropriate and the markets that may be suitable for trading.

The most basic form of technical analysis involves identifying specific price patterns (longer-term top and bottom formations like head-and-shoulders patterns or continuation patterns like triangles, as well as one-day patterns like spikes and gaps) and exploiting their probabilities.

Basically, charts allow you to identify trends and inflection points. Chart analysis is a visually based, subjective skill that nonetheless can yield excellent results when approached realistically, and it offers an alternative to mechanical, indicator-based techniques.

Point-and-figure chart

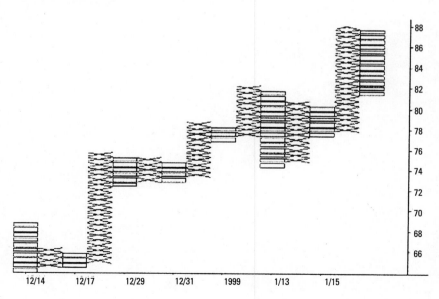

Finally, historical charts and price data allow you to test your ideas before you actually trade them. Luckily, computers and the Internet give you a great deal of power and flexibility in researching and analyzing charts and price data.

PART FOUR

Before You Start

swift ('swift) adj

1. Moving or capable of moving with great speed
2. Occurring suddenly or within a very short time
3. Quick to respond

synonym see FAST

27

A Personal Rant

Direct individual access has unquestionably affected the securities markets, but the jury is still out on what it all means. Major institutions and individuals alike wanted the liquidity that individual access to the markets could supply. But now that it exists, many are arguing for some sort of restrictions because of issues about volatility and balance of power. The media, encouraged by the powers that be, run shows on how greedy and awful traders are. But in reality, traders and speculators have been around since before the tulip days of 16th-century Holland. With transparent electronic access, one thing is for sure: Direct access to the markets is here to stay.

With the advent of sophisticated electronic communications networks like Archipelago, the very job and definition of market maker has changed. In fact, the very meaning of market has changed. Is it necessary, for example, to incur the legal responsibilities of making a market at a time when you can do virtually the same thing without the legal responsibilities?

The NASDAQ system took the first step in the electronic evolution of the markets when it created a virtual floor. Market participants from anywhere in the world could suddenly participate directly in the OTC market. Now, anyone with access to an ECN can enter orders through a computer with an Internet connection, 24 hours a day. What will this do to the market? What will be the meaning of "market hours" when humans are no longer required (or desired) to make markets?

I believe the securities markets are heading toward an electronic, ECN-dominated, 24-hour virtual floor, where anyone with a brokerage account will be able to buy and sell securities directly, without additional human intervention (in the form of a broker or trader), anytime, from anywhere in the world.

Supporting my conjecture is the fact that companies like Goldman Sachs and J.P. Morgan have taken major stakes in major ECNs. (I wouldn't bet against them.) And the NASDAQ is getting its proposed central order book online, via OptiMark. Additionally, many trading desks are evolving, as more and more institutions utilize the services of ECNs themselves, cutting out the traders and market makers.

What happens to brokers when individuals can sell their stock directly and can research companies for free over the Internet? Research reports put together by financial analysts will always be in need, since individuals will not have the specific knowledge (or time) to evaluate companies in the detailed way analysts do. So the analysts will always be around, and maybe in greater numbers, as more and more individuals enter the markets. But again, what about brokers?

It seems to me that it will be tougher and tougher for brokers. In the same way as the "travelling salesman" of the 1940s was edged out of existence by major department stores, where individuals could compare and make their own decisions, I think brokers will evolve out of existence. Sure there will be a few left. Some people will always need to speak with an individual and get a broker's thoughts before making a decision. But the job of broker will be distilled, as fewer and fewer are needed.

I can't help but feel sorry for the many individuals who make a living by recommending and facilitating the purchase of securities recommended to them in turn by their firms' analysts. I'm a licensed broker too, and if I listen really closely, I think I hear a bell somewhere.

SAILING UPSTREAM INTO THE WIND: SCALPING FOR AN EIGHTH OR SIXTEENTH IN THE FACE OF THE NEW ORDER-HANDLING RULES

I've already covered most of my thoughts regarding scalping as a business. Sure you'll occasionally find those quick eighths. But to trade with scalping as a modus operandi is in my opinion accepting tremendous risk for little to no gain. It is like being satisfied with a sardine fished at great expense out of the mouth of a huge tuna. If you're in these markets, it seems to me that scalping should be an occasional thing, not the primary plan of action.

Some people will say, "Yeah, but I can scalp 100 times a day, and make an eighth every time." This may be true in the short term. But you'll be paying such a huge percentage on commissions that it seems uneconomical to me. People will also say, "You're tripping over pennies on the way to dollars, worrying about transaction costs." To which I say, "Nonsense." If you're scalping 100 times a day, you know nothing about the stocks you're picking. What if you buy a stock and two minutes later the stock is halted? When it opens again, with terrible news, you're screwed. It happens frequently. That one lousy occurrence can set you back all of your gains.

What about all the big fish you're missing? Dozens of stocks move five points or more intraday. Sure these won't move in 30 seconds. But if you pick a few and watch them closely, you'll learn who the players are and how the stock tends to move. This information is very useful. You can use it to plan your strategies and remove as much risk as possible. Buying the intraday low and selling the high, or shorting the high and buying the low are strategies you can perfect. Holding overnight can be an excellent strategy, if you know the stock and circumstances surrounding it.

For example, one person I know bought E*Trade (EGRP) one day during incredible buying pressure. Many people got in and out for an eighth or a quarter, during the day, because the company had issued its earnings statement, and they were great. But this person bought the stock and held it overnight, for a possible gap-up. And gap-up it did. The next day it closed up $22. This person, who coincidentally has consistently earned amazing profits, over time, will not scalp and often holds overnight. If he is wrong, which he often is, he gets out quick, at a tiny loss. He employs stellar money-management techniques.

Consider the fact that, when scalping, you incur major commission costs and large losses when you're wrong. You need to trade size, often inappropriate size, to beat commissions when you're trading for an eighth. You are also subject to the vagaries of stocks you don't know. To get in and out of positions at a profit, you're subject to difficulties arising from the new order-handling rules. And finally, you make only a small profit when you're right.

When your plan is scalping, you are fishing for minnows in an ocean of big fish. You incur greater risk and greater expense for a smaller profit. With scalping as your main strategy, you will probably blow up.

Market makers hate day traders and scalpers. As soon as market makers are pegged as a buyer or seller of size, scalpers try to get in front of them. Scalpers make it harder for market makers to transact their large institutional orders profitably. Additionally, the volatility created by individual participation in the market makes it harder for market makers to do their jobs. They can't slack off, even for a moment. Finally, if market makers mess up and enter an incorrect price, some scalper will profit from their error almost instantaneously.

Scalpers create larger costs for market makers, since often they'll SOES them and transact many tickets for small numbers of shares. Market makers must often pay a ticket charge for each and every transaction, greatly reducing their overall profitability. Additionally, market makers are human and may have difficulty keeping up with their current positions, given the vast number of executions in such little time. But in the words of Frank Sinatra, "That's life!" You can talk about it all day, but in the end, market makers will just have to get over it and evolve, because the electronic revolution has only just begun.

The 24-hour, worldwide market is here. OptiMark (see Chapter 20) has recently stepped in as the call market of the NASDAQ. Orders entered into OptiMark will stay out there for the day and execute when marketable. This situation is not exactly what traders had in mind when the NASDAQ started talking about a central order book. But I think OptiMark has a good chance of evolving into just that. As time goes on, you can be sure that OptiMark will evolve to handle good-till-cancelled orders and the like. Call market in this case is just another way of saying order book.

Interestingly, OptiMark has just signed an agreement with the Tokyo Stock Exchange to fulfill the same role as it does on the NASDAQ and listed exchanges. What will it be like when Tokyo, the NASDAQ, and the NYSE can be played with one transparent order-entry system? The FTSE, DAX, and other world markets are sure to follow. Again, it is a brave new world.

Several years from now, with a laptop or a palmtop and a satellite phone (no doubt within the same device), it will be possible to aggressively trade all world markets from anywhere on the face of the planet.

28

Counterpoint

The following is a letter I received from a 20-year veteran of the U.S. stock market and full-time investor friend for whom I have a great deal of professional respect. He shares freely his opinions about investing versus day trading, using the Internet and email:

Dear Charles,

Here is a copy of the newsletter you asked me about. I put it out to all my stock market groupies and faithful followers. Feel free to share it with all your students and fellow day traders.

Dear Friends,

My aim in this report is to offer useful information to anyone who day trades, or anyone who wishes to day trade. Any suggestions, additions, corrections, would be appreciated. We do not encourage day trading, and, in our opinion, it is a fast way to lose money.

Day Trading—for the Hyperactive Trader

"Investors are trading up," writes Ted Fishman in *Worth* magazine. "Now they have the technology and access to buy and sell stocks like the pros." Online Investment Services suggests, however, that the real pros are the people who avoid day trading with the same determined attitude that they use to shun penny stocks and/or commodities.

Level I and Level II Quotes

Datek at the present time offers a streamer with Level I quotes. These are regular real-time quotes indicating the best bid and ask prices for stocks on all exchanges—NYSE, AMEX, NASDAQ, and other OTC. Most day trading firms offer in addition Level II quotes, which are for NASDAQ only, and they list all of the bid and ask prices for all market makers for

NASDAQ stocks only. Here's one comment: "The Level II feed shows the current bid/offer of every market maker in an issue. Unlike NYSE, where a single specialist determines the quote, NASDAQ is a competitive bidding process among a number of 'market makers.' With Level II, you're seeing the same information as the NASDAQ market makers see. Some believe that having the total view of all MM quotes and quantities gives a hint at the future near-term direction of an issue."

RealTick III and Level II Quotes

At MB Trading (and elsewhere), you can get a software package called RealTick III, developed by Townsend Analytics. With RealTick III, you can watch NASDAQ stocks tick by tick, follow each and every move, ask for any kind of chart you want, and search for all kinds of information. One of its features is a Level II market makers display screen, where you can find up-to-the-minute bid and ask offers on the stock. Much of the information is "colour-coded" so that you can see at a glance where the market buy and sell orders are. The information on listed stocks is rather shallow, but for NASDAQ it offers Level II quotes which tell you just about anything you want to know about the buying pressures under a stock, and the opposite selling pressures above it. In addition, the system offers charts (intraday, daily, weekly, monthly, candlestick, high-low bar, point and figures, overlays, stochastics, moving averages, etc.), Time of Sales reports, account history, and much more. Some custom versions of RealTick III include real-time updates of buying power.

The typical day traders are looking to scalp a quarter of a point here and a half a point there, possibly buying and selling the same stock several times in the same day. Ideally, they want a broker with low commissions, because even with discounters they are going to pay several hundred dollars a month in trading costs.

Frequent Traders Lose More Money Than Other Investors

University of California, Davis, researchers found that "a subset of investors who traded the most at a large discount brokerage firm between 1991 and 1996 had significantly lower returns than all the investors as a group. The annual returns, less transaction costs, of the 2 percent of investors who turned over their portfolios the most were about 10 percent, compared with 15 percent for the wider group, according to the study by Terrance Odean and Brad M. Barber" (*Wall Street Journal*, September 23, 1998, C21).

Most Day Traders Lose Money!

On the failure of the day trading firm Block Trading, investigators found that "the firm engaged in deceptive marketing to attract investors." It also found that "Of the 68 accounts at the Boston Block Trading office, 44 used borrowed money for trading and only *one* account made money during the year the office was open [our emphasis]." Both quotes here are from the *Houston Business Journal*. Other news reports are that the federal government is investigating day trading brokers because the losers are suing for losses of $40,000, $100,000, and more but have had little success in court. Day trading firms are supposed to disclose risk and have customers sign statements to such effect. Apparently day traders are like a lot of other stock traders; i.e., when they lose, they want to sue the brokers rather than blame themselves.

The day trading firms say that most of their customers do make money, at least after the first three months. One reporter found a trader who "expects" [i.e., "hopes"] to earn $300,000 this year, but most traders lose, even after they've taken day trading courses which cost US$1,500 to US$5,000. The manager of one firm said about "half of those who begin day trading wash out and never turn a profit." Another said: "It can be lucrative, but it can be devastating. You can lose a lot of money real fast."

One correspondent writes to me: "My advice to anyone considering day trading would be: (1) Don't plan on any significant profit for one to two years. (2) Use only money that you can afford to lose. (3) While developing the techniques, buy in blocks that are only large enough to validate the technique, i.e., minimize your 'at risk' capital during the learning period." Another writes: "Your blanket dismissal of instantaneous day trading is absurd. By all means spell out the very high risk—but for those who take the time to learn, and get the exceptional services and feeds now available, it is now possible [to successfully day trade] .... Why you perpetuate the myth that guessing long term is intrinsically less speculative than a one-minute stochastic, I have no idea." Obviously, my words are not going to discourage anybody!

High Cost of Data Feed, Charts, and News

Unfortunately, the typical day trading firm charges a steep price for all of its day trading dazzlements. MB Trading, Livetrade.com, and a number of others, want as much as $300 to $375 monthly for RealTick III data feed, news, and exchange fees. If you trade frequently, and that means 20 to 200 times monthly (50+ trades at MB Trading), you might get these services free.

Some brokers, like A.B. Watley, are starting to offer Level II systems free, although most of the brokers charge around $250 to $350 for the RealTick III or equivalent service. RT Trading, for example, charges $249/month for RealTick III and $62.50 for exchange fees, and MB Trading charges $375 per month ($300 for RealTick III and $75 for News Watch). Livetrade.com charges $324 per month ($299 for the RealTick III and $25 for News).

At one broker, Datek, you can get real-time quotes and automatic portfolio updating free, no matter how small your account. And the commission is only $9.99 per trade up to 5,000 shares. But you won't have anything as fancy as RealTick III. Some traders we know use RealTick III (or the equivalent) at a day trading firm, and then trade at Datek.

On the other hand, most of these brokers offer their Level II systems free with as few as 15 to 20+ trades per month. Watley offers its RealTick III system free, and Equity Trading offers the system free with 50+ trades/month.

These brokers are hard to compare and rank. Here is one letter: "I am not a customer of any trading company at this time, but in reading over your report you seem to emphasize Remote Trading's lower membership fee of $100 versus JRP and RML Trading. Your emphasis seems misplaced to me. If I am going to do business with one of these outfits I am probably going to make at least five round trip trades using limit orders per month. Thus with JRP my total cost for membership and commissions = $300, for RML = $399.50, for Remote $424.50—further, go look at RML's Web page—best training offer around for remote users it seems to me (2/1/99)." Obviously, this report can only provide the information. Traders will have to do their own comparisons.

In addition, you'll pay higher commissions per trade. MB Trading wants $22.95 per trade for up to 2,000 listed shares (or 10,000 NASDAQ shares), and you might compare that to Datek where you pay $9.99 per trade. At Datek you would get real-time quotes and the dynamic updating of your account on screen, but no RealTick III and (as yet) no Level II quotes.

What Day Traders Want in a Broker

The absolute necessities are (1) accurate real-time quotes; (2) automatic and immediate account updating; (3) fast executions; and (4) fast confirmations. In addition, day traders seem to want: (1) Web sites that do not time out: "Unfortunately," writes one trader, "most brokers have time out whenever you are not actively trading on their site, usually with a half hour." (2) A quick log-on procedure. (3) Reasonably low commissions. One day trader writes: "A large screen (20 inches or larger) is an absolute essential ... lots of windows active on the screen (graphs, waterfall tickers, an order window, a news window, an account window, etc.). Most of the tools you need are not available [with the ordinary Internet brokers] (4/27/99)."

Short Selling

If you want to sell short using an online Web broker, I find that Datek is by far the best broker to use; MB Trading is a good (but not excellent) second. Remember that brokers have to be able to borrow stock for you to sell short, and most brokers do not have a large inventory of shortable stock. Datek appears to have the best supply. Read the report carefully on Datek, however, as feedback lately, especially from day traders, is that Datek's servers are too often down and/or unavailable. Also, Datek has a short-selling rule that is quite difficult to fathom: Traders must issue short orders on an uptick, or else the order will be cancelled!

The Best Day Trading Brokers

If you must day trade, Appendix D includes some of the firms you ought to consider (we don't recommend any particular ones). Please note that, until you get into the relatively high-commission ones, you will not get the fancy stuff or the professional software like RealTick III. General consensus seems to be that the day trading firms are a lot better and a lot faster. Typical comment: "I don't think any of the [regular] discount brokers are fast enough for day trading." *

EPILOGUE

There you have it. My first attempt to formalize most of my knowledge about successful DAD trading in Canada. I hope this book helped you make a decision about whether DAD is right for you as a career.

Remember: Get an education before you begin. Good trading!

*Unfortunately my friend doesn't want his name and email address published for fear of a barrage of questions from readers. I can tell you that he uses fundamental and technical research and spends at least 80 hours a week, 52 weeks a year watching the market. I'd like to add my thanks for his permission to publish his comments as a counterpoint to day trading.

APPENDIX A:
50 CLASSIC TRADING RULES

1. Plan your trades. Trade your plan.

2. Keep records of your trading results.

3. Keep a positive attitude, no matter how much you lose.

4. Don't take the market home.

5. Continually set higher trading goals.

6. Successful traders buy into bad news and sell into good news.

7. Successful traders are not afraid to buy high and sell low.

8. Successful traders have a well-scheduled planned time for studying the markets.

9. Successful traders isolate themselves from the opinions of others.

10. Continually strive for patience, perseverance, determination, and rational action.

11. Limit your losses—use stops!

12. Never cancel a stop loss order after you have placed it!

13. Place the stop at the time you make your trade.

14. Never get into the market because you are anxious because of waiting.

15. Avoid getting in or out of the market too often.

16. Losses—not profits—make the trader studious. Take advantage of every loss to improve your knowledge of market action.

17. The most difficult task in speculation is not prediction but self-control. Successful trading is difficult and frustrating. You are the most important element in the equation for success.

18. Always discipline yourself by following a pre-determined set of rules.

19. Remember that a bear market will give back in one month what a bull market has taken three months to build.

20. Don't ever allow a big winning trade to turn into a loser. Stop yourself out if the market moves against you 20 percent from your peak profit point.

21. You must have a program, you must know your program, and you must follow your program.

22. Expect and accept losses gracefully. Those who brood over losses always miss the next opportunity, which more than likely will be profitable.

23. Split your profits right down the middle and never risk more than 50 percent of them again in the market.

24. The key to successful trading is knowing yourself and your stress point.

25. The difference between winners and losers isn't so much native ability as it is discipline exercised in avoiding mistakes.

26. In trading as in fencing there are the quick and the dead.

27. Speech may be silver but silence is golden. Traders with the golden touch do not talk about their success.

28. Dream big dreams and think tall. Very few people set goals too high. A person becomes what they think about all day long.

29. Accept failure as a step toward victory.

30. Have you taken a loss? Forget it quickly. Have you taken a profit? Forget it even quicker! Don't let ego and greed inhibit clear thinking and hard work.

31. One cannot do anything about yesterday. When one door closes, another door opens. The greater opportunity always lies through the open door.

32. The deepest secret for you as a trader is to subordinate your will to the will of the market. The market is truth, as it reflects all forces that bear upon it. As long as you recognize this, you are safe. When you ignore this, you are lost and doomed.

33. It's much easier to put on a trade than to take it off.

34. If a market doesn't do what you think it should do, get out.

35. Beware of large positions that can control your emotions. Don't be overly aggressive with the market. Treat it gently by allowing your equity to grow steadily rather than in bursts.

36. Never add to a losing position.

37. Beware of trying to pick tops or bottoms.

38. You must believe in yourself and your judgment if you expect to make a living at this game.

39. In a narrow market there is no sense in trying to anticipate what the next big movement is going to be—up or down.

40. A loss never bothers me after I take it. I forget it overnight. But being wrong and not taking the loss—that is what does the damage to the pocketbook and to the soul.

41. Never volunteer advice and never brag of your winnings.

42. Of all speculative blunders, there are few greater than selling what shows a profit and keeping what shows a loss.

43. Standing aside is a position.

44. It is better to be more interested in the market's reaction to new information than in the piece of news itself.

45. If you don't know who you are, the markets are an expensive place to find out.

46. In the world of money, which is a world shaped by human behaviour, nobody has the foggiest notion of what will happen in the future. Mark that word—nobody! Thus the successful trader does not base moves on what supposedly will happen but reacts instead to what does happen.

47. Except in unusual circumstances, get in the habit of taking your profit too soon. Don't torment yourself if a trade continues winning without you. Chances are it won't continue long. If it does, console yourself by thinking of all the times when liquidating early reserved gains that you would have otherwise lost.

48. When the ship starts to sink, don't pray—jump!

49. Lose your opinion—not your money.

50. Assimilate into your very bones a set of trading rules that works for you.

Appendix B: The Canadian Securities Commissions

ALBERTA

Alberta Securities Commission Agency
10025 Jasper Avenue, 20th Floor
Edmonton, Alberta
T5J 3Z5
www.albertasecurities.com
Tel: (780) 427-5201
Fax: (780) 422-0777

BRITISH COLUMBIA

British Columbia Securities Commission
200 – 865 Hornby Street
Vancouver, British Columbia
V6Z 2H4
www.bcsc.bc.ca
Tel: (604) 899-6500
Fax: (604) 899-6506

MANITOBA

Manitoba Securities Commission
1130 – 405 Broadway Avenue
Winnipeg, Manitoba
R3C 3L6
www.gov.mb.ca/cca/mbsecuri.html
Tel: (204) 945-2548
Fax: (204) 945-0330

NEW BRUNSWICK

Office of the Administrator

P.O. Box 5001

133 Prince William Street, Suite 606

Saint John, New Brunswick

E2L 4Y9

Web site unavailable at time of printing

Tel: (506) 658-3060

Fax: (506) 658-3059

NEWFOUNDLAND

Newfoundland Securities Commission

Department of Justice, Securities Division

400 – Confederation Building, East Block

St. John's, Newfoundland

A1B 4J6

Web site unavailable at time of printing

Tel: (709) 729-4189

Fax: (709) 729-6187

NORTHWEST TERRITORIES

Registrar of Securities

Department of Justice

Government of the Northwest Territories

3rd Floor Courthouse

5003 – 49th Street (P.O. Box 1320)

Yellowknife, Northwest Territories

X1A 2L9

Web site unavailable at time of printing

Tel: (867) 873-7490

Fax: (867) 873-0243

NOVA SCOTIA

Nova Scotia Securities Commission
1690 Hollis Street
2nd Floor, Joseph Howe Building
P.O. Box 458
Halifax, Nova Scotia
B3J 3J9
Web site unavailable at time of printing
Tel: (902) 424-7768
Fax: (902) 424-4625

NUNAVUT LEGAL REGISTRIES

Registrar of Securities and Legal Registries
Government of Nunavut
Bag 9500
Yellowknife, Nunavut
X1A 2R3
Web site unavailable at time of printing
Tel: (867) 873-7792
Fax: (867) 873-0586

ONTARIO

Ontario Securities Commission
Cadillac Fairview Tower
20 Queen Street West
Toronto, Ontario
M5H 3S8
www.osc.gov.on.ca
Tel: (416) 597-0681
Fax: (416) 593-8122

PRINCE EDWARD ISLAND

Registrar of Securities
Director of Corporations
Department of Justice
Shaw Building
500 – 105 Rochford Street (P.O. Box 2000)
Charlottetown, Prince Edward Island
C1A 7N8
Web site unavailable at time of printing
Tel: (902) 368-4550
Fax: (902) 368-5283

QUÉBEC

Commission des valeurs mobilières du Québec
Stock Exchange Tower
800 Victoria Square (P.O. Box 246), 22nd Floor
Montréal, Québec
H4Z 1G3
www.cvmq.com
Tel: (514) 940-2150
Fax: (514) 873-3090

SASKATCHEWAN

Saskatchewan Securities Commission
800 – 1920 Broad Street
Regina, Saskatchewan
S4P 3V7
Web site unavailable at time of printing
Tel: (306) 787-5645
Fax: (306) 787-5899

YUKON TERRITORY

Registrar of Securities
Department of Justice
Corporate Affairs J-9
Box 2703
Whitehorse, Yukon
Y1A 2C6
Web site unavailable at time of printing
Tel: (867) 667-5005
Fax: (867) 393-6251

APPENDIX C: DAY TRADERS' GLOSSARY

Accumulation   An addition to a trader's original market position.

Advance/Decline   Each day's number of declining stocks is subtracted from the number of advancing stocks. The net difference is added to a running sum if the difference is positive and subtracted from the running sum if the difference is negative.

All or None   An order sent to buy or sell a set number of shares. This order must be filled for the complete amount of shares requested or not at all. In other words, there can be no partial fills.

Arbitrage   The simultaneous purchase and sale of two different and closely related securities to take advantage of a disparity in their prices.

ARCA, ATTN, BTRD, ISLD, STRK, etc.   Short names for ECNs.

Ask (also known as offer)   The price at which a holder of a stock is willing to sell. In general, the asked price is the price you pay when you buy and is higher than the bid (see bid) price. In over-the-counter trading, securities dealers or market makers profit from the spread between these two so much that they are often willing to pay discount brokers for "order flow."

Ask Size (or offer size)   The number of shares associated with the current ask price or the number of shares, the seller(s) are offering for sale at the ask price.

Auction   A public sale of times to the highest bidders.

Average Daily Volume   The number of shares traded in a given number of days, divided by that number of days.

Axe   The key market maker in a stock who often directs the movement of price.

Bar Chart   A chart that displays a security's open, high, low, and close prices using one vertical line for each time period whether it is a minute, day, week, month, or year.

Basket Trades   Large transactions made up of a number of different stocks.

Bear Market (see bull market)   When stocks trend downward for a relatively long period of time. Depending on the type of trader/investor this can be a day, week, months, or years. The term comes from the way a real bear attacks, using a swift downward strike of its paw.

Bid   The price at which someone is willing to buy a security. This is the price you get when you generally sell a stock you currently are holding (see ask).

Bidding   The act of buying securities at the posted bid price or better.

Bid Size   The number of shares associated with the current bid price or the number of shares the buyer(s) are offering to buy at the posted bid price.

Breakdown   A sharp decline in price after the stock has traded sideways for a while.

Breakout   If a stock has traded in a narrow range for some time and then advances above the resistance level, this is said to be an upside breakout. Breakouts are suspect if they do not occur on high volume.

Bull Market (see bear market)   When stock prices have risen steadily over a period of time. Depending on the type of trader/investor this can be a day, week, months, or years. The term comes from the way a bull attacks. It rushes forward and holds its head low and gores upwards with its horns.

Bullet Trade   A trade that lasts only a few minutes or less.

Buy on Margin   The practice of buying stocks with money borrowed from a broker.

Call Option   A contract that gives the buyer of the option the right but not the obligation to take delivery of the underlying security at a specific price within a certain period of time.

Candlestick Chart   A chart that displays the open, high, low, and close prices of a stock for each time period much like a bar chart. Candlesticks, however, also illustrate the relationship between these prices by colouring the body of the candlestick dark or leaving it white.

Capital Preservation   Maintaining your trading capital by not allowing yourself to lose more than a certain percentage of your capital in any given trade.

Change   The difference between the preceding day's close price and the most recent transacted price of the stock.

Channel   When a stock trades around the same price for a certain period of time, it is said to be in a channel. On a chart, a channel will be recognized as a sideways line.

Chasing a Stock   Buying or shorting a stock after it has already made a large move. Chasing a stock is considered very dangerous, because one may buy at the top.

Close   The final trading price for a security at the end of the most recent trading day.

Closed Trades   Positions that have been liquidated.

Closeouts   Buying or selling enough shares to close out your position. Same as going flat.

Commission   A fee brokers charge for executing a transaction. The amount is usually based on the number of shares or the total dollar amount of the trade.

Common Stock   An ownership stake in a company. Holders of common stock shares are last in line in terms of their claim to dividends and assets.

Convergence   Two or more averages or indices draw closer together to help show confirming trends.

Correction   A sharp short drop in stock prices after which the market resumes an upward climb.

Covering   To cover means getting out of a short position. When one is short in a stock, one needs to buy back the borrowed shares to close out the trade.

Current Offer   The price at which the owner of a security offers to sell it at the posted ask price.

Daily Range   Intraday price volatility or the difference between the high and low price during one trading day.

Daily Volume   The average number of shares of a stock traded daily over the previous 13-week period.

Day Order   A trade order to buy or sell a security during the market hours in a trading day.

Day's High   The highest price of the stock during the current day's trading.

Day Trade   A trade that is closed within the same day.

Day Trader   A person who buys and sells stocks rapidly during the day in order to exploit the stocks' intraday price volatility.

Day's Low   The lowest price of the stock during the current day's trading.

Derivatives   Financial contracts, the value of which depends on the value of the underlying instrument commodity, bond, equity, currency, or a combination.

Direct Access Trading Terminals   Computer terminals located in day trading firms which day traders use to make direct trades with market makers and specialists.

Divergence   Two or more averages or indices fail to show confirming trends.

Diversification   An investing strategy that seeks to minimize risk by diversifying among many types of investments. Diversification and risk are directly related to each other. The more you diversify your portfolio, generally the less risk you have.

Dividend   The distribution of corporate earnings to shareholders.

Double Witching   A term used for the day when both options and futures expire.

Downtick   A downtick occurs when the bid price drops one level.

Earning the Spread   Due to emergence of alternatives to SOES in recent years, traders are now able to earn the spread by using ECNs instead of SOES. If you buy a stock on the bid (lower price) and sell it on the ask (higher price), you will have earned the spread. This trading technique is also called playing market maker.

ECN   Electronic communication network. ARCA, ATTN, BTRD, ISLD, REDI, and STRK are examples of ECNs.

Five-Minute Rule   You can only buy up to 1,000 shares of the same stock within five minutes if you are using SOES. If you want to buy more than 1,000 shares of the same stock on SOES, you have to wait five minutes before you can issue another buy order. However, if you bought 500 shares of a stock using SOES the first time, you may buy up to 500 shares more using SOES within the next five minutes. Note that if you use an ECN such as ISLD, you can always buy as many shares as you like of the same stock. The five-minute rule only applies to SOES! The same five-minute rule applies when selling or shorting a stock.

Flat for the Day   To close out all your positions before the end of the trading day. Day traders almost never hold positions overnight, because one has no control over which way a stock may gap.

FOK   Fill or Kill order. This is an order that will be filled or cancelled right away.

Futures   A future contract is an agreement between two parties in which one buys and the other sells something on a pre-arranged date. What day traders are mostly interested in are the S&P 500 futures. Stock prices follow futures prices. So watch the directions of the futures closely.

Gap   Difference between the closing price of the last trading day and the opening price of the next.

Going High Bid   Offering to pay more for a stock than the previous high bidder. This will narrow the spread.

Going Low Ask   Offering to sell a stock for less than the previous lowest seller. This will narrow the spread.

Good till Cancel   An order sent to buy or sell stock. These types of orders stay open until they are filled or cancelled by the sender.

Grinding   A trading technique that aims to continually grind out small profits such as 1/8 or 1/4 while keeping the downside risk under control.

GTC (good till cancelled order)   Your order will remain open until you cancel it manually.

Holding the Ask   Someone is preventing the price on the ask from going up even though there is a lot of buying of the stock.

Holding the Bid   Someone is preventing the price on the bid from going down even though there is a lot of selling of the stock.

Inside Market   Same as best ask or best bid. The highest bid and lowest ask currently available.

InstiNet   Private network that currently handles about 10 to 15 percent of the volume on NASDAQ. It matches buyers and sellers and often allows traders to buy and sell at prices between the ask and the bid.

Institutional Investor/Order   Banks, mutual funds companies, pension funds, or other corporate entities that purchase or sell stocks for themselves.

Intraday High   Today's highest price.

Intraday Low   Today's lowest price.

Intraday Range   The difference between today's high and low prices.

IOC (immediate or cancel order)   By using this order, whatever portion of your order which is not filled immediately will be cancelled.

Level II   Level II gives the trader much more detailed information than Level I. It lists all market makers and ECNs on the bid and the ask on a given stock, not just the top bid and top ask. One can also get much faster executions by using Level II direct access trading terminals.

Limit Order   An order to buy or sell a stock at a given price only. If the stock moves past your price before you get filled at your desired price, you will not get filled.

Liquidity   Liquidity is the ease with which a market can absorb volume buying and selling without dramatic fluctuations in price.

Maria Bartiromo   Commentator on CNBC, most watched and respected by the average day trader.

Market Maker   A representative of a brokerage house, like Goldman Sachs or Merrill Lynch, who buys and sells shares for a particular stock. A popular stock like MSFT has market makers from almost all brokerage houses, while less popular stocks only have a few market makers from smaller institutions. (MM is short for market maker.)

Market Order   An order to buy or sell a stock at given market conditions. Your order may get executed at different prices than what you envisioned.

Most Active   List of the most actively traded stocks.

Moving Average   Measures the past movement in price and allows one to see whether a stock is currently acting strong or weak compared to its past behaviour.

MSCO, GSCO, MONT, MLCO, SLKC, HRZG, FBCO   Symbols for market makers that one can see for NASDAQ stocks using Level II software. Note that stocks traded on the NYSE don't have these market makers.

NASDAQ 100 Index   The largest 100 NASDAQ domestic (U.S.A.) companies listed on the NASDAQ.

NASDAQ Composite Index   Measures all NASDAQ stocks, and each is market weighted.

Net Change   Difference between yesterday's close price and today's opening price.

NYSE   New York Stock Exchange. Rhymes with "wise."

Open Outcry   A method of public auction in which verbal bids and offers are made in the trading pits or rings. More to the point, a system of trading in which people standing in pits frantically wave and short out orders.

Options   An option is the right to either buy or sell a specified amount or value at a fixed exercise price. An option that gives the right to buy is a call option. An option that gives the right to sell is a put option. One needs to exercise the option before the specified expiration date. Stock options expire every third Friday of the month and can become absolutely worthless.

Pit   The area on the exchange trading floor where futures trading takes place. The area is generally octagonal with steps descending into the centre. Traders stand on the various steps, which designate the contract month they are trading. When viewed from above the trading area looks like a pit.

Range Trading   Similar to grinding, but one allows for more room for the stock to move. Range trades tend to take a little longer with both the gainers and losers being bigger than when grinding.

Relative Strength   An indicator that measures the past behaviour of a stock against all other stocks on a scale from 99 to 1, 99 being the strongest and 1 the weakest.

Resistance   When a stock has trouble breaking through a price area, it is said that a stock is up against resistance (e.g., it often trades just below $25, but can't move above $25).

Round or Board Lot   One hundred shares of a stock.

Run   When a stock has a quick change of price, it's said to be on a run.

S&P 500 Index/Futures   A list of 500 stocks picked by Standard and Poors which are traded on the NASDAQ, NYSE, and AMEX exchanges. The index is market-cap weighted and is regarded as the "broader market."

Scalper   A trader who uses scalping as a trading strategy.

Scalping   Trading quickly for small profits.

SEC   Securities and Exchange Commission. The U.S.A.'s federal agency that administers and protects the public with rules regarding the securities markets.

SelectNet   Operated by NASDAQ. One can try to get a better price than with using SOES, but there is no obligation for the other party to buy or sell the stock that you're interested in.

Shake Outs   A pullback in price before the stock continues in the same direction. Market makers love to shake traders out of their winning positions by creating wide trading ranges and big pullbacks.

Short Sale Rule   If the last tick was a downtick, you cannot short a stock at or below the bid price. However, you can still try to short the stock at any price above the bid price by offering it out on the ask.

Shorting a Stock   Shorting a stock can be very profitable in weak market conditions or when a stock has gotten way ahead of itself. The concept of shorting is that you sell a stock that you don't own (you basically borrow it from your broker) and expect to buy it back later at a lower price.

SOES   Stands for small order execution system, it allows you to buy (or sell) up to 1,000 shares from any market maker.

Specialist   Someone who handles all the transactions in a stock traded on the NYSE.

Spread   The difference in price between the bid and the ask.

Stock Split   The division of outstanding shares of a stock into a larger or smaller number of shares.

Stock Symbol   A one- to five-letter grouping assigned to represent a company that is publicly traded on a stock exchange. For example, MSFT is the NASDAQ symbol for Microsoft.

Stop   An order that becomes a market order to sell the current position once a certain pre-determined price has been reached.

Stop Limit   An order that combines both the stop and limit order.

Stop Loss   The worst price that you are willing to sell a stock for. Stop losses are very important to cut your losses when a trade has gone in the wrong direction!

Support   Happens when a stock won't fall below a price area. Opposite of resistance.

Swing Trade   A trade that usually lasts several day, as opposed to a day trade.

Tick   An important short-time indicator. It's the difference between the number of NYSE stocks that are on an uptick vs. the number of NYSE stocks that are on a downtick. E.g., if we have 2,000 stocks on an uptick and 1,800 on a downtick, then the tick would read +200.

Trading Chat Rooms   Usually IRC or Web-based chat rooms where information is given and posted in real time with fellow day traders. Highly dangerous to take trades posted here because most of the information is given out after someone has entered a trade.

Treasury Bond 30-Year   Is based on ten times the yield to maturity on the most recently auctioned 30-year U.S. Treasury Bond.

Trin   Measures the volatility and selling pressure. It's a ratio of the quotient of advancing stocks divided by declining stocks and up volume divided by down volume. Don't worry if you can't figure it out right away. The key is that a rising trin is bearish, and a falling trin is bullish.

Triple Witching   Occurs every third Friday of every third month (March, June, September, December). Options, futures, and options on futures expire.

Two-Sided Market   The obligation imposed by the NASDAQ that market makers must make both bids and offers in each stock they make markets in.

Uptick   This is when the bid price moves up a level.

Volume   The total number of shares traded in a stock exchange. Volume is reported slightly differently in the NASDAQ and the NYSE.

Witching   Occurs every third Friday of every month. Options expire this day.

Zero-Plus Tick   A zero-plus tick occurs when a stock upticks on a trade and the following trade is executed at the same price level.

APPENDIX D:
DIRECT ACCESS DAY TRADING FIRMS

BOLD typeface indicates Canadian Firms

Company	Web Site
All-Tech Investment Group	www.attain.com
Andover Trading	www.andovertrading.com
Bright Trading	www.stocktrading.com
Broadway Trading	www.broadwaytrading.com
Castle Online	www.castleonline.com
Cornerstone Securities	www.protrader.com
CyberBroker www.cybercorp.com	
Daylight Trading	www.daylighttrading.com
DirectTrade	www.d-trade.com
Edgetrade	www.edgetrade.com
The Executioner	www.executioner.com
Equity Trading	www.equitytrading.com
Harbor Securities	www.soes-trade.com
Landmark Securities	www.landmarksecurities.com
Livetrade	www.livetrade.com
Momentum Securities	www.soes.com
Navillus Securities	www.navillus.com
On-Line Investment Services	www.onli.com
On-site Trading	www.onsitetrading.com
Preferred Trade	www.preferredtrade.com
Remote Trading International	www.investors-street.com

Company	Web Site
Self Trading	www.selftrading.com
Summit Trading	www.summittrading.com
Swift Trade Securities Inc.	**www.swifttrade.com**
Tiger Investment Group	www.tigerinvestment.com
Van Vuren Securities	www.vbsecurities.com
Yamner and Co.	www.yamner.com

APPENDIX E: DOW JONES INDUSTRIAL AVERAGE (DJIA)

The Dow Jones Industrial Average (DJIA) is an index used to measure the performance of the U.S. financial markets. Introduced on May 26, 1896, by Charles H. Dow, it is the oldest stock price measure in continuous use. Over the past century the Dow has become the most widely recognized stock market indicator in the U.S. and probably in the entire world. The 30 stocks included in today's Dow are listed on the New York Stock Exchange, except for Microsoft and Intel, and are all large blue-chip companies that reflect the health of the U.S. economy. All but a handful of these have major business operations throughout the rest of the world, thus providing some insight into the economic well-being of the global economy.

The Dow has been repeatedly updated over the decades to reflect changes in corporate America. From the original 12 stocks used in 1896 it was increased to 20 stocks in 1916 and then 30 stocks in 1928. The most recent modification occurred on November 1, 1999, when Home Depot, Intel, Microsoft, and SBC replaced Chevron, Goodyear, Sears, and Union Carbide, respectively. Intel and Microsoft, which both trade on the NASDAQ stock market, are the first Dow 30 components that are not listed on the New York Stock Exchange since the Dow Jones Industrial Average was created in 1896.

Though it is only the unweighted average of 30 stock prices, over the long run the DJIA's tracking of market movements has closely paralleled more broadly based capitalization-weighted indices like the New York Stock Exchange Composite, the Standard & Poor's 500 and the Wilshire 5000. In 1896 the Dow was computed as the sum of the prices of 12 stocks divided by the number of stocks. Since then the divisor has been adjusted to compensate for stock splits and other distributions that would create distortions in the average that did not reflect a change in value of the stocks. The value of the adjusted divisor as of November 1, 1999, was 0.20435952. Its current value is printed in the *Wall Street Journal* every day.

The following are the companies that make up the Dow:

Company Name	Ticker Symbol
ALCOA Inc.	AA
AlliedSignal Inc.	ALD
American Express Co.	AXP
AT&T Corp.	T
Boeing Co.	BA
Caterpillar Inc.	CAT
Citigroup Inc.	C
Coca-Cola Co.	KO
Dupont Co.	DD
Eastman Kodak Co.	EK
Exxon Corp.	XON
General Electric Co.	GE
General Motors Corp.	GM
Hewlett Packard Co.	HWP
Home Depot	HD
Intel	INTC
International Business Machines Corp.	IBM
International Paper Co.	IP
J.P. Morgan & Co.	JPM
Johnson & Johnson	JNJ
McDonald's Corp.	MCD
Merck & Co.	MRK
Microsoft	MSFT
Minnesota Mining & Manufacturing Co.	MMM
Phillip Morris Co.	MO

Company Name	Ticker Symbol
Procter & Gamble Co.	PG
SBC Communications, Inc.	SBC
United Technologies Corp.	UTX
WalMart	WMT
Walt Disney Co.	DIS

APPENDIX F: DIRECT ACCESS DAY TRADING SOFTWARE PLATFORMS

Company Name	Web Site
AIQ Trading Expert	www.aiq.com
A-T Financial	www.atfi.com
Bloomberg	www.bloomberg.com
BMI	www.bmiquotes.com
CyberTrader	www.cybercorp.com
DTN Spectrum	www.dtn.com
First Alert	www.chartist.com
Metastock	www.equis.com
Omega Research Trade Station	www.omegaresearch.com
PC Quote	www.pcquote.com
Quote.com	www.quote.com
Real Tick III	www.taltrade.com
Reuters Quotron	www.reuters.com
S&P Comstock	www.spcomstock.com
Signal	www.dbc.com
Swift Trade	www.swifttrade.com
Telechart 2000	www.tc2000.com
Tradecast	www.tcast.com

APPENDIX G: STOCK RESEARCH SITES FOR DAY TRADERS

If you have any favourite sites please email them to me for future revisions of the book.

www.bloomberg.com

www.cnbc.com

www.cnnfn.com

www.dowjones.com

www.foxmarketwire.com

www.infobeat.com

www.instinet.com

www.investor.msn.com

www.isld.com

www.marketwatch.com

www.msnbc.com

www.nasdaq.com

www.nasdaqtrader.com

www.nasdaqnews.com

www.nyse.com

www.bigcharts.com

www.briefing.com

www.businesswire.com

www.dailystocks.com

www.einvestor.com

www.fool.com

www.investorguide.com

www.investorlinks.com

www.investorword.com

www.better-investing.org

www.forbes.com

www.fortune.com

www.inc.com

www.money.com

www.nasd.com

www.sec.gov

www.smartmoney.com

www.worth.com

www.quote.yahoo.com

www.news.com

www.pristine.com

www.quote.com

www.siliconinvestor.com

www.thestreet.com

www.tradealert.com

www.wallstreetcity.com

www.tdwaterhouse.ca

www.canada.etrade.com

www.actiondirect.com

www.investorline.com

www.canadatrust.com/ctsecurities

www.sdbi.com

www.investorlearning.ca

APPENDIX H: INTERNET BROKERS

BOLD typeface indicates Canadian firms

Company	Web Site
CIBC Investor's Edge	**www.investorsedge.cibc.com**
Scotia Discount Brokerage	**www.sdbi.com**
Ameritrade	www.ameritrade.com
Charles Schwab	www.schwab.com
Discover Brokerage Direct	www.discoverbrokerage.com
DLJdirect	www.dljdirect.com
TD Waterhouse Web Broker	**www.tdwaterhouse.ca**
E*Trade Canada	**www.canada.etrade.com**
Canada Trust CT Securities	**www.canadatrust.com/ctsecurities**
Royal Bank Action Direct	**www.actiondirect.com**
Bank of Montreal Investorline	**www.investorline.com**
National Discount Broker	www.ndb.com
AB Watley	www.abwatley.com
Bidwell	www.bidwell.com
Quick and Reilly	www.quick-reilly.com
Fidelity	www.fmr.com
My Discount Broker	www.mydiscountbroker.com
Wall Street Electronica	www.wallstreete.com
Wang	www.wangvest.com
Mr. Stock	www.mrstock.com

The following information is for sophisticated and experienced investors: low minimum opening balance, real-time quotes, ability to issue all types of orders, availability of options, rapid account updates, charts, news, and research information.

Company	Web Site
Swift Trade Securities	www.swifttrade.com
Brown and Company	www.brownco.com
Trading Direct	www.tradingdirect.com
Firstrade	www.firstrade.com
Investrade	www.investrade.com
Scottsdale	www.scottrade.com
AF Trader	www.aftrader.com
Vision Trade	www.visiontrade.com
Muriel Siebert	www.siebertnet.com
Tradestar Investments	www.4tradestart.com
Interactive Brokers	www.interactivebrokers.com
Suretrade	www.suretrade.com
Datek Online	www.datek.com

APPENDIX I: NASDAQ 100 INDEX

Company Name	Symbol	% of Index (Adjusted)
3Com Corporation	COMS	0.37
Adaptec, Inc.	ADPT	0.14
ADC Telecommunications, Inc.	ADCT	1.07
Adelphia Communications Corporation	ADLAC	0.31
Adobe Systems Incorporated	ADBE	0.67
Altera Corporation	ALTR	1.39
Amazon.com, Inc.	AMZN	0.62
American Power Conversion Corporation	APCC	0.55
Amgen Inc.	AMGN	1.35
Apollo Group, Inc.	APOL	0.09
Apple Computer, Inc.	AAPL	1.51
Applied Materials, Inc.	AMAT	2.02
Applied Micro Circuits Corporation	AMCC	0.74
At Home Corporation	ATHM	0.26
Atmel Corporation	ATML	0.38
Bed Bath & Beyond Inc.	BBBY	0.41
Biogen, Inc.	BGEN	0.52
Biomet, Inc.	BMET	0.3
BMC Software, Inc.	BMCS	0.39
BroadVision, Inc.	BVSN	0.51
Chiron Corporation	CHIR	0.56
CIENA Corporation	CIEN	0.83
Cintas Corporation	CTAS	0.43
Cisco Systems, Inc.	CSCO	8.67
Citrix Systems, Inc.	CTXS	0.55
CMGI, Inc.	CMGI	0.86

Company Name	Symbol	% of Index (Adjusted)
CNET Networks, Inc.	CNET	0.17
Comcast Corporation	CMCSK	0.88
Compuware Corporation	CPWR	0.13
Comverse Technology, Inc.	CMVT	0.66
Concord EFS, Inc.	CEFT	0.29
Conexant Systems, Inc.	CNXT	0.76
Costco Wholesale Corporation	COST	0.72
Dell Computer Corporation	DELL	2.5
Dollar Tree Stores, Inc.	DLTR	0.16
eBay Inc.	EBAY	0.76
EchoStar Communications Corporation	DISH	0.63
Electronic Arts Inc.	ERTS	0.19
Fiserv, Inc.	FISV	0.31
Gemstar International Group, Limited	GMST	0.48
Genzyme General	GENZ	0.24
Global Crossing Ltd.	GBLX	1.21
Herman Miller, Inc.	MLHR	0.09
i2 Technologies, Inc.	ITWO	0.92
Immunex Corporation	IMNX	1.28
Intel Corporation	INTC	7.54
Intuit Inc.	INTU	0.45
JDS Uniphase Corporation	JDSU	3
KLA-Tencor Corporation	KLAC	0.78
Legato Systems, Inc.	LGTOE	0.05
Level 3 Communications, Inc.	LVLT	1.09
Linear Technology Corporation	LLTC	1.13
LM Ericsson Telephone Company	ERICY	1.02
Lycos, Inc.	LCOS	0.26

Company Name	Symbol	% of Index (Adjusted)
Maxim Integrated Products, Inc.	MXIM	1.27
MCI WORLDCOM, Inc.	WCOM	2.26
McLeodUSA Incorporated	MCLD	0.5
MedImmune, Inc.	MEDI	0.52
Metromedia Fiber Network, Inc.	MFNX	0.76
Microchip Technology Incorporated	MCHP	0.2
Microsoft Corporation	MSFT	6.62
Molex Incorporated	MOLX	0.27
Network Appliance, Inc.	NTAP	0.89
Network Associates, Inc.	NETA	0.18
Network Solutions, Inc.	NSOL	0.49
Nextel Communications, Inc.	NXTL	2.48
NEXTLINK Communications, Inc.	NXLK	0.34
Northwest Airlines Corporation	NWAC	0.09
Novell, Inc.	NOVL	0.44
NTL Incorporated	NTLI	0.52
Oracle Corporation	ORCL	4.79
PACCAR, Inc.	PCAR	0.21
PacifiCare Health Systems, Inc.	PHSY	0.1
PanAmSat Corporation	SPOT	0.45
Parametric Technology Corporation	PMTC	0.17
Paychex, Inc.	PAYX	0.67
PeopleSoft, Inc.	PSFT	0.29
PMC - Sierra, Inc.	PMCS	1.25
QLogic Corporation	QLGC	0.29
QUALCOMM Incorporated	QCOM	4.72
Quintiles Transnational Corp.	QTRN	0.12

Company Name	Symbol	% of Index (Adjusted)
RealNetworks, Inc.	RNWK	0.28
RF Micro Devices, Inc.	RFMD	0.4
Sanmina Corporation	SANM	0.41
SDL, Inc.	SDLI	0.66
Siebel Systems, Inc.	SEBL	1.4
Sigma-Aldrich Corporation	SIAL	0.15
Smurfit-Stone Container Corporation	SSCC	0.17
Staples, Inc.	SPLS	0.32
Starbucks Corporation	SBUX	0.56
Sun Microsystems, Inc.	SUNW	3.34
Synopsys, Inc.	SNPS	0.17
Tellabs, Inc.	TLAB	0.6
USA Networks, Inc.	USAI	0.34
VERITAS Software Corporation	VRTS	2.2
VISX, Incorporated	VISX	0.05
Vitesse Semiconductor Corporation	VTSS	0.47
VoiceStream Wireless Corporation	VSTR	0.82
Xilinx, Inc.	XLNX	1.49
Yahoo! Inc.	YHOO	1.61

APPENDIX J: NASDAQ STOCK SYMBOLS

I frequently get asked the question of why some NASDAQ stock symbols have four letters and yet others have five. Here is the answer:

All NASDAQ stock symbols are represented by a minimum of four letters. Examples are MSFT (Microsoft), CSCO (Cisco), YHOO (Yahoo!), INTC (Intel), and so on. Occasionally you will see a fifth letter from A to Z tacked on the end of a NASDAQ stock symbol. The fifth character in a NASDAQ stock symbol identifies the issue as other than a single issue of common or capital stock. For example, in ERICY (Ericson) the Y denotes the stock as an American Depository Receipt (ADR) and therefore a foreign stock trading in the United States. Here is a chart illustrating the fifth character identifiers. Note that not all letters from A to Z are used.

Letter	Identifies the Stock as
A	Class A stock
B	Class B stock
E	Late in filing with the SEC
F	Foreign
G	First Convertible Bond
H	Second Convertible Bond
I	Third Convertible Bond
J	Voting
K	Non-Voting
L	Miscellaneous situations
Q	In the middle of bankruptcy
T	With rights and warrants
W	Warrants
Y	ADR—American Depository Receipt

APPENDIX K: SIGNIFICANT NASDAQ MARKET MAKERS

Market Maker Symbol	Firm Name
ABSA	Alex Brown and Sons Inc.
AGIS	Aegis Capital Corp.
BEST	Bear Stearns and Co. Inc
BTSC	BT Securities
CANT	Cantor Fitzgerald and Co. Inc.
CHGO	Chicago Corp.
CJDB	CJ Lawrence Deutsche Bank
COST	Coastal Securities
COWN	Cowen and Co.
DAIN	Dain Bosworth, Inc.
DEAN	Dean Witter
DOMS	Domestic Securities
EXPO	Exponential Capital Markets
FACT	First Albany Corp.
FAHN	Fahnestock and Co.
FBCO	First Boston Corp.
FPKI	Fox-Pitt, Kelton, Inc.
GRUN	Gruntal and Co., Inc.
GSCO	Goldman Sachs and Co.
GVRC	Gvr Co.
HMQT	Hambrecht and Quist, Inc.
HRZG	Herzog, Heine, Geduld, Inc.
JEFF	Jefferies Co., Inc.
JPMS	J.P. Morgan

Market Maker Symbol	Firm Name
KEMP	Kemper Securities, Inc.
LEHM	Lehman Brothers
MADF	Bernard Madoff
MASH	Mayer and Schweitzer, Inc. (Charles Schwab)
MHMY	M.H. Meyerson and Co., Inc.
MLCO	Merrill Lynch
MONT	Montgomery Securities
MSCO	Morgan Stanley and Co., Inc.
MSWE	Midwest Stock Exchange
NAWE	Nash Weiss and Co.
NEED	Neddham and Co.
NMRA	Nomura Securities Intl., Inc.
OLDE	Olde Discount Corp.
OPCO	Oppenheimer and Co.
PERT	Pershing Trading Co.
PIPR	Piper Jaffray
PRUS	Prudential Securities, Inc.
PUNK	Punk Siegel and Knoell, Inc.
PWJC	Paine Webber, Inc.
RAGN	Ragen McKenzie, Inc.
RPSC	Rauscher Pierce Refsnes, Inc.
RBSF	Robertson Stephens and Co. LP
SALB	Salomon Brothers
SBNY	Sands Brother and Co. Ltd.
SBSH	Smith Barney Shearson, Inc.
SELZ	Furman Selz, Inc.

Market Maker Symbol	Firm Name
SHWD	Sherwood Securities Corp.
SNDV	Soundview Financial Group, Inc.
SWST	Southwest Securities, Inc.
TSCO	Troster Singer Corp. (Spear Leads)
TUCK	Tucker Anthony, Inc.
TVAN	Teevan and Co., Inc.
UBSS	UBS Securities
VOLP	Volpe Weity and Co.
WARB	S.G. Warburg and Co., Inc.
WBLR	William Blair and Co.
WEAT	Wheat First Securities, Inc.
WEDB	Wedbrush Morgan Securities
WEED	Weeden and Co. LP
WERT	Wertheim Schroder and Co., Inc.
WSEI	Wall Street Equities, Inc.
WSLS	Wessels, Arnold and Henderson

INDEX